PRACTICAL THEOLOGY *and the*
ONE BODY OF CHRIST

THE BOOKSTORE

STUDIES IN PRACTICAL THEOLOGY

Series Editors

Don S. Browning
James W. Fowler
Friedrich Schweitzer
Johannes A. van der Ven

PRACTICAL THEOLOGY *and the* ONE BODY OF CHRIST

Toward a Missional-Ecumenical Model

Thomas John Hastings

WILLIAM B. EERDMANS PUBLISHING COMPANY
GRAND RAPIDS, MICHIGAN / CAMBRIDGE, U.K.

Published 2007 by
Wm. B. Eerdmans Publishing Co.
2140 Oak Industrial Drive N.E., Grand Rapids, Michigan 49505 /
P.O. Box 163, Cambridge CB3 9PU U.K.

Printed in the United States of America

-12 11 10 09 08 07   7 6 5 4 3 2 1

Library of Congress Cataloging-in-Publication Data

Hastings, Thomas John.
    Practical theology and the one body of Christ: toward a missional-ecumenical model /
    Thomas John Hastings.
        p.   cm.   — (Studies in practical theology)
    Includes bibliographical references.
    ISBN 978-0-8028-1760-0 (pbk.: alk. paper)
    1. Missions — Theory.   2. Theology, Practical.   I. Title.

BV2063.H37 2007
266.001 — dc22

                                                  2006039452

www.eerdmans.com

Contents

Series Foreword

In many countries around the world practical theology is gaining a new shape. It is stepping out of the shadow of being viewed only as the application of findings and guidelines developed by the so-called foundational theological disciplines of exegetical, historical, and systematic theology. Rather, the new practical theology is reminding all of theology of its practical nature, just as many of the great theologians of the past, from Augustine to Martin Luther and beyond, were in fact practical theologians.

In addition to the claim that all theology is practical, this movement is also asserting that practical theology is an academic discipline of its own and that its nature does not consist in merely being applied exegesis, dogmatics, or theological ethics, although it fully realizes the importance of its relation to these disciplines. This new identity of practical theology is not limited to a particular school of theology or to a particular country. Rather, practical theology has become the focus of an emerging international discussion that can be understood only by taking into account the various contributions from many countries and continents — North America, Europe, South America, Africa, and Asia.

Practical theology is a theoretical undertaking that builds on a practical basis. Although this discipline has much to learn from reflective practitioners — and in some of its forms actually begins with questions, problems, and descriptions from the field of religious practice — it is not an academic discipline to be identified solely with the processes going on in the field of religious practice nor with strategies and methods of stimulating these processes. The academic discipline of practical theology is a theory of the epistemological foundations, ethical norms, and general strategies of religious praxis in its various contexts. As a discipline, it should not be confused with the praxis itself, although it is highly relevant to all actual religious practice.

Practical theology should be understood as an empirically descriptive and critically constructive theory of religious practice. The empirical and descriptive dimension, which is pursued in close cooperation with other disciplines in the field of cultural studies, prevents practical theology from wishful speculative thinking and contributes to empirical theory building. The critical and constructive dimension, which is aimed at evaluating and improving the existing forms of religious practice, prevents practical theology from empiricism or positivism and contributes to a theology of transformation in the name of true religion.

Within the empirically descriptive and critically constructive framework of practical theology, religious practice may be studied on three different levels: with reference to society and culture, with reference to the church, and with reference to the individual. Christianity is not limited to the church, and practical theology should not be limited to a clerical paradigm. Its threefold focus is on ecclesial practices, on religious aspects of culture and society, and on the religious dimensions of individual life, including the interrelatedness of all three. Consequently, this series includes major pieces of work in all fields of practical theology, with an emphasis on the emerging international discussion.

The editors of this series are delighted to bring to publication Thomas Hastings' *Practical Theology and the One Body of Christ*. Although the Studies in Practical Theology Series has published authors from different parts of the world, this is the first book that takes the new practical theology discussion directly into the field of missions. Japan is the scene of the story. Religious education is the practical theology specialty at the center of the story. But the book is about the worldwide issues that Christianity faces as it confronts new cultures, thrives in some, withers in others, and struggles to find itself within the forces of modernization. Hastings calls his approach a "missional-ecumenical mode."

This book brings the best of the new practical theology to bear on the field of missions, presents telling critiques of past work, and opens new horizons worth studying by both those who venture into new cultures with their Christian witness and those who stay at home. In the end, the missional-ecumenical mode is relevant for both home and abroad.

Don Browning
James Fowler
Friedrich Schweitzer
Johannes van der Ven
Series Editors

Acknowledgments

This book is based on my doctoral dissertation, which I defended at Princeton Theological Seminary in December 2003. I first entertained the fantasy of doing doctoral studies as an undergraduate at Boston College when my beloved mentor, Dr. Adele Dalsimer, tried to convince me that I had a gift for reading Irish poetry. However, instead of continuing in graduate school, I met Carol, got married, and joined the Peace Corps. The next time I gave serious consideration to the terminal degree was at Wheaton College Graduate School when Dr. Lonna Dickerson, another supportive professor, suggested I apply to the University of Illinois for a program in linguistics. When my close friend Gabriel died soon after returning home to Nigeria to teach in a seminary, Carol and I opted to go to Japan as missionaries instead of pursuing doctoral studies at that juncture. After attending Princeton Theological Seminary as a special student from 1991 to 1992, my advisor Dr. James Loder suggested I should return to do the doctorate as soon as I had a chance. That chance finally came in the fall of 2000 due to the generous support of the Worldwide Ministries Division of the Presbyterian Church (U.S.A.), Tokyo Union Theological Seminary, and Princeton Theological Seminary. With recommendations from Dr. Loder and Dr. Richard Osmer, I enrolled as a Ph.D. student, finished my coursework in three semesters, took comps, wrote the proposal, and did the basic research for this dissertation before returning to Tokyo Union Theological Seminary (where I have taught since 1995) for the fall semester, 2002.

First and foremost, I want to express my deep gratitude to Dr. Loder who, in addition to challenging me to think with theological and scientific clarity, had a gift for being fully attentive to his students and the Holy Spirit at the same time. Just a few days before his sudden death in November 2001, he called me into his office and said he wanted to discuss my dissertation. After I rambled on for a few minutes about my tentative plans, he turned and gently encouraged me: "Focus, Tom!" Since I had to write while teaching a full course load at Tokyo Union, that simple advice turned out to be exactly what I needed. I also want to thank Dr. Osmer for his wise and faithful guidance. He granted me the freedom to frame and develop my ideas while checking to make sure I did not go too far afield. I am also deeply grateful to Dr. Andrew Walls, who taught me more about historical research in one semester than I had learned in many years of history courses in university, graduate school, and seminary. I want to express a special thanks to Ajit Prasadam, general secretary of the India Sunday School Union, my constant friend and conversation partner during our doctoral residency. Finally, I know that I could never have done this without the loving support and patience of Carol and our four children, Rose, Paul, Sarah, and Katie. I dedicate this book to my father-in-law, mentor, and friend, the late Rev. William Gray Tolley (PTS class of 1955).

CHAPTER ONE

Introduction

In practical theology the disciplines that will help us understand human action must be put into a constructive relationship with the disciplines that enable us to understand who God is from God's self-disclosure. The systematic task of practical theology, then, is to preserve the integrity of such disciplines and . . . relate them so as to gain a more comprehensive understanding of the phenomenon in question than any one such discipline may be able to provide by itself. At the same time, such a relation should enrich both sides of this interdisciplinary endeavor.

JAMES E. LODER,
"Normativity and Context in Practical Theology"

The Cultural Captivity of Contemporary North American Practical Theology

In the wake of the modern encyclopedic splitting of *theologia* into discrete and increasingly autonomous academic disciplines, the question of the interdisciplinary relation between the non-theological and theological disciplines has been a particularly vexing issue for practical theology.[1] While the distinctive epistemic traditions that have emerged within modern biblical studies, church history, and systematic or dogmatic theology necessarily manifest variable degrees of academic interdisciplinarity (i.e., between theology and philology, archeology, linguistics, literature, historical studies, philosophy, psychology, sociology, anthropology, etc.), practical theology has become

1

particularly sensitized to the interdisciplinary problematic since this branch of the theological encyclopedia must, by definition, devise coherent methodologies for negotiating the complex trafficking between modes of rationality pertaining to both theoretical and practical domains of understanding and action. By contrast, interdisciplinarity in modern biblical, historical, and systematic theology may legitimately be, and in fact often has been, restricted to the level of theory alone.

In other words, while scholars in the three so-called "foundational" theological disciplines may, according to personal persuasion, ignore or express a passing or genuine interest in contemporary ecclesial or trans-ecclesial fields of Christian practice, practical theologians must carefully consider both the best past and present theories and practices concerning worshiping, preaching, catechizing, caring, serving, evangelizing, etc., always with an eye toward better guiding the ongoing understanding and performance of these actions within a particular social, political, and cultural context. Because practical theology must traverse both epistemic fields of theory and practice, the issue of interdisciplinarity can never be adequately resolved in either a purely theoretical or purely practical mode of rationality. In order to continue being both practical and theological, this discipline must intentionally engage in dialogue with biblical, historical, or systematic theology as well as a wide range of non-theological disciplines. In short, practical theologians cannot circumvent the complex relations between ecclesial or trans-ecclesial Christian practice and theoretical (theological and non-theological) reflection.

The need for a careful integration of theory and practice at the core of this discipline requires practical theologians to consider and relate theoretical and empirical factors at every turn in their specific investigations. This daunting task is easier said than done. As I will attempt to show below, the kind of disciplinary integration required by practical theology has been unwittingly but seriously undermined by the culturally specific modes of rationality that have dominated the modern West. Given this particular cultural milieu, it is not surprising that Western practical theologians in the twentieth century have often given in to the temptation to opt for theory over practice or practice over theory. Epistemologically, placing theory over practice or practice over theory tends to undermine a holistic grasp of the phenomenon under investigation. The ongoing intellectual struggle between analytical/dualistic and synthetic/unitary (not monistic) modes of thought is by no means unique to practical theology, nor is it new in the history of the Christian church. In fact, this dilemma is probably an inevitable outcome of serious engagement with the radical universalism (catholicity) of the Christian message within the strict limitations of social, political, and cultural existence.

To illustrate this dilemma, it seems helpful to draw an analogy between the practical theological temptation to choose theory over practice or practice over theory and the Trinitarian and Christological debates of the first centuries of the Christian church. Theory-centered practical theologians who take inadequate notice of actual cases of Christian praxis easily err in the direction of what may be called a transcendent idealism analogous to the various forms of gnosticism that attended the spread of the gospel. Conversely, practice-centered practical theologians who focus only on certain instantiations of Christian praxis easily err in the direction of what may be called an immanent realism analogous to Arianism. Just as the theological grammar of the Nicene *homoousion* or the Chalcedonian *hypostasis* emerged from the missional tension between the biblical and apostolic witness to Jesus as the Christ and the reigning modes of thought, feeling, and action in the Greco-Roman culture, a parallel tension is necessarily recapitulated every time Christians wrestle with the core problematic of the gospel within the rational, affective, and volitional limitations of their particular culture.[2] While few today would dispute the assertion that practical theologians must be conversant with both theology and actual ecclesial and trans-ecclesial situations of Christian practice, I want to show that such interdisciplinary correlations between theoretical and empirical dimensions of knowledge have become particularly problematic in the modern West since the rejection of metaphysical certainty and our subsequent turn to the autonomous human subject as the primary or even sole locus of knowing.[3]

In this book, I will begin by showing how certain stubborn and theologically problematic Western cultural norms have tended to dominate this field. Further, I will argue that practical theologians who are personally engaged in intercultural praxis and reflection are more likely to have some of their own controlling tacit cultural norms exposed for critical, interdisciplinary reflection. In support of these two conclusions, I will present a two-tiered argument involving (1) a critical exploration of three leading contemporary North American models of practical theology; and (2) a case study of Tamura Naomi (1858-1934), a first-generation Japanese Protestant pastor and pioneer in the field of religious education. Because of both his local (missional) and cross-cultural (ecumenical) engagement in Japan and North America, Tamura's case offers a very different perspective on the religious education movement from the story commonly recounted by practical theologians in North America or Europe.[4] This alternative narrative may be instructive for contemporary North American Protestant practical theologians who are beginning to take seriously the question of the mission of congregations who increasingly feel marginalized within their own social, political, and cultural situations.

For the sake of clarity, I will set out my approach in the first chapter in outline form here. Drawing on Richard Osmer's "consensus model" which describes practical theological models in terms of four core tasks *(descriptive, interpretive, norms of practice,* and *rules of art)*, I begin by teasing out some of the governing epistemological, theological, and ecclesiological "norms of practice" guiding three leading North American approaches to this field as well as exploring some of the positive intradisciplinary developments that attempt to overcome the limits of some of these norms.[5] Firstly, in dialogue with James Fowler's article "Practical Theology and Theological Education: Some Models and Questions,"[6] I explore the norms informing the *critical theoretic correlations*[7] model. Fowler's article presents a serious and largely unanswered challenge to the leading representatives of this model. Secondly, I consider Rebecca Chopp's article "Practical Theology and Liberation"[8] as a good example of a *critical praxis correlations*[9] model. As an attempt at intradisciplinary development, Chopp criticizes the *critical theoretic correlationalists* and tries to expand the investigatory horizon of practical theology by privileging the praxis of oppressed communities. Thirdly, I introduce the *transformational*[10] model outlined in James E. Loder's article "Normativity and Context in Practical Theology."[11] Reformulating the core problematic of the entire discipline, Loder constructs an interdisciplinary approach grounded in theological rather than philosophical discourse that tries to overcome some of the limitations of both correlational models. I spend the most time on Loder since I believe that his theologically oriented approach has the greatest potential for moving this discipline forward in an intercultural direction. Finally, I will draw some initial conclusions based on this discussion and conclude by making the charge that, in spite of their differing approaches to practical theology, these theorists show little or no consciousness of the missional task or ecumenical makeup of the Christian church.

The Critical Theoretic Correlational Model

Following his publication of several initial articles and books on his theory of faith development,[12] James Fowler has been a major influence on developments in the practical theological field of Christian religious education since the mid-1970s.[13] After enjoying a wide-ranging, but by no means universal reception of his own theory,[14] Fowler wrote a thought-provoking and self-critical article in 1985 in which he reflected on the state of the field of practical theology. First, he offers the following four positive points of convergence found in the work of certain leading North American theorists (Edward

Farley, David Tracy, Don Browning, and Fowler himself) within the emerging academic discussion of practical theology: (1) a dialectical approach to the theory-practice relation; (2) an implicit "concept of truth as both dialectical and emergent"; (3) a sophisticated hermeneutical orientation to methodology; and (4) an interest in personal and social transformation.[15] Fowler briefly examines the work of each of these leading theorists and places them all under Matthew Lamb's *critical theoretic correlations* rubric.[16]

He then points out the following "two deep sources of concern and reservation" regarding these leading approaches to practical theology: (1) their failure to account for divine agency; and (2) their imprisonment in an Enlightenment rationality. Fowler explains what he means by his first reservation.

> There is no clear affirmation or examination of the priority and objectivity of divine initiative as the ground, the tendency, and the backdrop of situations of contemporary interpretation and response. This omission results in a subtle but dangerous tendency to abstract from actual contexts and issues of praxis, and from risky correlative existential-historical interpretation of the dialectic of divine and human action, and to focus instead on meta-theoretical issues of method.[17]

While exempting his own positive attempts to embrace both theological (i.e., H. R. Niebuhr and Paul Tillich) and social science (i.e., Piaget, Kohlberg, etc.) resources and norms in his own work, Fowler accuses the other three leading theorists of failing to offer "what we might call a critical and correlational 'theory of divine praxis.'"[18]

On the one hand, while this seems a grave indictment of the "norms of practice" in a discipline which is by definition theological, the failure of these practical theologians to seriously tackle the issue of divine agency may be understood as a natural reflection of the tacit cultural assumptions adhered to within their various North American universities. I deliberately use the phrase "tacit cultural assumptions" here because, in spite of the modern Western quest for the holy grail of some non-contingent, objective universality in the construction of theories, the pre-reflective *habitus* that infuses the cultural location of any theorist clearly exerts a strong, even if not determinative influence on his or her mode of investigation.[19] As Fowler rightly suspects, even those modes of rationality that are the most scrupulously refined by post-Kantian epistemologies can never completely transcend the contingencies of a particular cultural context.[20]

When he turns to his second charge of a captivity to an Enlightenment epistemology, Fowler does not exempt his own theory of faith development.

He composes a satirical rhetorical triad about *reason trying to conquer reason by reason* to underline his own frustration with the degree to which these North American university-based practical theologians appear to be caught in a closed-circuited modernist epistemology. "Most fundamentally, I believe, these theologies remain trapped in a dialectic in which critical reason tries to overcome the limits of critical reasoning by the mediation of reason alone."[21] Drawing on Johann Baptist Metz's trenchant critique of the "middle-class citizen" birthed by the Enlightenment, Fowler details this second criticism.

> The indictments represent the endpoint of a line of reasoning that goes, in extremely abbreviated form, something like this: (1) The Enlightenment gave rise to the creation of a new human self-image and reality — the self-critical epistemological (and axiological) *Subject.* (2) Correlative with and fundamental to this new self-image are critical reason and volitional autonomy. (3) Reason, in service of responsible freedom, is taken to be the prime mediator of the Subject's relations to tradition, to human relations, and to the claims of ethical and religious ultimacy. (4) Severed from the possibility of metaphysical knowledge, critical reason learned to approach truth by the rational, transcendental establishment of *method.* (5) Method, primarily hermeneutic in character, then, becomes the fulcrum on which the lever of interpretation can rest, and it becomes the arbiter of the interpretation of tradition, of the present situation, and of actors' self-other understandings.[22]

In an essay that traces the evolution of the modernist epistemology from Descartes, Newton, and Kant, T. F. Torrance further nuances Fowler's critique in his description of what he calls the "constructivist mentality" of the modern mind which assumes (1) "the transfer of intelligibility to the human (a priori) pole of the knowing relation" and (2) "the rise and development of the masterful idea that we can understand only what we can construct for ourselves."[23]

While Fowler unfortunately does not ponder the close, if not causal relation between his "two deep sources of concern and reservation," one might legitimately wonder how he might ever expect to find any "critical and correlational theory of divine praxis" when the so-called "Enlightenment rationality" *ipso facto* presumes an unbridgeable breach between God and the world. In other words, how could Fowler expect insights about God's interaction with human beings from university-situated practical theologians whose culture of belonging is highly suspicious of any theological assumption or conviction? Especially in light of his own positive attempts to describe the interaction of human and divine praxis in and beyond his work on faith development theory, one might expect Fowler to be even more critical and ask whether or not the reticence of Farley, Tracy, and Browning on the topic of divine agency may be an outcome of their captivity to the modernist epistemology and axiology.

Reinhard Hütter neatly summarizes the two characteristic modernist modes of thinking discernible in the work of the practical theologians Fowler criticizes. On the one hand, we find Schleiermacher's post-Kantian theology in which "There may be intimation of the divine as poietically construed by pious consciousness, but there is no genuine knowledge of God."[24] On the other hand, we find the Hegelian conflation, within the epistemic field of the human spirit, of the distinction between Creator and creation. Here, "There is a knowledge of a 'God,' who has essentially ceased to be God."[25] Referring to Robert Jenson's article titled "How the World Lost Its Story," Barry Harvey similarly says that modernity tried to preserve a "universal story without a universal storyteller."[26]

> In short, the project that is the modern world sought to sustain its inherited faith in a narratable world while at the same time withdrawing allegiance from "the God who was that faith's object" (Jenson 1993:21). The understanding of the limits of knowledge, the humility that must accompany the quest for truth, also went by the wayside in this new, brave universe.[27]

In addressing biblical and systematic theologians who more or less share the same *field-limiting epistemic conditions* as the practical theologians Fowler criticizes, T. F. Torrance charges that modernity's critical mode of rationality has underwritten "a fatal deistic disjunction between God and the world."

> Yet it is, strangely, some notion of non-cognitive revelation, and correspondingly of non-cognitive faith, deeply embedded in their presuppositions, that appears to govern the approach of many contemporary scholars and theologians, reflecting a *fatal deistic disjunction between God and the world* that does not allow for any real Word of God to cross the gulf between God and the creature or therefore to permit man in space and time any real knowledge of God as he is in himself. Since it declines to accept any objectively grounded revelation of God or any knowledge of God objectively grounded in himself, biblical and theological interpretation of this kind is regularly trapped within the fallacies of socio-cultural relativism and linguistic nominalism. (italics mine)[28]

Torrance makes a strong case that, in the post-Einsteinian scientific world, this radically dualistic frame of mind is being overturned in favor of a more unitary approach. He also charges that theologians and those in the humanities and social sciences have been slow to respond to this fundamental shift in thinking. I will return to this issue later.

While a more detailed examination of the cultural assumptions shared by the practical theologians Fowler criticizes is beyond the scope of this book, a summary of the norms that have allowed these theologians to maintain a quiet niche within some North American research universities would include the following three: (1) the acceptance of a stark, if not absolute analytical distantiation between *the individual theorist-as-subject* and *contexts of practice-as-object;* (2) the acceptance of dualistic modes of modern theological discourse (i.e., *Geschichte* vs. *Historie, kerygma* vs. *didache,* the Jesus of history vs. the Christ of faith, etc.); and (3) the acceptance of a non-cognitive, existential, or experiential-expressivist[29] view of revelation and faith. Taken together, these "tacit cultural assumptions" virtually necessitate the silence of these practical theologians on the key question of divine agency. Thus, what Fowler calls their "dangerous tendency" to focus on abstract issues of methodology is a logical consequence of accepting the critical norms that infuse their community of belonging. If the suspicions and critiques of Fowler, Hütter, Jenson, Harvey, and Torrance are accurate, making positive theological statements about the agency of God in the practices of the contemporary church would be suicidal for practical theologians within the halls of many modern universities, where self-censorship on such questions is a virtual requirement of faculty membership.

The Critical Praxis Correlational Model

Next, by turning to an example of what we might expect to be a more epistemically and ecumenically open-ended approach to practical theology, I want to suggest that the critical issues that worry Fowler are not limited to the exemplars of the *critical theoretic correlational* methodology.[30] Rebecca Chopp's article entitled "Practical Theology and Liberation" is a fine example of Lamb's *critical praxis correlational* model. The key distinction between Chopp and the thinkers Fowler examines is an ideologically informed shift from a theory-normed to a praxis-normed approach to correlation. She begins her article by critiquing the theoretical correlationalists, whom she calls "liberal revisionists," charging that their mode of rationality ignores and even excludes the situations of concrete praxis of liberation theologians, critical theorists, and feminists like Chopp herself.

This liberal-revisionist response to critiques such as mine reveals two important presuppositions of the revised correlation approach to practical theology: (1) that there is a progression in the hierarchy of order from fundamental through systematic to practical theology, and (2) that the congregation has some privileged primacy for correcting the errors of theologians.[31]

The first criticism ("progression in the hierarchy of order") is aimed most clearly at David Tracy's neo-Schleiermacherian parsing of the theological encyclopedia[32] but also, by extension, may include Fowler's invariant stage theory of faith development or Groome's shared-praxis model of religious education. For Chopp, such hierarchical, structuralist, and ontological approaches are not only a legacy of the Enlightenment epistemology but they also reflect the deeply entrenched Western political *habitus* of male domination.

In her second criticism, Chopp refers specifically to Dudley's case study of Wiltshire United Methodist Church[33] to expose some of the unexamined sociocultural presuppositions behind what she calls the liberal-revisionist "subtle romanticization of the congregation."[34] Referring to the conspicuous disconnect that members of that "liberal congregation" experience between the categories of Christian religious and secular languages, she offers a trenchant critical description of Wiltshire's thorough enculturation in a secularized, middle-class, North American subculture.

> Theologians will discover no magic formulas, different questions, or naïve religious experience in this congregation: indeed the Wiltshire case is enough to convince anyone that secularized culture, privatized religion, and the crisis of truth, meaning, and meaningfulness of religious language is the burden not only of modern theologians but also many congregational participants. The issue, then, is not that theology should be related in closer fashion to the church; this solution tries to reverse the first presupposition about the hierarchical order of theology. Rather, the problem lies on another level, for both the church and theology find it difficult to speak of God in a society whose ideology and politics demand strict adherence to secularistic language that places experiences such as religion on the margins of public life in the realm of the private. As the voices of liberation theology will soon suggest to us, liberal-revisionist theology and the modern church are manifestations of their culture, twin manifestations that disclose the constitution of Christianity in bourgeois society as individualistic, existentialistic, and privatistic.[35]

Chopp is surely correct to point out that an "individualistic, existentialistic, and privatistic" *habitus* characterizes the cultures of congregations like Wiltshire and the guild of North American practical theologians who study them. Fowler's references to Metz show that he, too, is sensitive to the charge of a tacit middle-class politics. Chopp is also right to charge that, because such congregations and the middle-class practical theologians who examine them share the same tacit sociocultural values, it is patently disingenuous for them to think they will discover anything beyond felicitous attestation of their theories by focusing on such congregations. While I do not want to deny the value of empirical congregational studies, especially when they are conducted across a broad spectrum of the *ecumene,* her point, that this kind of congregational navel gazing is a failed attempt to compensate for the problematic hierarchical assumptions of the field, is particularly persuasive. While she does not adequately consider the implications of this important critique, Chopp's suspicions of practical theologians who privilege the local congregation point helpfully to the need for a broad ecumenical ecclesiology that seriously takes into account the local variations in Christian understanding and practice.

Unfortunately, while she seeks to replace the middle-class, "universal" "cognitive claims" of liberal-revisionism with what she sees as the broader, open-ended, emancipatory praxis of certain marginalized "victims of history," Chopp also unwittingly reflects the same middle-class epistemology she criticizes in the liberal-revisionists. Just like the practical theologians whom Fowler criticizes, Chopp also seems to "find it difficult to speak of God," failing to offer any account whatsoever for divine initiative. She fails to draw upon a single biblical or theological norm (even liberation theology's vision of the kingdom of God). Does she really imagine that Latin American communities of faith are somehow free from the deep tensions between their own kinds of cultural captivity and their understanding of the gospel? In terms of Osmer's consensus model, Chopp wants to shift the "norms of practice" for practical theology from the rarified deliberations of middle-class academia and their affiliated congregations to those social and political contexts that oppress certain groups of people. In place of theorizing in ivory towers, what "ought" to be going on is political struggle on the ground.

Tragically, the only alternative "norms of practice" she offers for overcoming the faults she finds with the liberal-revisionists is an alternative philosophical accounting for ecclesial praxis. In place of Kant, Schleiermacher, and Hegel, she draws on "contemporary retrievals of Aristotle and Marx,"[36] and in place of middle-class congregations, she privileges the economically oppressed Latin American "base communities" which are far removed from her own sociocultural location as a feminist practical theologian working within a North American academic institution. Thus, in spite of its promise of a more liberating ecumenicity, Chopp's critique amounts to an idealization of distant, victimized communities.

Though Chopp helpfully expands the locus of theoretical authority from the individual reflections of academic practical theologians and middle-class congregations to include communities of the marginalized, she is by no means free of the Enlightenment rationality Fowler decries in himself and his peers. Her "praxis" approach is also thoroughly normed by the modernist epistemological hesitancy to posit any "theory of divine praxis."[37] This again shows the deep mutual relation between the epistemological and theological questions raised by Fowler. On both accounts, she exemplifies the same abstract middle-class rationality she criticizes in her opponents. This example illustrates James E. Loder's statement that practical theological approaches "that are non-theological in their baseline do not meet the central problematic of the field and present, thereby, a displacement of practical theology from its theological center."[38] While pointing to the need for practical theologians to consider the broader *ecumene*, Chopp's approach fails to challenge the anti-theological bias of the North American university.

In addition to Fowler's two reservations, I have made the further claim that both of these approaches to practical theology strongly reflect the tacit intellectual *habitus* of the North American university. This charge of cultural captivity is brought into clearer relief when we consider how these two seemingly different practical theological approaches actually view the Christian church in strikingly similar ways. While the *theoretic correlationalists* tend to focus on middle-class North Americans in their empirical case studies, the *praxis correlationalists* focus on the practice of politically and economically marginalized faith communities. In other words, by riveting their empirical or ideological gaze on relatively homogeneous Christian communities, neither group exhibits any consciousness of the theological import of the staggering cultural diversity of the contemporary global *ecumene*. I have also charged that the catastrophic equivocation of both groups on the question of divine agency is a logical consequence of the epistemological fracture that occurred in the foundations of Western thought beginning with the scientific revolution of the sixteenth century. In this book, I will try to show how a broader intercultural appreciation of the Christian churches and a post-critical epistemology that takes serious account of the contingency of the created order may greatly enrich this discipline.

From this admittedly limited analysis of these models, it seems that both the *critical theoretic* and *critical praxis correlational* approaches to practical theology have been unable to overcome the specific cultural *habitus* of contemporary North American academia wherein interdisciplinary methodologies that treat theological questions are only deemed legitimate when carefully transposed into inoffensive philosophical terms. As examples of this tacit *tertium quid* methodology, Loder lists the existentialism of Tillich, the phenomenology of Farley, the cultural-linguistic approach of Lindbeck, the structuralism of Fowler, the ontological approach of Groome, and the process approach of Browning.[39] If, as I have charged, such models reflect the local cultural bias, or what Loder calls the *ethos*[40] of the North American academy, how can they speak authentically to situations of Christian practice in non-Western cultures? I will return to this important question in Chapter Two.

The Transformational Model

Since his own work attempts to consider both theological and epistemological questions at every turn, I will now introduce the transformational model of James E. Loder by referring to one of his most sophisticated descriptions of that model in a paper entitled "Normativity and Context in Practical Theology." At the outset, I want to say that I have some serious, lingering questions about Loder's approach which I will address later. I will begin, however, with a positive evaluation of how his transformational model seriously wrestles with theology and epistemology without seeking refuge in some repristinated premodern mode of rationality.

In this paper, Loder sets out, in characteristically ironic and paradoxical Kierkegaardian fashion, to completely shift the disciplinary focus of practical theology. Instead of entering into the endless disputes about the relative priority of *theoria* or *praxis* that leave little or no place for theological questions, Loder proposes a complete figure-ground reversal that brings theological confession into the very center of practical theological reflection, without diminishing in any way the importance of questions posed by the human sciences. In essence, in a move that attempts to be faithful to the biblical witness and, in some ways, deliberately flies in the face of the modernist epistemology described above, he sets out to positively relate the epistemological question to the theological grammar of the Christian gospel.

Repudiating the view of practical theology as a discipline that sets its gaze primarily on "how to" issues of application, Loder begins this key paper by stating that the core issue for practical theology "is not in its practices, congregations, or functions, but in why these, and related phenomena, are a problem."[41] In terms of Osmer's "consensus model," Loder's model begins with a bold interpretive move, based on his own convictions about the field's proper "norms of practice," in shifting the main emphasis from "how" to "why" questions. His proposed solution to this "why" problematic intentionally pushes the boundaries of practical theology to include intentional reflection on the field of divine and human reality that the ecumenical churches (Roman Catholic, Orthodox, and Protestant) confess as cohering in the one person of Jesus Christ.[42] For Loder, inasmuch as the Christian churches continue to confess Jesus Christ as the paradigmatic case in which human and divine existence and action are perfectly correlated under the limitations of space and time, the "why" questions in practical theology are far more consequential than the "how" questions.

Loder states his own solution to the discipline's core problematic with an elegant simplicity that bears the marks of deep contemplation. "Such phenomena combine two incongruent, qualitatively distinct realities, the Divine and the human, in congruent forms of action."[43] Loder's formula reflects his conviction that all proposals in this field must be constructed and evaluated in intentional conversation with both the divine and human realities upon which they claim to reflect. By proposing a more intentionally theological and therefore open-ended approach to this field, he seeks to subvert the closed epistemology of *reason trying to overcome reason by reason* descried by Fowler. Put another way, for Christian practical theological theories to claim to be theological as well as practical, Loder insists they must seriously consider the "ultimate paradox" of the union of divine and human being and action in the person of Jesus Christ.

In place of purely critical, transcendental, *a priori* modes of thinking that are, in Fowler's terms, "severed from the possibility of metaphysical knowledge" and consequently centered on "meta-theoretical issues of method" or *praxis,* Loder proposes a post-critical, *a posteriori* mode of practical theological thinking that foregrounds the "incongruent and qualitatively distinct realities" of God and humanity without dismissing the relative importance of issues of methodology and actual situations of Christian practice. Loder's figure-ground reversal significantly ups the ante of what is at stake in practical theology by opening the door to the free, sovereign working of the Spirit of the Triune God, revealed in the person of Jesus Christ, within the limited conditions of space and time. In effect, it is a solution which is also a non-solution in that it grants central place to the mediation of divine agency within the multiple spheres of Christian practice upon which practical theological reflection revolves.[44]

Since practical theology must propose rational theories of action that describe the divine and human dynamics of Christian formation and transformation and suggest "rules of art" that sponsor and guide the ecclesial and trans-ecclesial practices of formation and transformation, Loder insists that those approaches that conflate the necessarily open-ended tensions between theology and the human sciences, in favor of either "field of reality," are *ipso facto* inadequate.[45] By positing a mutually constructive interdisciplinary relationality, Loder seeks to overcome these either/or solutions.

Loder's proposal attempts to bring "theology and the human sciences into a transformational interaction." Of this approach, Osmer says, "Here, theology and its non-theological dialogue partners are conceptualized as standing in an asymmetrical bipolar unity that is analogous to the Christological formulations of the Council of Chalcedon."[46] Loder carefully describes what he intends by the cryptic term "asymmetrical bipolar unity."

> where human science understandings (or their equivalents) negate the Divine reality, this negation is negated and these understandings are reappropriated in terms of cognate theological concepts; where theological concepts negate the legitimacy of human science insights as elements in the transformational interaction, this negation must also be negated. However, the direction of the transformational dynamic, manifesting its inherent spiritual quality, is always to establish a bipolar asymmetrical relational unity between the human science understanding and its more comprehensive theological cognate, thus reflecting the Chalcedonian model.[47]

In order to understand Loder's proposal, I must briefly introduce the work of T. F. Torrance and Michael Polanyi, two thinkers with whom he was in constant dialogue in his later work. While his proposal may appear at first glance to be an arbitrary theological *coup d'état,* Loder has no interest in trying to restore theology to its premodern status as the "queen of the sciences" or to reduce complex, contemporary scientific theories about the world and persons to theological categories. His proposal of a figure-ground reversal is, at heart, a serious attempt to overcome theological liberalism's "translation" approach[48] by also making the theological "field of reality" an explicit focus of practical theological deliberation from beginning to end. Even though Loder does not address the problem of natural theology directly, his transformational model is one of the first serious attempts to consider some of the implications of T. F. Torrance's post-Barthian reformulation of natural theology for practical theology.[49]

In order to show how Loder relies on Torrance, I need to touch upon how Torrance reconceives natural theology without losing Barth's radical emphasis on the otherness of God. First of all, Torrance is in full agreement with Barth's rejection of any *theologia naturalis* which is conceived of as a "revelation-independent" knowledge of God that is generically accessible to human reason.

> It seems evident, then, that Barth's opposition to the traditional type of natural theology, which is pursued as an independent system on its own, antecedent to positive or revealed theology, rests upon a radical rejection of its dualistic basis and constitutes a return to the kind of unitary thinking we find in classical Christian theology as exemplified by Athanasius, in which theology is committed to one coherent framework of thought that arises within the unitary interaction of God with our world in creation and incarnation, and in which we are unable to make any separation between a natural and a supernatural knowledge of God.[50]

Torrance's use of the phrases "unitary thinking," "coherent framework of thought," and "unitary interaction of God with our world in creation and incarnation" underlies his apologetic concern to overcome what he sees as the modern mind's capitulation to the above-mentioned "fatal deistic disjunction between God and the world."[51] Torrance reconceives of natural theology as that which is "*natural* both to theological and natural science" when both disciplines are comprehended "within their common sharing of the rational structures of space and time conferred on the universe by God in his creating of it, and within their common sharing in the basic conceptions of the unitary rationality of the universe, its contingent intelligibility and contingent freedom."[52]

While Torrance readily acknowledges that the investigational trajectories of science are distinct from those of theology, he also insists that both disciplines share the same key "field limitations" of the *unitary rationality of the universe,* its *contingent intelligibility,* and *contingent freedom.* Torrance tries to make the historical case that an understanding of these three pivotal limitations operative in both science and theology did not and could never have arisen independently either within Hebraic or Hellenistic culture. Rather, he claims that it was the early church's theological reflection on the incarnation of Jesus Christ the Son of God and the relation of that singular revelation to the Hebraic doctrine of Creation *ex nihilo* that provided the historical impulse for the rational, scientific investigation of the created universe. Under the weight of the Word becoming flesh, the world with all of its seemingly inexplicable quirks began to be seen as a field laden with immense exploratory potential and pointing contingently toward a mysterious but knowable ultimacy because the eternal Creator God had once entered into the conditions of space and time in the person of Jesus of Nazareth. According to Torrance, the consequences of this rational correlation between the doctrines of incarnation and creation were immense. Because the One God has entered the very space and time in which we live and has fully assumed our humanity in Jesus Christ, the "intelligible structures" of space and time have been decisively transformed and opened up to our rational minds to reveal their contingent intelligibility and freedom in relation to the Creator. In other words, in the vicarious humanity of Jesus Christ, actual knowledge of God has once and for all been communicated within the epistemic limits of human experience.

> If God is really God, the living Creator of us all, not only is he intelligibly accessible to our understanding but actively at work within the world in revealing himself in cognitive ways to those whom he has made for communion with himself.[53]

Torrance contrasts this approach which grounds our knowledge of God in the union of divine and human being and agency in Jesus Christ with modernist approaches to the New Testament witness which cut a deep gulf between our "knowledge" of God and knowledge of God in himself. Such reductionistic approaches leave us with what Torrance calls a

> non-cognitive revelation, detached from the intelligible structures and the objectivities of space and time within which the Word was made flesh in Jesus Christ. . . . Since it declines to accept any objectively grounded revelation of God or any knowledge of God objectively grounded in himself, biblical and theological interpretation of this kind is regularly trapped within the fallacies of socio-cultural relativism and linguistic nominalism.[54]

For Torrance, what is at stake here is nothing less than the truth claims of the gospel and whether or not the biblical writings can continue to be read as conveying any real word of God. Torrance strongly denounces the demythologizing, existentializing turn that biblical studies took with Bultmann. In place of this non-cognitive approach, he suggests what he claims is "a more scientific approach" to the relation between scripture and doctrine, proper for both biblical scholars and theologians, that "does not automatically exclude the ontological unity of form and being, or of structure and material content, in their investigation and interpretation of the Holy Scriptures."[55]

Torrance goes to great lengths to show how theology has been threatened in the ancient, medieval, and modern periods by a variety of philosophical dualisms that have, in one way or another, undermined this conviction of a unitary approach to theoretical and empirical knowledge.[56] Because Loder sees practical theology mired in precisely this kind of hopeless either/or debate about theory and practice, his transformational model insists on holding tenaciously onto both theoretical and empirical resources. Contrary to those approaches which are centered in either the *a priori* structures of the mind (à la Kant) or subjective religious experience (à la Schleiermacher), Torrance and Loder begin with the claim that the universe's order is grounded in the

> uncreated and creative Logos, in whose image, by the grace of God, we ourselves have been created, so that as we contemplate the rational order in the creation, we are directed above and beyond ourselves to the one God, the Lord of creation.[57]

Thus, Torrance rejects what he sees as the disastrous split in modernity between theoretical and practical knowledge and goes to great lengths to show how the emergence of scientific inquiry in the West is actually rooted in the early Christian struggle "to break through the pagan outlook upon the world with its identification of cosmology and theology, and often the identification of God and the world."[58] Again, according to Torrance, the key issue for the early church in its *pathic* intercultural, missional encounter with conflicting accounts of God and the world was how to give rational articulation to the relation between the doctrines of creation *ex nihilo* and incarnation.[59] Torrance asserts that the precarious history of the Nicene-Constantinopolitan formulation and reaffirmation of the *homoousion* had epochal public epistemological consequences, issuing in "a radical reconstruction of the foundations of ancient philosophy, science and culture."[60] He says that the *homoousion* shattered

> the dualistic structures of the ancient world, with their bifurcation between what is real and eternal and changeless and what is unreal, apparent, and evanescent. . . . There was a head-on clash at essential points in the basic structures of thought.[61]

The result of this clash was a unitary conception of the universe, where the intelligible order and freedom of creation is understood to be in contingent relationality to divine intelligibility and freedom.

This brings us to a core apologetic conviction that infuses Torrance's entire opus and is reflected in Loder's transformational proposal for the discipline of practical theology. Torrance and Loder[62] are convinced of a felicitous analogy between the unitary view of the universe constructed under the restraint of the truth of the gospel in the early church and the contemporary search in physics for a unified theory of the universe that was opened up, but not closed, by Einstein's theory of relativity. While his argument for a deeper dialogue between science and theology is resolutely theological, missiological, and apologetic, Torrance carefully resists the temptation of reducing theology to science or science to theology. Following Barth, Torrance and Loder are faithful to the Chalcedonian Christology which confesses Jesus Christ as "one person in two natures, without separation or division and without confusion or change." For Torrance and Loder, the divine/human relationality which coheres perfectly in Jesus Christ alone functions as the "constitutive" and "regulative" ground[63] for the analogy between natural science and theological science. In analogical relation to this mystery, the various spheres of rational investigation are reconceived within this deeper, more comprehensive unity without losing their individual integrity and distinctions.

> However we consider it, it seems clear that theological science and natural science operate within the medium of space and time, which are the bearers of contingent order or intelligibility in which all created realities share. Within that medium, natural science is concerned to explore the stratified structures of contingent existence, and theological science inquires of God their Creator who reveals himself through them.[64]

Beyond his basic theological position, Loder's proposal for practical theology also draws on Torrance's post-critical epistemology. In articulating the epistemology for theological science, Torrance says that science and theology share two basic criteria that he learned from his reading of Barth and Michael Polanyi. The first is the criterion of an *a posteriori objective realism*. In keeping with Barth, Torrance rejects all speculative attempts to get in front of, above, or behind the given "datum of revelation." While this realism or actualism is the point where Barth's theology appears to invite the charges of a "positivism, objectivism or foundationalism of revelation," Torrance defends this approach, with the help of Polanyi, as epistemologically more consonant with the methods of contemporary science. The key idea here is that each field of investigation must be known according to its own inherent intelligibility and not from any external, independent, or disinterested perspective.

Like Torrance, Loder believes that theology and human sciences share the same epistemic and linguistic limitations, meaning that theology has no intrinsic superiority, as one form of rational human expression, over the human sciences. However, as he learned from Torrance and Polanyi, the specific "objects" or "field of reality" under investigation in theology (God-world-humanity) and the human sciences (world-humanity), while overlapping at certain points, are also distinct in fundamental ways. Torrance describes this post-critical epistemology most clearly in *The Mediation of Christ.*

> We develop a form of inquiry in which we allow some field of reality to disclose itself to us in the complex of its internal relations or its latent structure, and thus seek to understand it in the light of its own intrinsic intelligibility or *logos*. As we do that we come up with a significant clue in the light of which all evidence is then reexamined and reinterpreted and found to fall into a coherent pattern of order. Thus we seek to understand something, not by schematising it to an external or alien framework of thought, but by operating with a framework of thought appropriate to it, one which it suggests to us out of its inherent constitutive relations and which we are rationally constrained to adopt in faithful understanding and interpretation of it.[65]

Seen in this way, the crucial determinative differences between theological and human science investigations do not lie in their ways of knowing and rational expression but in the specific, indeterminate "fields of reality" to which they turn their gaze (i.e., God-world-humanity vs. world-humanity).

According to Polanyi's post-critical view of personal knowing, all serious inquiry, whether in science or theology, requires that a self-involved investigator or community of investigators wait patiently for the "field of reality" under examination to disclose how it is to be best known and described. Stated negatively, to hastily claim either to know or describe some "field of reality" in categories that are foreign to the "intrinsic intelligibility or *logos*" of that field, as when theology imposes its own *logos* on the human sciences or vice versa, cannot contribute to the advancement of knowledge within or between cognate fields. In other words, the theologian, like the scientist, must resist the temptation to impose some alien theory or frame of reference onto the field under investigation. Torrance sees Barth as a towering exemplar of this *a posteriori objective realism.*[66]

The second shared epistemological criterion in science and theology, which Loder also picked up from Polanyi and Torrance, is what may be called the *pathic self-investment of indwelling.*[67] Loder and Torrance subscribe to Polanyi's view that all instances of human knowing are self-investing and therefore necessarily involve tacit, affective, and fiduciary dimensions.[68] Because the self-disclosure of the "object" always exercises a primary, marginal control in any epistemic event, there is an inescapable dimension of *pathos*, in the sense of an "undergoing," "suffering," or "bearing with" on the part of the serious inquirer which cannot be circumvented on the way to new discovery and insight.[69] In other words, the *inherent constitutive relations* which pertain within each investigational field of reality can only be carefully teased out by means of this participatory form of knowing. This view, of course, flies in the face of the modernist presupposition of a necessary distantiation between *the subject as investigator* and *the object as investigated.*

The pathic self-investment of indwelling* is the disposition of one who has freely submitted himself or herself in service to some indeterminate "field of reality" which, because of the dynamics of freedom and contingency, is always open to be more fully known and described. Characterized by trust, risk, testing *(tentatio)*, meditative patience, and intuitive alertness, pathic knowing events necessarily embrace the entire epistemic repertory of cognition, affect, and action. This disposition is evident in the work of both theologians and scientists who approach their inquiries with an attitude of passionate and attentive receptivity, conscious that the in-breaking of new insight and discovery is contingent upon the field's self-disclosure of its own inherent intelligibility or *logos*. This disposition is an essential element of Loder's proposal for a figure-ground reversal in practical theology.

> Because this problematic (the above stated "why" issue) implies an inclusive theory of action, the articulation of any answer given must necessarily reflect in itself the substance of the answer given. A disengaged mind or a detached solution is thereby excluded. Addressing this problematic requires an interdisciplinary methodology that establishes a relationship between theology and the human sciences, and is, at the same time, self-involving.[70]

Having introduced Loder's basic position and his conversation partners, I will now turn to my critique. While Loder's proposal of a Christocentric, relational, and pathic view of interdisciplinarity offers a viable, nuanced, post-critical alternative to the dichotomous correlationalist preferences for either theory or praxis, his transformational model also unwittingly continues to reflect the local Enlightenment epistemology and undermines the witnesses of Christian scripture and theology on two key points which I will now address. *Firstly, in Loder's portrayal of the bipolar relationality of the human spirit and Holy Spirit, the experience of the discrete individual is portrayed, in spite of his many positive statements about the import of the ecclesia, as the primary epistemic sphere of Christ's redeeming and sancti-*

fying (transforming) work. On the one hand, Loder positively claims that the field "in which practical theology becomes most visible and manifest"[71] is the worshiping community of the church.

> The living centre of this field, as a discipline, is worship in which the methodology thus articulated is expressed in prayer and praise, and the liturgies of Word and Sacrament. Here the methodology is taken up into the reality from which it has arisen and toward which it points.[72]

On the other hand, there is a preponderance of examples that could be given of Loder's much stronger emphasis on the experience of the transformed individual. The following are two examples from the article I have been examining:

> When the human spirit is awakened and empowered by the Creator Spirit, the human intensity is transformed into Christ's passion for the world, and the human imagination becomes his vision of the world.[73]

> The dynamic relationality between *praxeis* and *theologia* is sustained by the Spiritual Presence of Christ working in and through the human spirit.[74]

What besides the discrete individual could possibly be intended by the term "human spirit"? This individualistic experientialism is in sharp contrast to the New Testament's overwhelming accent on the translocal and transtemporal "one body of Christ" as the locus of the ongoing mission of the Triune God.[75] Whereas Loder emphasizes the Spirit's recapitulation of Christ's benefits as taking place primarily within the consciousness of an awakened individual, Paul sees this recapitulation as taking place primarily within the eschatological communion of the "one body of Christ." In effect, by focusing on the subjective experience of the individual, Loder's masterful description of the logic of transformation reverses the biblical ordering of the *pro me* and *pro nobis* dimensions. This is not an insignificant theological problem.

Without denying the secondary or derivative importance of the *pro me* dimension of transformation in the Spirit, whenever it is portrayed as the primary epistemic sphere wherein Christians consciously experience or discern the mysterious workings of divine agency, a serious question mark is cast over what scripture portrays as the primary, corporate meaning and significance of the entire church within the mission of the Triune God. Torrance helps us clarify this important *pro nobis–pro me* ordering principle in the relation of Christ and the church and, by extension, the individual believer.

> That "great mystery," as Paul described it, of *the union between Christ and his Church is primarily and essentially corporate in nature*, but it applies to all individual members of his Body who are ingrafted into Christ by Baptism and continue to live in union with him as they feed upon his body and blood in Holy Communion. Since the Church is rooted in the hypostatic and atoning union embodied in the person of the mediator, the description of the Church as the Body of Christ is not a figurative way of speaking of some external moral union between believing people and Jesus Christ, but an expression of the ontological reality of the Church concorporate with Christ himself, who not only mediates reconciliation between man and God but constitutes and embodies it in his own divine-human Reality as Mediator.[76] (italics mine)

While Loder's five-step depiction of the logic of transformation is a brilliant theological interpretation of Dewey's scientific method,[77] when that logic is applied to the Christian experience of transformation in the Spirit of Christ, it dangerously obscures the decisive biblical accent on the community of faith as the primary participant in the ongoing *missio Dei*. While Loder was rightly challenging North American "mainline" Protestantism's tragic loss of the personal conviction of faith, gazing too intently at the *pro me* dimension can reduce the community and its core practices to little more than instrumental, and therefore ontologically inconsequential occasions for personal charismatic experience.

This individualistic experientialism is evident, for example, in Loder's problematic use of the classical mystical pattern of *awakening, purgation, illumination,* and *unification* to explicate the transformations he observed in the course of his counseling practice.[78] Here Loder ignores, for example, Barth's strong rejection of mysticism and the corresponding temporal sequencing expressed by the Protestant scholastic *ordo salutis (illuminatio, regeneratio, sanctificatio,* and *glorificatio)*. Barth rightly cautions that this kind of approach always has the regrettable effect of psychologizing the doctrine of sanctification into some theory of "steps" or "stages," and thereby undermining the once-and-for-all-ness proclaimed by scripture.[79]

Without wanting to discredit Loder's brilliant examination of psychospiritual development in *The Logic of the Spirit,* I believe that, by giving too much weight to the subjective, individual experience of transformation, he unwittingly obscures the biblical priority granted to the intercultural *ecclesia,* and not the discrete individual, as the decisive space-time participant in and witness to the ongoing mission of the Triune God. Further, and for contemporary Protestant theologians a bigger issue, by narrating individual transformational experience in terms of the classical mystical sequence, Loder sabotages the anthropology expressed by the *totus* and *simul* of Luther's *totus simul iustus et peccator*.[80] Isn't there a way to interpret transformational dynamics in conversation with a more biblical view of sanctification? In spite of his regular cautions about charismatic abuses or his often-expressed maxim that all transformational experiences of the Spirit properly "belong to the church," Loder's problematic view of the relation between the experience of the Christian individual and the community of faith does not seriously wrestle with the radical directionality of this relation in Paul or other New Testament writers.

In a discussion with Allen Verhey on the question of how the New Testament describes Christian ethical action, Richard Hays says,

> the NT does certainly offer moral exhortation and guidance for individuals. Nonetheless, I stand by the statement that the corporate obedience of the community is the primary concern of the NT writers. This concern differs so markedly from the usual individualistic assumptions of Western liberal culture that strongly worded guidelines are necessary in order to recall to us the NT's ecclesially oriented perspective.[81]

For those nurtured in modern Western culture who have never lived in a premodern "non-Western" society, it is admittedly a difficult if not impossible task to grasp that Paul and the other New Testament writers were nurtured within such a world. Since we all filter our reading of the biblical texts through our local cultural assumptions about the relation between persons and communities, we need the kinds of "strongly worded guidelines" Hays suggests.

For practical theologians who want their work to reflect a serious wrestling with the canonical texts of scripture as well as engagement with contemporary issues, such "strongly worded guidelines" are nowhere as desperately needed as on the issue of anthropology. In spite of the universalist presumptions of modern Western theories, the modernist anthropology has not unseated the traditional anthropologies of non-Western cultures, even in societies like Japan that have experienced protracted contact with the West. Scholars from the West who have spent sufficient time in Japan have encountered this radical contrast in anthropology firsthand. A notable example is psychoanalyst Alan Roland, who conducted clinical intercultural psychoanalytic research during the 1970s and 1980s in Japan and India. Roland discovered that he had to completely revise the normative cultural understanding of the self he had learned as a North American psychoanalyst.[82]

Drawing on the work of the Dutch psychologist of religion Hans Fortmann, Gerben Heitink comments on some of the consequences of modernity's radical analytical distinction between the individual and the collectivity, which is evident in the work of all of the practical theologians I have
examined thus far.

> In archaic cultures one hardly finds any distinction between the individ-
> ual and collectivity, between I and not-I, between subject and object, be-
> tween the inner and the outer, between the conscious and the uncon-
> scious (Fortmann, 1971, 29). Everything participates in everything. . . .
> Fortmann maintains that in the last few centuries Western culture has
> moved in the direction of separation and distinction. The "I" begins to
> live a life of its own. This leads on the one hand to autonomy and self-
> realization, but on the other hand to isolation and disintegration. There is
> an enrichment but also an impoverishment, since the reflecting con-
> sciousness gets separated from its unconscious roots, from the maternal
> womb of collectivity, and thus loses its potential to participate and sym-
> bolize. . . . This development has its consequences in the area of religious
> experience as well as in that of spiritual health.[83]

Without denying the significant gains of the Enlightenment, which include
legal protection of the rights of racial and ethnic minorities, children, and
women, practical theology must also address the disastrous consequences of a
notion of human being in which maturity is understood as distancing oneself
from one's nurturing community. The almost complete absence of a positive
ecclesiology in the correlationalists and Loder reveals the depth of practical
theology's captivity to the Enlightenment anthropology.

For Paul and the other writers of the New Testament, the maternal
nexus of the Christian collectivity is always primary. It would be no exaggeration to say that Paul did not have a conception of the person *qua* individual.
In his commentary on the Pauline ethics of 2 Corinthians, Richard Hays
characterizes the church community as the "sneak preview of God's ultimate
redemption of the world."[84]

> This eschatological transformation of the community explains Paul's ex-
> traordinary affirmation that the purpose of God's reconciling work in
> Christ is "that we might become the righteousness of God" (5:21). He
> does not say "that we might know about the righteousness of God," nor
> "that we might believe the righteousness of God," nor even "that we
> might receive the righteousness of God." Instead, the church is to *become*

the righteousness of God: where the church embodies in its life together the world-reconciling love of Jesus Christ, the new creation is manifest. The church incarnates the righteousness of God.[85]

Notice it is the mission of the entire transformed community of faith in all of its rich intercultural expressions, not the experience of the transformed individual, that is the proleptic sign or witness to God's ultimate purposes for all creation. By clarifying the New Testament perspective, it is not my intention to deny the personal experience of transformation. I only wish to point out that the scriptural accent is clearly and wisely on the far broader field of the *ecclesia* — in its almost infinite ecumenical variations — as the primary space-time locus and sign of God's saving and sanctifying work.

If we are to faithfully bring Chalcedon to bear on our deliberations in practical theology as Loder proposes, the *pro me* consequences of the mission of the Triune God always need to be comprehended and criticized within the much wider horizon of the *pro nobis.* This discussion of the *pro nobis* and *pro me* relationality brings us to an important question. Is it possible that the way contemporary non-Western Christians understand the self-community relation may be in some respects closer to the biblical imagination than the way this relation has evolved in the post-Enlightenment West? If this is the case, the Western churches, which have been in the position of missionary teacher and evangelist for the past two hundred years, may need to be taught and evangelized by non-Western missionaries today.

The second place in Loder's work where I see the persistence of the modernist epistemology that is both contrary to the witness of scripture and his own Chalcedonian model of practical theology is in his casting of the dialectic between socialization vs. transformation. Again, in spite of his insistence that socialization and transformation always belong together and that socialization is always "unto transformation," Loder invariably casts socialization or enculturation in negative terms and transformation in positive terms. While many examples could be brought forth to show this opposition,[86] I will introduce just one from the present article. In a passage that describes the transformational shift from *theoria* to *theologia* and *praxis* to *praxeis,* Loder says that *theologia,* under the effects of the mediation of the Spirit's transformation, "exercises marginal control over *praxeis.*"

> Together in the Spirit, then, these polarities in their relationality constitute a Christological reality that erupts from within and beyond the field of human action, creating no passing rebellion nor romantic revolution, but gives rise to a Christological order that shakes the very foundations of

socialization and its repressive and oppressive grip upon human consciousness and action.[87]

While not wanting to deny the potentially destructive effects of human socialization, one wonders why Loder always casts socialization in negative terms, especially considering the many positive New Testament words used to describe the specifically *ecclesial* actions or practices of socialization.[88] I think he derives his negative conception of socialization or enculturation from at least the following two sources: (1) Søren Kierkegaard's radical critique of Christendom; and (2) Talcott Parsons's four-sphere model of human action.

Commenting on Kierkegaard's statement that "All Christian education is based upon a sheer lie,"[89] Loder says,

> It is not sufficient to socialize persons into the use and practice of established Christian truths. Christianity will not yield to habit, however well ingrained it may be. The dynamics of habituation and socialization are not sufficient — and sometimes look bizarre — in their efforts to be bearers of Christian truth.[90]

Kierkegaard's view, which of course was forged within the very different sociocultural conditions of the *corpus christianum* that still persisted in his early nineteenth-century Denmark, was especially attractive to Loder in light of his own disappointment with the directions of post-1960s "mainline" Protestantism in the United States. This dissatisfaction only intensified following his own personal experience of transformation in 1970, which he brilliantly narrates and interprets in *The Transforming Moment*. As generations of his students will attest, there is a sense in which Loder saw his transformational critique of socialization as his primary vocation.

Another source of Loder's emphasis on subjective experience and his negative view of socialization is his appropriation of Parsons's model of the four spheres of human action (biological, psychological, social, and cultural).[91] While he introduces transformation into the model as the force that undoes the "tension-reduction and pattern-maintenance" dynamics of enculturation or socialization,[92] he does not ask how theological resources might positively criticize the analytical determinism of this model. For example, precisely in light of the Chalcedonian relationality he suggests, one question that could be asked is whether or not it is possible to parse the biological, psychological, social, and cultural spheres of human action as starkly as required by Parsons's model. If relationality is at the very heart of Loder's proposal, why doesn't he consider the interrelations between the biological, psychological, social, and cultural spheres of human action? As his model which describes transformation in multiple contexts shows,[93] he seems to have more interest in proving how the logic of transformation takes place within discrete spheres of action rather than wondering how the four spheres interrelate.[94]

Further, Loder does not consider Parsons's model in light of the biblical vision of the *ecclesia* as a very peculiar kind of community that offered, according to Rodney Stark,

> a coherent culture that was *entirely stripped of ethnicity.* All were welcome without the need to dispense with ethnic ties. Yet, for this very reason, among Christians ethnicity tended to be submerged as new, more universalistic, and indeed cosmopolitan, norms and customs emerged.[95]

While Christians necessarily belong to some local society and culture, even today when the boundaries between cultures appear, on the surface, to be blurring with increasing globalization, we also belong to the divinely created and sustained translocal society or culture of the "One, Holy, Catholic, and Apostolic Church." Even without the ecumenical dimension, the horizons of Parsons's model need to be expanded to include the "world" or "humankind" along the lines of Roland Robertson's model of the "global field."[96]

Serious problems arise when Loder's views of transformation and socialization are considered in relation to the practical theological model he himself constructs. The core problem here is a confusion in Loder's portrayal of the epistemic boundary conditions or field limitations wherein Christian socialization and transformation are thought to take place. In contrast to transformational knowing, which embraces the world, the self, the void, and the holy, Loder consistently portrays the systems of socialization as functioning only within the flatland two-dimensionality of world and self.[97] Again, while Loder draws on biblical and theological resources to ground his view of transformation, he fails to bring biblical and theological resources to bear on his understanding of socialization. Thus, he sets a positive theological concept in stark opposition to a negative human science concept, failing to bring theology and human science into the kind of "transformational interaction" that his own model proposes.[98]

Again, in spite of his use of the corrective category "marginal control," transformation exercises decisive control in Loder's work. In place of the correlationalists' option for *theory* or *praxis,* here we are presented with the options of *transformation* or *socialization.* By consistently portraying transformation "in the Spirit" as the power that negates the deleterious effects of socialization, and never seriously wondering what "socialization in the Spirit" might look like in light of the strong New Testament accent on the formative practices performed by the *ecclesia,* Loder comes close to embracing precisely the either-or dualism that his Chalcedonian model seeks to overcome.

In Loder's apotheosis of transformation there may be more of Plato than the New Testament, Nicea, and Chalcedon, which presents us with a serious theological problem. While I am sure that Loder never intended such a consequence, a blanket exultation of transformation or denigration of socialization undermines the ontological significance of the humanity of God in Jesus Christ. Is the world completely or only tentatively embraced in the *exitus-reditus oikonomia* of the Triune God?[99] Does the New Testament ever present the incarnation as a *deus ex machina* for some higher stage of spiritual liberation? As well as its radical discontinuity, doesn't the incarnation also ensure a radical continuity between the old and new creations? Doesn't the incarnation signify for the church the hope of transformation within all dimensions of human life, including the mundane practices of socialization and enculturation?

From the perspective of Chalcedon, to even suggest a correlation of Christian transformation with divine agency and a reduction of Christian socialization to human agency is highly problematic. While Loder rightly insists on the dynamics of transformation "in the Spirit," scripture also speaks with confidence about what might be called ecclesial practices of socialization "in the Spirit."[100] The astounding claim here is that the Triune God continues to work within and through the limitations of space and time, not for the sake of some higher integration that negates the significance and limitations of space and time, but as a means of witnessing to the divine purposes within the limitations of space and time.

In the above discussion, I have tried to show the integral relation between the operative theological, epistemological, and ecclesiological norms of some of the leading North American practical theologians. It appears that in all three cases, the modernist epistemology continues to exercise a strong influence on their approaches to theology and ecclesiology. Because of the intellectual *habitus* of the university culture, the correlationalists have, for the most part, been less than forthcoming on the vital theological question of divine praxis. For practical theologians who seek to maintain some continuity with Christian scripture and premodern theology, this reticence is problematic if not fatal. On the other hand, Loder's transformational model boldly presses the sticky and unpopular question of how the Spirit of the Triune God continues to transform persons in conformity with Jesus Christ. While not, in any way, wanting to deny the importance of the work of theologically concerned correlationalists, like Fowler and Browning, who dare to swim against the governing *ethos* of their own spheres of belonging, I think Loder's model, in spite of the serious reservations I have pointed out, goes a long way toward reconstruing practical theology as an interdisciplinary and inter-cultural theological discipline entrusted with the responsibility of reflecting on and guiding Christian practice in and beyond the churches.

To conclude this introductory chapter, I want to underline a two-dimensional ecclesiological problematic that the correlationalists and Loder have almost completely overlooked because of their cultural locations. The first dimension of this ecclesial problematic that these leading practical theo-logians have overlooked is the consciousness of the deep, inescapable "missional" tensions that inevitably arise between the Christian gospel, the church, and its social, political, and cultural location.[101] As a double inheri-tance of European Christendom and the long-lived, but currently waning so-cial, political, and cultural hegemony of Protestantism in North America, there still seems to persist, in both conservative and liberal Protestant circles, a stubborn and naïve hope in the possibility of some unambiguous contiguity or even synthesis between the gospel and the North American churches and culture. This stubborn and theologically naïve hope, which fails to take the religious and cultural pluralism of North America seriously, is implicit in these leading approaches to practical theology. While communitarians, tak-ing their cue from Stanley Hauerwas, are proclaiming that the North Ameri-can churches are already in a post-Constantinian situation, and a new genera-tion of missional theologians, drawing on the work of Lesslie Newbigin, are wondering whether or not North America can be converted, most practical theologians have still not seriously addressed the hitherto unthinkable prob-lematic of how to understand and guide Christian practice within their own post-Christian social, political, and cultural context.[102]

The second dimension of this ecclesiological problematic is seen in the waning consciousness of the time-space-transcendent "ecumenical" unity or catholicity of the profoundly diverse Christian churches in the world today. Practical theologians have shown little awareness of the *ecumene* as either an intercultural or theological actuality. Perhaps this ecclesial provincialism is in part a consequence of the postmodern "turn to the local," but is it not a tanta-lizing irony that the loss of any ongoing consciousness of the *ecumene,* a loss that is especially strong in contemporary North American Protestant churches, has occurred precisely while the North American "mainline" de-nominations and their theological institutions were trying to distance them-selves from what they saw as the generally negative legacy of the modern mis-sionary movement?[103]

CHAPTER TWO

Biblical, Theological, and Missiological
Grounds for a Missional-Ecumenical
Approach to Practical Theology

In light of Chapter One, I will begin this chapter with a reading of Paul's
imaginative exposition, in Romans 12, of the relation of divine and human
agency within the singular missional-ecumenical "body of Christ." I will then
briefly describe the global situation of the churches in relation to the North
American churches and introduce the "gospel-church-culture model" of
missional theologian George Hunsberger. This chapter is intended to provide
a normative, descriptive, and interpretive bridge between the discussion in
Chapter One and the "missional-ecumenical" case study of Tamura which
begins in Chapter Three.

Charismatic, Missional, Ecumenical Praxis
Within the "One Body of Christ"

I appeal to you therefore, brothers and sisters, by the mercies of God, to
present your bodies as a living sacrifice, holy and acceptable to God,
which is your spiritual worship. Do not be conformed to this world, but
be transformed by the renewing of your minds, so that you may discern
what is the will of God — what is good and acceptable and perfect. For by
the grace given to me I say to everyone among you not to think of yourself more highly than you ought to think, but to think with sober judgment, each according to the measure of faith that God has assigned. For
as in one body we have many members, and not all the members have the
same function *(praxin)*, so we, who are many, are one body in Christ, and
individually we are members one of another. We have gifts *(charismata)*

that differ according to the grace given to us: prophecy, in proportion to faith; ministry, in ministering; the teacher, in teaching; the exhorter, in exhortation; the giver, in generosity; the leader, in diligence; the compassionate, in cheerfulness. (Rom. 12:1-8)

In this rich, paranetic passage from Romans 12, Paul, the Jewish apostle to the Gentiles, gives practical theological expression to the broad Christocentric unity of the geographically dispersed and culturally disparate churches. When this exhortation is read in light of the entire letter, we find that Paul is making some normative "proto-missional" and "proto-ecumenical" claims about the "one body of Christ." One of those claims is that, as each local instantiation of the "one body of Christ" seeks, in its worship of the God revealed in Jesus Christ, to discern the will of God in their own place and time, they will necessarily encounter tensions with their own native culture. To foreshadow the missional discussion of gospel, church, and culture tensions that will follow my reading of Romans 12, George Hunsberger speaks of this initial missional encounter as one in which Jesus Christ "is introduced as one who bursts open the culture's models with the power of a wholly new fact."[1] Further, the tacit "proto-ecumenical" claim we discover here and elsewhere in Paul is that each local expression of the church is intimately bound to all other local expressions of the church as the "one body in Christ." The theological implication is that, in order to more fully discern the praxis of God in the world today, churches in one place need the kind of mutual challenge and encouragement that can only be provided by active ecumenical engagement with churches in different places.

Now I will try to draw out some of the implicit missional and ecumenical claims in this text. Though Paul had not yet met the Jewish and Gentile Christians in Rome, he addresses "all God's beloved in Rome" (Rom. 1:7) with a level of familial intimacy that would have been considered radical given the sociocultural boundaries of ancient Greco-Roman filial piety.[2] In spite of the fact that Paul had not personally communicated the evangel to the Romans, he portrays himself and the distant Roman Christians as inextricably bound together in Christ's body as "members one of another." Further, he states in the salutation his desire to visit Rome "so that we may be mutually encouraged by each other's faith" (Rom. 1:12). This expresses Paul's conviction that Christian communities, whose relational unity is found in Christ alone, have much to gain from active engagement with Christian communities in other places.

Since Paul is free of any pastoral need to defend personal challenges to his apostolic ministry to the Christians in Rome, we may have in this letter, if not a full-blown doctrine of the church, one of the clearest expressions of his ecclesial ideal. He imagines a worship-centered, mission-directed, and ecumenically connected community wherein the space-time distinctions between here and there, now and then, are completely relativized. The members of the "one body of Christ" are called to commitment to and consciousness of (1) the *mission* of God within a situated Christian community; and (2) the *ecumene* of other Christian communities who equally share in the operation of divine grace across space, time, and sociocultural boundaries. This *missional-ecumenical* communal ideal is simultaneously local and global. This bipolar, relational unity between locality and globality calls to mind Andrew Walls's brilliant description of the relation between what he calls the "indigenous" (missional) and "pilgrim" (ecumenical) principles. Walls says that these two principles

> are not in opposition, nor are they to be held in some kind of balance. We need not fear of getting too much of one or the other, only too little. . . . It is a delightful paradox that the more Christ is translated into the various thought forms and life systems which form our various national identities, the richer all of us will be in our common Christian identity.[3]

Though he does not use the term "bipolar relational unity," Walls's description of this creative tension is actually a more faithful example of the Chalcedonian logic than Loder's oppositions of socialization and transformation, which we spoke about in Chapter One.

As a consequence of the gospel mission that took Paul and others beyond the boundaries of Palestine and Judaism, the churches gradually began to identify themselves as local communities joined inextricably to communities in different places by God in Christ. Indeed, this local-global identity made the church an anomalous, "cosmopolitan" collectivity that was often suspected of undermining the traditional loyalties of local societies, cultures, and polities. Drawing on the second- or third-century *Epistle to Diognetus,* Barry Harvey describes the early church's self-identity as an *altera civita,* "a distinct *politeia* within and for the sake of the world."[4] Such a view is implicit in Paul's vision of this Christocentric, charismatic, missional, and ecumenical community where, as a witness to the generosity of God toward all peoples, local sociocultural distinctions are simultaneously enhanced and relativized.

In hindsight, we may say that Paul is giving early expression to the faith in the catholicity of the church.[5] In more contemporary terms, Paul is advocating a Christocentric, charismatic community that pathically embraces both local differences and global unity. Whereas in chapter 12 of 1 Corinthians, he employs the metaphor of the "one body" to address specific pastoral issues within the bounds of one local community of faith, here in Romans the geographical dimension of the "one body" is extended to encompass a wider circle of Pauline churches and churches founded by other missionaries. This explosion of ecclesial horizons implicitly includes the Christian church wherever, whenever, and among whomever it appears.

While he does not address the issue directly here, one of Paul's major themes throughout the letter has been the gospel's transformation of the relative status of Jews and Greeks before God and, consequently, their relation to each other. The dual nature (divine-human and human-human) of Christ's reconciliation, a theme that finds its most explicit statement in the deutero-Pauline Letter to the Ephesians,[6] is already implicit in Paul's exhortation to the Romans. From this vision of the radical transformation of the relation of Jews and Greeks in Christ, we may characterize the church, again in more contemporary terms, as a translocal and transtemporal unity of faith communities that function together corporately and individually, each "according to the measure of faith God has assigned" (Rom. 12:3), in their witness to the redemptive mission of Christ. This is a very comprehensive formulation of the parameters within which the church practically functions, under the divine agency of the Holy Spirit, as a participant in and witness to the reconciling mission of God in Christ for the world.

In contrast to the reticence of contemporary practical theologians on the question of divine agency, it is astounding to discover that Paul not only sees reconciliation as a divine gift, but he also sees the Spirit as presently at work in the discrete, public ecclesial "functions" (*praxin*, Rom. 12:4) that participate in and bear witness to Christ's reconciliation within the contingencies of space and time. In other words, Paul asserts an unambiguous correlation between divine gift *(charisma)* and ecclesial practice *(praxis)*.

The specific list of *charismata* in this passage includes prophecy, ministry, teaching, exhortation, giving, leadership, and compassion (Rom. 12:6-9). Paul's positive, pneumatological view of these public, communal practices contrasts with Loder's unfortunate tendency to restrict the epistemic sphere of the transformational Spirit-spirit relation to subjective experience and his consistently negative view of socialization. In the view expressed in Romans, ecclesial socialization is transformational precisely because of the conviction of the real mediation of divine agency operative in the "one body of Christ." An important implication is that the operational field of divine agency, the missional and ecumenically engaged "one body of Christ," is simultaneously local and global. In other words, the divine gifts and their ecclesial functions are dispersed locally and across this broad range of communities in ways that are known only to God. In this vision of how divine gift and ecclesial function operate, Paul leaves no latitude for human hubris. "For as in one body we have many members, and not all the members have the same function *(praxin),* so we, who are many, are one body in Christ, and individually we are members one of another. We have gifts *(charismata)* that differ according to the grace given to us" (Rom. 12:4-6). This verse may be read today as a rejection of any Christian ideology that overemphasizes local autonomy at the expense of the kind of translocal mutuality Paul is hoping to establish with the Christians in Rome.

When compared with similar lists of *charismata* in the Pauline corpus (i.e., 1 Corinthians 12), it is unlikely that Paul intends the present list to be exhaustive.[7] In other words, while suggesting some common pattern in the correlation of *charisma* and *praxis* across geographical and temporal boundaries, Paul is acknowledging the decisive priority of divine freedom in the contingent ways that *charismatic praxis* will function within each community; "according to the proportion of faith," "in (the) teaching," "in (the) ministry," "in (the) encouragement," etc. In the "one body in Christ," the church's local particularity and translocal unity are both initiated and supported by the gracious and free distribution of divine *charisma* via the core ecclesial practices which participate in the mission of God within and beyond a specific place and time. Given the temporal-transtemporal, local-translocal operation of God's grace within the ever-expanding body of Christ, it becomes an evangelical imperative for churches and theologians to actively engage in serious historical research[8] and dialogue with contemporary Christians beyond their own social, political, and cultural spheres. If we take Paul seriously, such engagement may significantly broaden our understanding of the workings of divine grace in situations of ecclesial and trans-ecclesial Christian practice today.

Keeping in mind Walls's comment of not having too much of the indigenous or pilgrim principles, in this wide-angled Pauline vision of divinely initiated and sustained missional-ecumenical ecclesial practice, the translocal and transtemporal unity of the "one body in Christ" does not undermine the distinctive witness of Christian practices within a local cultural or historical setting. Nor, on the other hand, does the distinctive witness of Christian practices within a local cultural and historical setting undermine the translocal and transtemporal unity of the "one body." Within this local-translocal vision of the "one body of Christ," worship is seen as the central epistemic sphere of ecclesial practice. Here the mind of the whole community, and not only or even primarily the discrete individual, is renewed in order to better discern the will of God.[9] Worship, as the core practice that unites the *ecumene,* is also the epistemic sphere wherein the entire community more faithfully discerns the will of God.

Of course, the rationale for Paul's joining of the One in the many and the many in the One is theological. The local and translocal, temporal and transtemporal forms of the "one body in Christ" are correlated to the singular revelation of the unity of divine-human act and being, person and word, eternity and time in Jesus Christ.[10] The Lord God's initiative revealed and fulfilled in the history of the people of Israel and Jesus Christ and carried forth by the Spirit in the witness of the churches is the sole ground and ongoing source of Christian identity. In Christ, every alternative social, cultural, or political ground or source of Christian identity is radically relativized. In Paul's portrayal of the church to his distant sisters and brothers in Rome, ecclesial unity and diversity are bound together in the kind of asymmetrical bipolar relational unity that Loder's Chalcedonian model asserts.[11]

The new and decisive fact for Paul and the Christians in Rome is their mutual participation and belonging in Christ, in whom God's promises to Israel are realized and expanded. The gospel proclaims that the new community of those who have been baptized into Christ's death and resurrection is no longer "under law" but is now "under grace."[12] For Paul, this radical shift in God's dealings with humanity results in a new community that is inclusive of Gentiles as well as Jews. Thus, both the church's unity and diversity are embraced and preserved whenever this One is recognized in the others of the gathered and scattered community, and whenever the others of the gathered and scattered community are recognized in this One.[13] This Christocentric communal identity marks the expanding *ecumene* from the earliest stage of the Gentile mission.

Since the crucified and risen Jesus Christ alone is the ground, ongoing basis, and eschatological *telos* of Christian unity and diversity, that which is local and temporal within the church will always be apprehended, under the boundary conditions of space and time, in pathic tension with that which is translocal or transtemporal. Beginning in the third chapter, we will explore this pattern of local-translocal, temporal-transtemporal tensions in my examination of Tamura's work as a first-generation convert and practical theologian in Meiji, Taisho, and early Showa Japan. The recognition of the church's complete dependence on divine grace for its present witness to and the ultimate fulfillment of the mission of God is behind the apostle's admonition "not to think more highly than you ought to think, but to think with sober judgment" (Rom. 12:3). While the church's ecumenical unity in the "one body" both embraces and transcends every cultural or temporal expression of the "one body," the consciousness and experience of this unity are never depicted as a *fait accompli*.[14]

35

To state Paul's vision of the missional and ecumenical church and its practical ministries in more theological terms, we may say that the unity of ecclesial translocality and locality is initiated, sustained, and perfected only by the freedom of divine-human agency enacted on behalf of the whole world in the history of Israel and fulfilled in the person of Jesus Christ. In other words, the revelation of God in the history of Israel and Jesus Christ, in the messianic expectation, incarnation, and proleptic *parousia* through the power of the Holy Spirit, sets the space-time field limitations of the church and the churches. Since ecclesial unity has no other basis and expression than in the unity of God's being and act revealed in the history of Israel and in Jesus Christ, Christian unity must be continually renewed and experienced by faith as the gracious gift of God. By faith in Jesus Christ, the worshiping community together discerns "what is the will of God" and is empowered by the Holy Spirit with the necessary *charismata* to function simultaneously as a local and global participant in and witness to the ongoing mission of God in and on behalf of the world. The *charismata*, the divine authorization of ecclesial praxis, serve no other agenda than the mission of the Triune God for the world.

Thus, from the perspective of practical theology, we may say that the space-time-contingent ecclesial practices (worshiping, preaching, teaching, caring, serving, leading, evangelizing, etc.) serve and participate in the unconditional unity of divine and human practice revealed in the One Lord of the church or, conversely, the One Lord of the church presides over, through the agency of the Holy Spirit, all of the performative practices of his church.[15] Instead of being an occasion for individual religious experience, the church as the One Body of Christ is a theater where Christ himself administers his sacraments, preaches and teaches his Word, shepherds his people, serves the poor, confronts the powers, and transforms the world. On the one hand, the *charismata* are tragically misunderstood whenever seen as the possession of certain privileged members of the *ecclesia*, whether in the institutional form of a hierarchical magisterium, the social, cultural, or political convictions of some local community, or the case of certain spiritually gifted individuals.[16] On the other hand, the core practices of the church (worshiping, preaching, teaching, caring, serving, leading, evangelizing, etc.) are equally misunderstood when they are completely severed from the *charismata* and reduced purely to objects of empirical description or prescription. While the first caution recalls my critique of the individualistic emphasis in Loder's transformational model, the second caution anticipates the critique I will offer later of the scientific positivism of Tamura and the religious education movement.

What has become so difficult for modern Christians to grasp is that all

Christian communities, regardless of time and place, are implicit in all other Christian communities on the basis of their divinely gifted participation in the mission of the Son, to the glory of the Father, in the power of the Spirit, on behalf of all creation. While the mission of the church as an *altera civita* necessarily takes place within particular social, political, and cultural contexts, the missional-ecumenical church that Paul envisions, while being inevitably influenced by the particular *habitus* of the locality in which it finds itself, no longer grounds or seeks its primary identity within its particular social, political, and cultural context. The church's divinely ascribed identity is nothing less than participation in and witness to the mission of the Triune God. Precisely because of its primary identity as a worshiping community that participates in the ongoing *oikonomia* of the Triune God, the church will never escape the experience of serious, prophetic tensions with the dominant *habitus* of the local culture where it attempts to live as witness.

Because of the bipolar, missional-ecumenical identity of this eschatologically authorized community, the church is called to bear a divine question in relation to every settled human answer. As Jürgen Moltmann put it in *The Theology of Hope,*

> Those who hope in Christ can no longer put up with reality as it is, but begin to suffer under it to contradict it. Peace with God means conflict with the world, for the goal of the promised future stabs inexorably into the flesh of every unfulfilled present.[17]

Paul expresses this unavoidable tension between the church and its local *habitus* in his exhortation to "not be conformed to this world (age) but be transformed by the renewing of your minds" (Rom. 12:2). In worship, the church is renewed in its discernment of the divine will. One important aspect of discerning the divine will is for the Roman community to begin to recognize itself as part of a much broader, divinely sustained community, a community whose ever-growing boundaries are expressed by the metaphor of the "one body of Christ." Following his admonition to spiritual worship, Paul immediately reminds the Roman Christians of their need for sober self-assessment in light of the rich diversity of the "one body of Christ" (Rom. 12:3-5). In other words, one consequence of the transformation that takes place in the self-understanding of the church is the consciousness of being constantly drawn beyond the narrow horizon of its own cultural locality in humble recognition of its need of being enriched by the spiritual gifts of Christians in differing cultural spheres of the *ecumene.* The incipient ecclesiology Paul is sketching here suggests that, inasmuch as each local church is an expression or sign of the "one body of Christ," they will be conscious of and intentionally engaged with churches in other spheres of the *ecumene* in order to more faithfully discern, participate in, and witness to God's mission in and for the whole world.

This, of course, is an ecclesiology that flies directly in the face of the *de facto* "congregation-centeredness" that has become increasingly typical of North American Protestant churches and practical theology today. In Chapter One, I pointed out that the practical theological "turn to the congregation," which Chopp rightly criticizes, may subtly underwrite a parochial ecclesiology that, especially with the eclipse of the modern missionary movement, has little if any consciousness of being inextricably united in Christ, as local-global participant-witnesses, with Christians in other places and times. In her critique of the middle-class practical theologians, Chopp unfortunately never ponders the rich biblical metaphor of the local-translocal and temporal-transtemporal "one body of Christ," a far more inclusive and potentially radical proposal than the philosophical alternative she posits. As I pointed out in Chapter One, in place of middle-class expressions of the church, she privileges the distant, marginalized communities of Latin America. Further, we saw that her reticence on the subject of divine agency is every bit as apparent as the practical theologians whom Fowler criticizes.

In the churches and among the theologians of the West, the missional tension Paul describes between each church and its particular social, cultural, and political location and the need of each church for ongoing ecumenical enrichment has long been obscured by the legacy of Christendom and the Enlightenment.[18] Since I have already touched upon the consequences of the Enlightenment for practical theology in Chapter One, I will only comment briefly here on one striking legacy of Christendom for the Protestant churches. One only has to recall the social, political, and cultural context in which Protestantism was birthed to realize that the Pauline vision of the missional and ecumenical church was completely overlooked by the magisterial reformers who continued to take the church-culture synthesis of medieval Europe for granted.[19] While the humanist reformers were masterful exegetes of the texts of scripture, they had no firsthand experience of the missional tensions between gospel, church, and culture that characterized the Pauline intercultural context of the expanding Gentile mission of the first-century churches. Within the context of the *corpus christianum,* it is not surprising that the reformers focused on preaching and sacraments as the marks of the true church. Paul surely would have also added local missional discernment and ever-expanding ecumenical engagement as true marks of the "one body of Christ."

It is my conviction that the church's loss of consciousness of this divinely initiated and sustained missional-ecumenical horizon has meant a tragic impoverishment in our appreciation of the unique ways that Christ has been, is being, and will yet be revealed through the witness of the world's culturally diverse peoples. However, as the churches and theologians of the West slowly begin to acknowledge that we too are living in a post-Christendom or post-Constantinian social, political, and cultural situation which in some ways has a closer affinity with the situation of Paul (and, as we will see later, Tamura) than the reformers, perhaps we have a new and unprecedented opportunity to begin to seriously reflect on the church's missional-ecumenical vocation.

Before turning to the case study of Tamura, I want to clarify why I think missional and ecumenical questions are so pressing for practical theologians in North America today. I will touch upon two momentous global trends that are just beginning to receive some long-overdue attention in most North American seminaries and university divinity schools. The related trends I have in mind are the dramatic demographic transformation of global Christianity and the twilight of "mainline" Protestant foreign mission programs. Then, in conversation with British missionary theologian Lesslie Newbigin and certain North American "missional" theologians, I will introduce Hunsberger's model that attempts to sort out the multiple tensions that missional churches inevitably encounter between the gospel, church, and culture.

The Demographic Transformation of World Christianity and the Twilight of "Mainline" Protestant Foreign Missions

As I have mentioned elsewhere,[20] while the failure to consider the question of the contemporary Christian church's staggering cultural diversity would be inconsequential if North American theorists had no relation to Christians in different cultures, the mere fact that many non-Western churches continue to privilege North American and European theologies and send their best students to study in either North America or Europe makes such a failure problematic if not irresponsible. Ironically, it is often in those universities and seminaries where the story of the modern missionary movement has been repudiated for being triumphalistically Westerncentric and therefore expunged from institutional memory that a quick glance at theological curricula and faculties reveals that a thoroughgoing Westerncentrism often dominates. As Newbigin also discovered when he returned to his native England from years in India, many "mainline" Protestant seminaries and university theology departments have courses on the history of mission and various third-world theologies but offer little or nothing on the theology of mission.[21] While such trends may also reflect the "turn to the local" that has come in the wake of the postmodern rejection of modernity's obsession with the "universal," they are also an indication of the waning consciousness of the missional and ecumenical identity and calling of the churches.

In light of the discussion in Chapter One, I invite the reader to imagine what happens when the best students of the non-Western churches are sent, especially for doctoral studies, to the Western centers of theological education. Having spent many years studying alongside some of these sisters and brothers, I have observed that too often these foreign students' distinctive cultural experience and understanding of God in Christ and the church are overlooked, ignored, or deliberately demeaned as they are obliged to conform to an alien culture, rationality, and rhetoric that will earn them the vaunted degree while taking them farther and farther afield from the actual issues confronting their native churches and societies. This is a particularly painful experience for students of practical theology since this discipline must carefully consider the social, cultural, and political situations wherein discrete Christian practices are performed. With few exceptions,[22] these students will find little or no curricular emphasis on non-Western Christianity or an even-handed treatment of missionary history, and they will soon learn that most members of the theological faculty have never had any significant level of personal interaction with Christians outside of their own cultural-linguistic setting; and this at a time when the churches of Asia, Africa, and Latin America account for two-thirds of the world's Christian population![23]

There are, of course, a number of complex factors behind this lamentable situation. For example, by every sociological measure, the former "mainline" Protestant churches of North America have themselves experienced continuing demographic decline and diminishing influence within their own social, political, and cultural setting since the 1960s.[24] Also, according to Newbigin, one underlying epistemological factor behind this decline is what he calls the "plausibility structure" of modernity in which "facts" have come to be associated with the publicly verifiable, "objective" canons of science while "values" are increasingly seen as properly belonging to the private sphere of "subjective," individual opinion and religion.[25] The current disjunction between personal "spirituality" and institutional "religion" and the inability of many "mainline" Protestant churches to transmit their Christian faith to the next generation, both important issues for practical theology, are contemporary examples of the churches' unwitting capitulation to this "public fact-private value" dualism. Confirming Newbigin's suspicions, sociologists like Robert Bellah and Robert Wuthnow conclude that whatever shared religious consensus may have existed previously, questions of ultimacy have come to be framed purely in terms of individual preference in most middle-class North American communities today.[26] Recalling my criticism in Chapter One, the correlationalists' reticence on divine agency or Loder's negative appraisal of "public" socialization and positive appraisal of "private" transformational experiences are indications that practical theologians are by no means immune to this fact-value dualism.

During the post-1960s era which has also witnessed the slow but certain decline of the "mainline" Protestant missionary movement, "mainline" church leaders and theologians have tended to privilege only certain non-Western ecclesial trends or theologies that have ideological coinage within their particular conservative, liberal, or progressive coteries. Chopp's option for Latin American base communities is an excellent example of this highly selective ecumenism. Occasionally, as in the recent decision of the Episcopal Church to ordain an openly homosexual bishop, the church is alerted to a recognition of the existence of an immense chasm between the convictions of some Western and non-Western Christians, but generally, in this post-missionary era, Western church leaders and theologians have been free to pursue their local academic or ecclesial agendas without taking to heart and mind their distant sisters and brothers in Christ, while forgetting that their very introduction to the Christian faith was most likely a direct or indirect result of the missionary agency of their own churches!

In such a situation, it seems legitimate and perhaps even imperative to wonder what the local situation of the North American Protestant churches looks like in relation to the radical transformation of the global *ecumene*. While "mainline" Protestantism has been declining in North America, global Christianity has undergone a dramatic demographic reversal. In 1900, two-thirds of the world's Christians were found in Europe, the former Soviet Union, and North America and one third in Africa, Asia, and Latin America. By 2000, these figures were completely reversed with one-third in Europe, the former Soviet Union, and North America and two-thirds in Africa, Asia, and Latin America.[27] How can this development be ignored by the "mainline" Protestant churches in the West, especially when, as I have already mentioned, it was mostly those churches who confidently dispatched and enthusiastically supported thousands of missionaries throughout the world during the modern missionary movement?

How have the Western churches and practical theologians in particular responded to this demographic reversal? On the one hand, in an essay titled "The Coming of the Third Church," Walbert Bühlmann acknowledges that

"It is now an incontrovertible fact that the West has been dismissed from its post as centre of religious cultural unity for the whole of Christianity."[28] Clearly, at least a passing awareness of this "incontrovertible fact" is one factor behind the recent trend to try to include the issue of globalization, for example, in discussions of North American theological education. Using the key words "theological education" and "globalization," I located 140 articles, published between 1986 and 2002, on the ATLA Religion index. In this literature, the efforts of the Association of Theological Schools are particularly noteworthy.[29] On the other hand, again calling to mind my discussion in Chapter One, the import of this "incontrovertible fact" has not yet entered into the deliberations of most practical theologians in the West.[30]

Musing on the potential consequences of this extraordinary transformation in the cultural makeup of the *ecumene*, Scottish historian of Christian mission Andrew Walls says,

> We now live at a time when the Church is multicultural. I think that the fullness of the stature of Christ will emerge only when Christians from all these cultures come together. If I understand what Paul says in Ephesians correctly, it is as though Christ himself is growing as the different cultures are brought together in him.[31]

With Walls, I want to suggest that the Western churches that originally sent out missionaries to plant churches, schools, and hospitals in Africa, Asia, and Latin America now have a pressing, pragmatic rationale and perhaps even a sacred obligation to explore and reflect on how Jesus Christ has been and is being experienced in new lights by non-Western Christians in the former "mission churches." Such a "coming together" of Christians will require that we in the West suspend our pendulous obsession with the universalizing and relativizing rationalities of both modernity and postmodernity, and begin to seriously investigate and appreciate the distinctive, local ways that peoples with differing conceptions of the constitutive relations between persons, communities, creation, and ultimacy actually experience and articulate their participation in Christ and his church within the social, political, and cultural conditions in which they live out their witness.

In the heyday of the modern missionary movement, the churches of North America clearly saw themselves as "senders" and the so-called "younger" churches of Asia, Africa, and Latin America as "receivers." Today, in the twilight of that movement, the Western churches have yet to awaken to the fact that, partly because of and partly in spite of the missionary movement, Christianity, which "is itself increasingly marginal to Western intellectual discourse," is now "a non-Western religion."[32] Given this new situation, Walls also suggests, "Perhaps there is now an obligation of Christians to 'use means' better fitted for two-way traffic, fellowship, for receiving, than have yet been perfected."[33] Through the case study on Tamura that begins in the next chapter, I will try to show how such "two-way traffic" has important and yet unconsidered consequences for practical theology and, by implication, other theological disciplines as well.

Given the contemporary Western church's growing experience of cultural displacement or "exile"[34] in which Christians may no longer expect their surrounding culture to be able to recognize Christian ways of thinking, feeling, and acting, or even to tacitly embody some vestige of a Judeo-Christian *ethos,* we may have something valuable to learn from the "exile narratives" that have shaped the identity of the so-called "younger churches" of the former "mission lands." Partly as a result of the efforts of our own nineteenth- and twentieth-century missionary and theological forebears, those churches were birthed, formed, and transformed through their struggle to bear witness to the gospel within a non-Christian culture, often as distrusted or despised religious minorities, in the face of the daunting tensions between their allegiance to Jesus Christ, their home culture of belonging, and modernization (Westernization). From such conversations with Christians in places where the churches have never enjoyed anything even remotely resembling "Constantinian"[35] status, we may experience, not a confirmation or affront to our own conservative or liberal politics, or some temporary psychological lift that helps us "feel better about things as they are,"[36] but a new vision of the crucified and risen Christ who calls the church into mission in each place and promises to remain with, sustain, and transform his people in both the verdant and wilderness places of their "afflicted but well-equipped witness"[37] within and on behalf of the world.

Non-Western Christianity still remains a largely unexplored but potentially fertile field of inquiry and reflection for Western biblical, systematic, historical, and practical theologians. Such inquiry will require new and creative methodologies and curricula. Theologians with a consciousness of and commitment to the global *ecumene* have much to learn, for example, from the creative methodology of scholars like Rodney Stark, who has examined the emergence of Christianity in the Greco-Roman world in conversation with contemporary studies of new religions.[38] Through such studies, we may be surprised to discover that the experience and self-understanding of the non-Western churches shed new light on the experience of the earliest Christian churches, since many of the same critical tensions between the gospel, church, and culture have been and are being recapitulated in their experience.[39] Another fruit of such investigations may be an increased awareness of and sensitivity to the ways some of our most treasured epistemological and theological convictions are also not untainted by our own local cultural *habitus*.

Facing Up to the Tensions Between the Gospel, Church, and Culture

Charging that the "mainline" Protestant churches have succumbed, sometimes consciously and sometimes unconsciously, to the above-mentioned fact-value dualism, a growing group of Newbigin's disciples are calling the North American churches to reconstrue their current "exile" as a new kind of *missional* opportunity that requires serious theological reflection on the relationship between the gospel, the church, and the particular cultural milieu in which the church is called to live out its witness. Craig Van Gelder examines this new missional situation in light of the "third disestablishment" of Protestantism in the United States. The "first disestablishment" refers, of course, to the constitutional decision of the nation's founders to separate church and state. The "second disestablishment" was an unanticipated outcome of the massive immigrations of Roman Catholics, Jews, and Orthodox Christians in the late nineteenth and early twentieth centuries. The current "third disestablishment" is expressed in the increasing consciousness of the "reality of pluralism" and is rooted in the critical social movements of the 1960s and 1970s.[40]

Wanting to avoid the extremes of capitulation and sectarianism that have often characterized the church's engagement with culture, this group of church-minded scholars envisions a missional church as one that self-consciously engages the tensions it experiences in its common life between the gospel and the social, political, and cultural modes of rationality and rhetoric that dominate the local culture. Practical theologians who are similarly committed to the church have much to learn from and contribute to this conversation.

As a way of clarifying these tensions, George Hunsberger has developed a helpful "triangular model of gospel-culture relationships" that correlates the following three axes: (1) a "conversion encounter axis" between gospel and culture; (2) a "reciprocal relationship axis" between gospel and church; and (3) a "missionary dialogue axis" between church and culture.[41] Since I will utilize Hunsberger's model in Chapter Three to analyze Tamura's work within the situation of early Japanese Protestantism, I will introduce it briefly here.

The Conversion-Encounter Axis
Between Gospel and Culture

Hunsberger characterizes the encounter between the gospel and culture along the first axis in terms of a "challenging relevance" that creatively combines elements of discontinuity and continuity. As the narratives of missionary history attest, in order for the gospel to take root in any culture, it must be "embodied in the terms by which people of the culture have learned to understand their world."[42] On the other hand, the theological conviction here is that Jesus Christ is never completely reducible to the noetic framework of any culture but "is introduced as one who bursts open the culture's models with the power of a wholly new fact."[43]

I would like to briefly suggest how this dynamic of a "challenging relevance" might relate to my criticism of contemporary practical theology in Chapter One. There I referred to Walls's masterful description of this gospel and culture encounter as a relentless, irreducible tension between what he calls the "pilgrim principle" and the "indigenizing principle." To repeat, Walls says that these principles

> are not in opposition, nor are they to be held in some kind of balance. We need not fear of getting too much of one or the other, only too little. . . . It is a delightful paradox that the more Christ is translated into the various thought forms and life systems which form our various national identities, the richer all of us will be in our common Christian identity.[44]

Walls's studied observation that you can only have "too little" of either culture or the gospel sheds some important light on the cultural captivity of the North American practical theologians I criticized in the first chapter. Their reticence on divine agency, construction of "tertium quid" methodologies, and capitulation to an individualistic-expressivist religiosity, as well as the loss of any consciousness of the missional and ecumenical charter of the Christian church, all bear witness to the loss of evangelical nerve within North American "mainline" Protestantism today. Contrary to the claims of conservative evangelicals or communitarians, the problem I see with "mainline" Protestant churches and theologians is not "too much" culture. I believe we should be commended for being engaged rather than withdrawn, for trying to maintain a positive, ongoing conversation with the resources of contemporary culture. Rather, our weakness, as I see it, has been "too little" gospel.

The Reciprocal Relationship Axis
Between Gospel and Church

Hunsberger describes the second axis of "conversion" between the gospel and the church as a "hermeneutical circle." Drawing on Newbigin, he says, "A community is established for whom 'the Bible is the determinative clue to the character and activity of the one whose purpose is the final meaning of history.' But this community that is 'a people of the book' is also the community that bears the Bible as its own testimony."[45] This axis places church traditions and practices in a dynamic interpretive dialogue with scripture. On the one hand, tradition inevitably "shapes" the church's reading of scripture, while on the other hand, the church, under the ministry of Word and sacrament, is continually reshaped by its reading of scripture. However, lest this dialogue between the community and the book be misunderstood as a closed symmetry, Hunsberger posits the *telos* of this dialogue in the ecclesial and trans-ecclesial practices of witness to the One whom scripture discloses.

> The church's commitment to the Bible's authority, embodied in active discipleship, enables the hermeneutical circle between Bible and church itself to become the hermeneutic of the gospel among the cultures of the world.[46]

Christomorphic witness, characterized by self-giving love and grace, is the *sine qua non* that the church is a faithful, public bearer of the Word of God.

In *The School of Faith*, T. F. Torrance describes the reformed churches' practice of catechesis in a way that helps explicate what Hunsberger has in mind in his description of the hermeneutical tensions along this gospel-church axis. Torrance says that, as the church is carefully nurtured into a dynamic relation with the Truth of God in Jesus Christ, we always stand under the gracious judgment of this Truth. This necessitates what Torrance calls *the adaptation of our capacities to the nature of that Truth.* Torrance says,

> when we encounter the Truth in Christ, we discover that we are at variance with the Truth, in a state of rebellion and enmity toward it, so that the way of knowledge is the way of surrender and acknowledgment through self-denial and repentance.[47]

Surrender, self-denial, and repentance are the forms of "active discipleship" that are a fruit of the church's ongoing encounter with scripture. In the light of the liberating gospel Word, the church is transformed into an incarnate-iconic witness, within its particular social, political, and cultural space and time, to the Truth of God in Christ.

In addition to Torrance, the recent work of biblical scholars and theologians such as Stephen Fowl and David Yeago also adds depth to Hunsberger's scripture-discipleship hermeneutic along the gospel-church axis. These post-critical scholars are calling for a renewal of an ecclesial-based practice of scriptural interpretation that attempts to overcome the limitations of both liberal historical criticism and conservative plenary verbal inspiration. For example, in conversation with the statement of St. Hilary that "Those who are situated outside the church are not able to acquire any understanding of the divine discourse," Yeago makes a case for scriptural interpretation as "a practice *intra ecclesiam*."[48]

> Scripture functions as a quasisacramental instrument of the Holy Spirit, through which the Spirit makes known the mystery of Christ in order to form the church as a sign of messianic dominion. The church's knowledge of Scripture as inspired therefore has interpretative consequences; it calls for a specific art, or perhaps a concatenation of arts, of faithful reading, exposition, and application by which Christ is glorified and the church built up in its distinctive life and mission.[49]

The kind of "arduous and countercultural"[50] interpretive ecclesial practices (arts) called for here will inevitably bring the community of faith into real tension with the dominant social, cultural, and political powers of the situation in which it finds itself. As I will show below, such deep tensions along this gospel-church axis figure prominently in the experience of the first generation of Japanese Protestants.

The Missionary Dialogue Axis Between Church and Culture

Here Hunsberger sees a need for a conscious vision of a "multiplex church in full ecumenical dialogue among its own members in the variety of human cultures."[51] On the one hand, the missionary church honors what Newbigin calls "the radical independence of the new convert (and newly converted church) vis-à-vis the missionary church through which the message has come."[52] However, the church's cultural discontinuity and independence can never be absolute since "the new church takes its place alongside the other churches of the world in the necessary ecumenical conversation between the various inculturations of discipleship."[53]

This joining of the local and translocal expressions of the *ecclesia* is given clearer theological articulation by Walls, who speaks of the "dual nationality" of every Christian. On the one hand,

> The Christian has all the relationships in which he was brought up, and has them sanctified by Christ who is living in them. But he also has an entirely new set of relationships, with other members of the family of faith into which he has come, and whom he must accept, with all their group relations (and "disrelations") on them, just as God has accepted him with his.[54]

Further, since the "history of Israel is part of Church history," Walls says,

> The adoption into Israel becomes a "universalizing" factor, bringing Christians of all cultures and ages together through a common inheritance, lest any of us make the Christian faith such a place to feel at home that no one else can live there; and bringing into everyone's society some sort of outside reference.[55]

There will always be a tension between what Walls calls the old and new relations, since no Christian church has ever arisen spontaneously, that is, without the historical background of Israel in addition to the practical agency of some other church. Especially in light of what Walls calls the "universalizing" factor of the church's "adoption into Israel," this church-culture dynamic implies both the historical and theological facticity, whether recognized or unrecognized, embraced or denied, of a catholic union of all local churches within the global *ecumene*. This local-translocal relationality is reflected in the early church's self-identity as an alternative *polis*. Again, as Barry Harvey puts it,

> There was from the beginning, however, one major difference between the pilgrim city of Christ and all others. This parallel *polis,* unlike every other city, had no walls, for it had no territory to defend. Its assembly *(ekklesia)* of citizens was not gathered together in one place, but was dispersed throughout the empire and beyond.[56]

Hunsberger's model envisions the church as a local (missional) and global (ecumenical) community of faith. Whether in a "post-Constantinian" situation like North America or in a "pre-Constantinian" situation like Japan, I believe that the churches have much to gain by engaging in intercultural conversations about ways to live more faithfully as the "One Body of Christ" in light of the perduring and daunting tensions between gospel and culture, gospel and church, and church and culture. This book is intended to suggest what such an intercultural, missional-ecumenical conversation might mean for practical theology.

In light of the discussion up till this point, I will turn in Chapter Three to the case study of Tamura Naomi,[57] a first-generation Japanese Christian who helped introduce the contemporary North American theories of religious education in the turbulent social, political, and cultural climate of early twentieth-century Japan. The missional and ecumenical tensions Tamura experienced are highly instructive for practical theology today because his case shows how practical theological theories, which were forged within the Protestant hegemony of North America, were interpreted by a non-Western practical theologian within the very different situation of a former "mission land." Tamura's case shows how both active missional and ecumenical engagement may enrich the practical theological discipline of religious education within and across social, political, and cultural contexts.

Through Tamura's pioneering work in the field of religious education in Japan, I want to show how this kind of practical theological research may (1) enrich our understanding of and appreciation for the profound tensions that characterize a missional encounter between the Christian gospel and a non-Christian social, political, and cultural context; (2) bring to clearer light some of the problematic cultural assumptions that continue to influence our Western approaches to practical theology; and (3) aid us in the construction of theories and rules of art that are more open to the wide range of faith expressions within the global *ecumene*. Through my analysis of Tamura's work, I hope to show how practical theology and its subdisciplines may benefit greatly from a "missional-ecumenical" model that builds on the positive gains of Loder's transformational model. Finally, at the beginning of Chapter Six, I will bring the lessons learned from the case study back into conversation with the contemporary discussion and provide an example of the kind of direction in which I think practical theology needs to move today if it is to more faithfully serve the divine and human praxis of the Trinity of Love revealed in the person of Jesus Christ and participated in by Christians around the world. Given the limitations of this book, I do not propose a full articulation of this broader direction but only some possible ways forward.

CHAPTER THREE Gospel, Church, and Culture Tensions
in Meiji Japan

In this chapter, I will begin my detailed case study that examines how the practical theological theories and practices of the North American religious education movement were introduced in Japan by Tamura Naomi (1858-1934), a first-generation Protestant pastor and the first Japanese graduate of Princeton Theological Seminary (class of 1886). In this case study, I will employ, in an *ad hoc* fashion, Hunsberger's model in tandem with Osmer's "consensus model" as heuristic tools for unpacking some of the tensions experienced by Tamura in his attempt to introduce the theories of religious education in the dynamic missional and ecumenical context of late Meiji, Taisho, and early Showa Japan (1900-1934). Through my presentation of Tamura's story, I will show that some of the same modernist norms that I criticized in Chapter One were also dominant in the work of the early North American leaders of the religious education movement.

Tamura Naomi and His Times

The Reverend Tamura Naomi, career pastor of Sukiyabashi Church[1] and pioneer of Japan's religious education movement, begins *The Guide of Religious Education* (1928)[2] by reflecting on his days as a seminarian in the United States at Auburn Theological Seminary (1882-1885) and Princeton Theological Seminary (1885-1886). He reports that he had never once read or even heard the phrase "religious education" while studying in the United States, and though he was unsure about the exact origin of the phrase, he describes "religious education" as a revolutionary conceptual truth that had burst upon the North American scene around the turn of the century. The religious education movement, which had already entered or was about to enter its second phase in the United States and Germany[3] when Tamura wrote his *Guide* in 1928, suggested to Tamura a positive way for the missionary-founded Japanese Protestant churches and their Sunday Schools to finally escape from what he saw as an unnecessary bondage to premodern, pre-scientific habits and conceptualities and emerge with a robust, modern, and rational Christian self-understanding that could effectively and unembarrassingly withstand the searchlight of the new evolutionary paradigm and thereby contribute significantly to the Christian transformation of Japanese society and culture.

In the first chapter of his *Guide,* Tamura bemoans the tenacious mutual antagonism that continued to overshadow the relations between educators and religious leaders in Japan at that time, and he expresses the utmost confidence that the new paradigm of religious education offered the definitive solution to this dichotomous impasse. Describing this church-culture tension, Tamura says that Japanese educators generally viewed religion as "an outdated superstition" that would eventually disappear with the triumph of positivistic modern science, while religious leaders tended to scorn education as "a snake with which it should not get too entangled."[4] The proper domain of education was thought to be the head, while religion was concerned only with the heart.

Tamura disagreed strongly and believed that the new paradigm of religious education, which sought to integrate the latest findings of psychology and education with the convictions of a more enlightened, contemporary expression of Christian faith, would overcome this unnatural antipathy between the head and heart, and even the deepening rift between modern science and Christian faith. Reflecting the buoyant optimism that was also characteristic of the early pre–World War I days of the religious education movement in the United States, Tamura proclaimed that education and religion, which had formerly been in a relation of mutual enmity, had now been happily married together and were giving birth to a new word of truth embodied by the term "religious education."[5] He was fully confident that religious education offered the way toward a positive integration of these woefully fragmented aspects of modern life. While he never suggested what could be called a sophisticated methodology for practical theology, and while his work needs to be examined critically, Tamura creatively and intuitively engaged in what I will call a missional-ecumenical model of practical theology.

In order to appreciate Tamura's personal development which led to this optimistic faith in the religious education movement and the complex historical, sociocultural, and political developments behind the bifurcation between religion and education to which he refers, I must touch upon Japan's profoundly ambiguous experience of modernization following its coerced reopening to the world by U.S. "gunboat diplomacy" in 1856, the collapse of the 250-year Tokugawa Bakufu (shogunate), the ideological teeter-tottering of the Meiji government (1868-1912), and the arrival of the first Protestant missionaries and other Westerners beginning in the late 1850s.

The era of Tamura's childhood[6] leading up to and following the establishment of the Meiji government in 1868 has been called a "period of bewildering confusion" *(konmeiki)* by the Japanese historian of Christian education Kobayashi Koichi.[7] With the arrival of Commodore Matthew Perry and his four warships in 1853 and his prompt return in 1854 with eight warships, the Bakufu was overwhelmed by the threat of the superior military power of the United States and had no choice but to accept the terms of the letter from U.S. President Franklin Pierce for Japan to treat shipwrecked American sailors humanely, allow American ships to enter Japanese ports, and open bilateral trade relations.[8] This traumatic "opening" not only ended Japan's long self-imposed isolation, but in the words of Hane Mikiso, it also "signaled the beginning of the end of the Tokugawa Bakufu, for its opponents and critics could now begin to intensify their attacks against it, criticizing its inability to stand against the Western powers."[9] One momentous symbol of this change was the samurai (warrior) class's loss of their right to wear the sword in 1876. It is not an insignificant fact that Tamura and most of the other early Protestant leaders came from disenfranchised samurai families.

Under the feudal ideology of the Tokugawa period (1603-1867), Japan had developed a strong self-confidence about the inherent superiority of Asian culture, imagining the countries of the West as vastly inferior, even "barbaric." This deeply ingrained view was suddenly capsized with the arrival of Perry's "black ships." Thus, the uninvited confrontation with the West amounted to a colossal loss of self-confidence for the Japanese, who now felt themselves to be vastly inferior to those Western nations they had formerly perceived to be "barbarian," especially in military, technological, and political terms.

In his comparative analysis of modern Western and Japanese expressions of nationalism, Matsumoto Sannosuke says,

> Nationalism in Japan was very much the result of "external pressure" by which she was forced into the West-centered family of nations and which in turn caused her people to harbor strong fears and anxieties about their new contact with the alien world.[10]

Having been rudely awakened to the reality of the towering technological power of the West, the new Meiji government doggedly set out in pursuit of its stated policy of "Wealthy Nation, Strong Military" *(Fukoku Kyohei)* in order to quickly build a modern nation-state capable of standing shoulder to shoulder with the West. Kobayashi lists the following three pillars of this national policy:

1. The quick adoption of European civilization (especially industry, technology, military affairs, and education);
2. The promotion and protection of capitalism; and
3. An emphasis on nationalism.[11]

Matsumoto points out that, in the wake of the French Revolution, nationalism had become the shared political principle by which modern Western countries defined themselves.

> "National interest" provided the principal rationale as well as the key motivating factor for a country's external and internal behavior. Similarly, national symbols and national consciousness proved to be indispensable assets for the state authorities in the process of political integration. Modern Japan was no exception to this worldwide trend. Indeed, as a late starter in modernization Japan was compelled to be even more nationalistic than the advanced countries of the West.[12]

Naturally, nationalism took a culturally particular form in Japan. Building on Maruyama Masao's thesis that Japanese nationalism was essentially a self-preserving reaction to the invasion of European Christianity and industrialism, Japanese theologians Furuya Yasuo and Ohki Hideo conclude that

> From the outset, Japan's nationalism had the character of an anti-Christian nationalism. Thus, Japan's pre–World War II nationalism took the form of an ultra-nationalism that was self-consciously distinct from the nationalism shared by the modern Western nations.[13]

Not surprisingly, the collapse of the Bakufu was accompanied by a significant rethinking of the religious and philosophical foundations for the polity of the new, "modern" Japan. In place of the Buddhist and Confucian synthesis that had provided the ideological basis for the Tokugawa polity, the leaders of the new Japan drew inspiration from the nativist, Shinto writings of Yamazaki Ansai, Motoori Norinaga, and Hirata Atsutane and other repre-

sentatives of the Mito school and the School of National Learning
(Kokugakusha) as a more distinctively Japanese tradition upon which to build
the national polity.[14] In light of the Bakufu's impotence in the face of the new
global political realties, the *Kokugakusha's* Shintoist critique of Buddhism
seemed especially prescient.

Thus, under the perception of a heightened threat from the West, Japan
was thrust into a reflexive quest for the most salutary domestic and imported
sources of cultural capital upon which to erect the new nation. In the twenty-
one years between the establishment of the Meiji government (1868) and the
promulgation of the Meiji Constitution (1889), Japanese leaders eventually
constructed what Helen Hardacre has fittingly called the "invented tradition"
of modern State Shinto, which carefully wedded the "supercharged symbol-
ism" of Japan's ancient imperial mythology with a predominantly Confucian
ethic and the Western idea of an absolute monarch.[15] Given Japan's particular
cultural and intellectual history, it is not surprising that the ancient imperial
mythology emerged as the most emotionally evocative, distinctively Japanese
symbol for centering and promoting the identity of the new nation-state.
However, the path leading up to this premodern-modern synthesis was anything but straight.

At the same time that the basis for Japan's national polity was undergoing this ideological transformation from a Buddhistic/Confucianist to a Shin-
toistic/Confucianist orientation, a torrent of new and often conflicting religious and secular ideologies such as Christianity (in its Roman Catholic,
Orthodox, and various Protestant expressions),[16] Darwin's theory of evolution, and British utilitarianism were being introduced through foreign missionaries and teachers, Japanese who had returned from studying abroad, and
the rapidly growing number of translated foreign books.

The Protestant missionaries embodied both the "interdenominational"
consensus of the Evangelical Alliance[17] and their particular denominational
traditions. At the same time, other Westerners, like the naturalist Edward
Morse who introduced Darwin's theory of evolution in a series of lectures in
Tokyo in 1877, promoted scientific rationalism, materialism, and historical
relativism as new truths that were believed to undermine the traditional doctrines of Christian faith.[18] As more and more Japanese intellectuals seized
upon this modern European skepticism to repudiate their country's need for
Christianity, the missionaries began to realize that the current intellectual
trends in the West were perhaps a bigger obstacle to evangelization than the
traditional religions of Japan.[19]

Faced with this confusing ideological rivalry, some leading Japanese educators thought it prudent to make Shinto the foundation of the nation's ed-

ucational system while others suggested the adoption of a more pragmatic and utilitarian (*sic* Western) approach. From a tactical standpoint, the government knew that the quick achievement of the first goal of its *Fukoku Kyohei* policy (the adoption of European civilization, especially industry, technology, military affairs, and education) would require a highly literate populace. Thus, the Education Ordinance *(Gakusei)* of 1872, which established Japan's modern educational system, shows that the government initially chose pragmatic utilitarianism over nationalistic ideology. Reflecting the influence of the father of modern education, Fukuzawa Yukichi, the original structure of Japanese schools was modeled on the French system while the curriculum was derived mainly from America.[20] While moral education *(Shushin)* was a subject in government primary and secondary schools from the time of the *Gakusei,* the actual content of the *Shushin* course was originally left up to individual teachers.[21] In spite of this initial Western-leaning educational policy, the deep tensions within the government between Shinto conservatives and progressives like Fukuzawa did not disappear. I will return later to the subject of moral education.

At this juncture, I want to mention the not insignificant role played by the schools, especially the schools for girls, founded by the missionaries. The subject of much curiosity, the mission schools naturally embodied and implicitly modeled current Western educational theories and practices within Japan. By 1883, the missions reported the existence of thirty-one schools with a total of 1,091 students, and by 1900, those numbers had increased to sixty-seven schools with a total of 4,958 students.[22] Unfortunately, this missionary contribution is consistently left out of Japanese textbooks that treat the history of education in early modern Japan.[23]

Tamura came of age during this era of educational experimentation. After being adopted when he was eleven by a wealthy Kyoto samurai family and attending a military academy there, he moved to Tokyo in 1873. There he started to study English with a single missionary named Miss Park who worked with Christopher and Julia Carrothers, missionaries originally affiliated with the Presbyterian Church in the United States of America.

Tamura was well known among his peers as a rowdy student with strong opinions, and his classmates were reportedly shocked when he suddenly announced his decision to be baptized by Carrothers in April 1874. In *Fifty Years of Faith,* Tamura later recounted his Christian understanding at the time of his baptism.

> I was a thorough-going nationalist and did not become a Christian because of any deep conviction. I had not yet had even the slightest taste of

spiritual Christianity. It was simply because Christianity was the religion of civilized nations, making Shinto and Buddhism useless. I was only convinced in my heart that without Christianity Japan could never become civilized like the Western countries. While I had some conception of God, my heart was completely oblivious to spiritual issues such as Christ or Christ's salvation. I think all of the members of the Tsukiji Band who became Christians with me were the same type of believers. Nevertheless, my reception of baptism was a revolution that capsized my entire life. My teachers paid attention to me because I loved being a student. Also, my own sense of becoming a Christian helped me achieve better self-control. My present spiritual age is fifty. The one difference between becoming a Christian then and now (in 1924) is that you could not receive baptism unless you were prepared to be rejected by your parents or ridiculed by your friends. I am one who underwent such bitter experiences. However, I am thankful that whenever I look back on those days, I feel like something of a hero.[24]

Five years later, after graduating in 1879 from the *Tokyo Icchi Shingako,* an early forerunner of Tokyo Union Theological Seminary, Tamura was ordained by Guido Verbeck, a first-generation missionary luminary from the Reformed Church in America. In 1880, at the age of twenty-two, he was installed as the first Japanese pastor of the First Presbyterian Church in Tokyo (Ginza).

Tamura met with controversy the first time in 1882 when, while away on an evangelistic mission with Verbeck, a former geisha who had become a Christian accused the young pastor of engaging in sexual relations with her. Maintaining his innocence, Tamura appealed his case to the Presbytery. The night before the Presbytery was scheduled to review his case, the woman withdrew her accusations, and the Presbytery concluded that the accusations had been "part of a vendetta against Tamura by a faction within the congregation."[25] Nevertheless, because of the commotion this accusation had stirred up in his congregation, Tamura decided to resign. In August of the same year, he left for the United States to pursue further studies at Auburn and Princeton.

By the time of his departure, the era of Japan's educational experimentation was already grinding to a halt. Perceiving the dangerous encroachment of alien Western values through the pragmatic, utilitarian approach to education, nationalists like Eifu Motoda began to assert their ideological influence on Japan's schools. This change in direction was underwritten by imperial authority in a document called "The Outline of Learning" (*Kyogaku Taishi*) that was signed by the Emperor Meiji in 1879. Concerning this reactionary shift, Hanae says,

A conscious effort was made to replace the more libertarian, individualistic values that were taught in the school with traditional virtues such as loyalty to the Emperor, filial piety, and benevolence and righteousness.[26]

Beginning in 1886, these nationalistic reforms were instituted under the direction of Mori Arinori (1847-1889), the minister of education, who was, ironically, later assassinated by ultranationalists on the morning of February 11, 1889, the day the new constitution was proclaimed.[27]

Not surprisingly, the progressives, led by Fukuzawa, disagreed strongly with both the diagnosis and remedy of the nationalists. Given the rapid transformation of Japanese society, they believed that a certain degree of social, political, and cultural instability was inevitable and that it should not be blamed on the recent introduction of Western educational theories and practices.[28] In spite of Fukuzawa's opposition, the Meiji government turned from French and American models and looked more and more to the German tradition of moral education, exemplified by Johann Friedrich Herbart, for guidance on how to effectively implant the emperor-centered piety in the heart of every imperial subject. Thus, while the early years of the Meiji Era saw a rise in interest in the enlightenment ideas of individualism and freedom, by the end of the 1880s there was an overwhelming consensus that an austere, monolithic communal morality based on an emperor-centered filialism was in Japan's best national interests.

Tamura and other leaders among the first generation of Japanese Christians expressed a variety of responses to these complex tensions between the teachings of the Christian faith, the contemporary interpretations of the inherited capital of Japanese culture, and the increasingly secular, scientific spirit of the modern West. For example, together with Uemura Masahisa, who would later become his nemesis, and Kozaki Hiromichi, Tamura helped launch the apologetic and progressive magazine *Rikugo Zasshi* in 1880 as a public forum to discuss the intersection of these complex issues. Around the same time, Uchimura Kanzo, who eventually founded the Non-Church Movement *(Mukyokai)*,[29] was reported to have undertaken a serious study of the "relation of biology to Christianity."[30] Not surprisingly, there was a range of attitudes toward recent sociocultural trends among the missionaries. While some were implacable in their rejection of modern science, others, like Verbeck, who had ordained Tamura, expressed an open-minded orthodoxy that was not perfunctorily closed to the findings of science. For example, in an 1884 lecture, Verbeck said that Christianity and science "treat of entirely different departments of human knowledge and are necessary adjuncts to each other."[31]

To further complicate matters for both the missionaries and the new Japanese converts, the American Unitarian Association sent Arthur Knapp in 1887 to Japan to give speeches on the Unitarian approach to the relation of religion and science. Notably, these lectures influenced the pragmatic Fukuzawa, who had previously been very skeptical of Christianity. Since Fukuzawa's son Ichitaro had been a boarder in the Knapps' home while he was studying in the United States, Fukuzawa invited Knapp to speak to his students at the *Keio-gijuku*. As a result of Knapp's lectures, Fukuzawa softened his former opposition to Christianity and remarked that the Unitarian "negation of miracles, the humanness of Jesus, and the rational development of morality by human endeavor were all agreeable to him."[32]

However, on the question of the relation of Japan's traditional religions to its current national ambitions, Knapp may have unwittingly given support to the ultra-nationalistic direction of the Japanese government. Robert Schwantes quotes from Knapp's speech at the English Law School, as follows:

> That which you have always reverenced, the virtues, the honor of your ancestors . . . instead of being despised and cast out, ought to be made the very foundation of . . . the higher religion of your future. . . . Civilization means and demands of you, not imitation, not uniformity, not subserviency, but the utmost development of your national individuality.[33]

While the degree of impact that these Unitarian ideas had on the government or the subsequent development of the faith of the Japanese churches is still debated by scholars today,[34] it is telling that the 1890s witnessed a significant decline in church growth, with many prominent Christians abandoning their faith.

Education from Above

On February 11, 1889, Japan's first modern constitution, which guaranteed freedom of religion within the strictly defined limits of national interest, was promulgated by the emperor. Next, the Imperial Rescript on Education (*Kyoiku ni Kansuru Chokugo*),[35] which set an inviolate Imperial (Shinto) Household at the core of Japanese personal, familial, communal, educational, vocational, and national morality, was also promulgated by the emperor on October 30, 1890. Commenting on the Rescript's creative synthesis of Shinto, Confucian, and Western elements, Klaus Luhmer says,

Reference to the Shinto mythology surrounding the origin and status of the Imperial family in the eyes of its authors did not violate the principle of separation of Church and State. It was used as a medium for giving expression to the paternalistic foundations of the identity feeling of the Japanese nation — a family with the Emperor as family head.[36]

Some had suggested a Buddhistic or even a Christian religious grounding for the Rescript, but in light of the misgivings about Buddhism with the collapse of the Bakufu and the daunting ambiguities attending the introduction of nineteenth-century Western Christianity, the Shintoist imperial mythology was thought to be the only shared cultural symbol capable of eliciting the "identity feeling" thought to be necessary for uniting the nation.

Practically speaking, the comprehensive moral vision promulgated by the Rescript was impressed upon the hearts of all Japanese children by means of regular, affectively charged ritual performances that took place in all Japanese schools. Luhmer describes this practice as follows:

> The Rescript was treated with quasi-religious reverence, kept together with the picture of the Emperor and Empress in a special safe, recited solemnly in front of the entire student body on national feast days, entrance and commencement exercises, and similar occasions. Elderly Japanese even now remember it by heart. The story goes that some principals committed suicide when they mispronounced a word in reciting the Rescript or when it perished in a fire.[37]

Until Japan's defeat in World War II in 1945, the Rescript served as the hallowed nationalist creed and moral foundation of modern Japanese identity.

As these ambiguous but interrelated developments cutting across the spheres of national polity, religion, morality, and education attest, the Meiji government utilized the Rescript to foster a spirit of unquestioning loyalty to the emperor as the means of achieving its pragmatic political and economic goals. Of the enforcement of this "nationalism from above," Kobayashi says that, since it was unrealistic to expect a spontaneous and active sense of civil solidarity to arise from the people, education was mobilized to serve a nationalist agenda. While the "ethnic spirit" of the people was successfully transformed into a "national spirit" using the characteristic pattern of "revolution from above" or "modernization from above," the people generally had little awareness and understanding of the nation state.[38]

Matsumoto attributes this lack of civic consciousness to the intellectual and historical differences behind Western and Japanese nationalism. He says that Japan had no "universalist cultural tradition" akin to the medieval *corpus christianum* or any notion parallel to "the universal, abstract, and rational individual" that arose out of the renaissance and reformation testing of the medieval consensus. Lacking any civic tradition of freedom for rational, individual expression or any democratic tradition of "government by consent," Matsumoto says,

> From the very outset, Japan's modern state pursued political integration along nationalistic rather than democratic lines. The rational, dynamic approach which attempts political integration through free expressions of divergent individual opinions and through adjusting conflicting interests did not take root in practice. Instead, the Japanese state relied more on the emotional approach which, in appealing to the national consciousness, dramatized the unique character of the nation and the racial homogeneity of the people to effect a national unity. The absoluteness of the emperor's personal authority and the idea of imperial sovereignty were, of course, pivotal for the Japanese pattern of national integration.[39]

Under the sway of this policy of "education from above," internal and external affairs tended to strengthen the feelings of nationalism among the people. Drummond comments on the chilling effect that these political and sociocultural developments had on Christianity.

> These documents (the Meiji Constitution and the Rescript) expressed essentially the political, social, and cultural aspirations not only of the ruling classes but also the bulk of the nation. As they came to be interpreted and applied in the light of this background, they occasioned a new form of Japanese cultural confrontation with the transcendent claims of Christianity. The issue came to be formulated by the proponents of the Japanese cultural tradition *(kokusui)* and social-political structure *(kokutai)* as the irreconcilability of Christianity with the mainstream of historic Japanese life.[40]

While the first generation of Japanese Protestants were all nationalists to one degree or another, it is important to remember that they were all educated before the promulgation of the Rescript. It was only a matter of time for the monolithic national *ethos* to clash with the more individualistic expression of Christian conscience. In 1891, the well-known *Lese Majesty Incident (Fukeijiken)* involving Uchimura Kanzo occurred.[41] Uchimura was eventually forced to resign from his teaching post at the First High School in Tokyo for refusing to bow during the school's first ceremonial reading of the Imperial

Rescript on Education. Katoh describes this momentous event in the history of modern Japan.

> Uchimura was third in line to mount the platform to pay his respects. With virtually no time to think about what he was doing, Uchimura proceeded before the Rescript, and plagued by doubts, slightly bowed his head but did not worship (which required clapping three times and bowing deeply). Though he had no theoretical conviction about his own actions, in that terrifying moment, he simply followed his conscience as a Christian and felt as if he were treading onto thin ice.[42]

This unknown young Christian suddenly became the target of enraged ultra-nationalists who publicly taunted him as a "blasphemous boy" *(fukeikan)* and "public enemy" *(kokuzoku)*. Uchimura's action was interpreted as "a lack of respect for the imperial family, and it greatly stimulated attacks on Christians who were accused of being unpatriotic."[43]

While Uchimura's true intentions have been the subject of much subsequent debate, the *apologia* of a contemporary Christian published in 1906 sheds some light on the complexities of being a Christian in Japan during the early 1890s. On the one hand, Yamaji Aizan claimed that Uchimura had been a hapless victim of ultra-nationalist conservatives. He also takes pains to show that Uchimura himself was a thoroughgoing, albeit Christian patriot.[44] Trying to disassociate Uchimura from the missionaries and those Japanese Christians, like the early Tamura, who had developed more favorable relations with the missionaries, Yamaji writes,

> Even if at that time there was no great gap between Uchimura and the Christians, he was an enthusiastic patriot because he most bitterly hated the foreign missionaries.[45]

As even further evidence of Uchimura's love of his country, Yamaji recounted a lecture that Uchimura had delivered in 1889, two years prior to the *Lese Majesty Incident,* on the emperor's birthday at *Toyo Eiwa Gakko,* a mission-founded school in Tokyo's Azabu district.

> He (Uchimura) pointed to the chrysanthemum (the symbol of the imperial family) that adorned the podium and said that the flower was one of nature's special blessings to Japan. It is a famous flower unique to Japan. "Ladies and gentlemen, look out the window and see Mount Fuji, which rises in the western sky. This is also splendid scenery bestowed upon our

country by heaven. Students, please remember, however, that in Japan, the greatest and most mysterious thing, which surpasses all things in the world, is, in reality, our Imperial Household." He said, "Our Imperial Household, like heaven and earth, has no end. It should be the only pride of the Japanese people."[46]

Whatever the real nature of Uchimura's paradoxical loyalties to Jesus and Japan, there is no doubt that his action galvanized the nativist attacks on Christianity and the educational institutions founded and still largely administered by the missions.

The *apologia* for this nationalist offensive was expressed most clearly in Tokyo Imperial University's Inoue Tetsujiro's 1893 essay titled "The Collision of Education and Religion" *(Shukyo to Kyoiku to no Shototsu).* Inoue's straightforward attack consisted of three main points recounted by Yamaji:

1. Education in our country must be based on the Imperial Rescript on Education.
2. The Imperial Rescript is statist and based on filial piety. Christianity is based on internationalism not statism. It teaches that there should be no discrimination in love, and it does not teach loyalty to the state. It teaches that above our lord (the emperor) there is God and Christ, and thus it is opposed to loyalty and filial piety.
3. For this reason religion and reason are in collision.[47]

In the wake of the assaults of Inoue and others, government authorities were emboldened to take a more aggressively critical approach toward Christianity. Perhaps the most unequivocal example of the government's antipathy toward Christianity came in 1899 with the "Ministry of Education's Directive Number Twelve" *(Monbusho Kunrei Daijunigo).* This law was intended as a direct hit on the Christian schools. Signed by Count Kabayama, minister of education, it read:

It being essential from the point of view of educational administration that general education should be independent of religion, religious instruction must not be given, or religious ceremonies performed, at Government Schools, Public Schools, or schools whose curricula are regulated by provision of law, even outside the regular course of instruction.[48]

In 1926, reflecting on this time of bitter testing for the churches and mission schools, August Karl Reischauer says,

Many, even ministers of the Gospel, grew indifferent and some turned violently against Christianity . . . the old charge was revived that Christianity is the enemy of the state since it demands supreme loyalty to Christ.[49]

Following this general description of the missional and ecumenical situation of Meiji Japan, I will now turn to a highly politicized and traumatic event that forever changed Tamura's life and the direction of his work as a practical theologian.

The *Japanese Bride* Incident

In 1893, two years after Uchimura's *Lese Majesty Incident,* a forgotten but perhaps even more significant incident in the history of Japanese Christianity took place involving Tamura and his recently established church, the Church of Christ in Japan (Presbyterian). In 1886, just after returning from the United States with a joint master's degree from Princeton Theological Seminary and Princeton University, Tamura had published a small book in Japanese called *Beikoku no Fujin (American Women),* which criticized what he perceived to be the miserable plight of Japanese women in light of the relatively more favorable situation of women he had witnessed firsthand in the United States. Flowing from his normative understanding of Christian social ethics, the book touts the doctrine of the equal rights for women and men and urges the need for the construction of a new kind of family in Japan. Tamura believed that this familial ideal, in which, for example, the mutual sexual fidelity of men and women would be maintained, and through which the social status of women would gradually be improved, was only possible by the power of Christianity.[50] Very much in keeping with the spirit of the age of Westernization described above, *Beikoku no Fujin* was evidently well received inside and outside the Japanese churches.[51] According to Tamura's own account, not a single person "raised any questions about the content of the book nor about his personal character."[52]

However, after returning from a trip to the United States in 1892 to raise money for his boarding house for poor students *(Jieikan),*[53] Tamura slightly revised his *Beikoku no Fujin* for an English audience with the help of a classmate from Auburn Theological Seminary. The book was published in English in 1893 by Harper & Brothers as *The Japanese Bride.*[54] Recounting the events that unfolded subsequent to the English publication, Tamura wrote that he had been ominously forewarned by his missionary friend David Thompson[55] not to go through with the publication of *The Japanese Bride.*

> When he heard that this book was going to be published in the United
> States, Thompson visited my home and told me, "In the current situa-
> tion, to clearly reveal the Japanese situation in an English writing would
> not only be a dangerous but an unwise action. For your own safety, I
> think it would be best to abandon the idea."[56]

While expressing his gratitude for Thompson's kind concern, Tamura reportedly told him that he was convinced of his duty as a Christian and lover of the
truth to speak openly about the shortcomings of the Japanese, even if he had
to endure the world's attack.[57]

The eight chapters of *The Japanese Bride* are titled as follows: (1) Why
Do We Marry?; (2) Courting; (3) The Go-Between; (4) Preparation for the
Wedding; (5) The Wedding Ceremony; (6) The Honey-Moon; (7) Bride and
Bridegroom at Home; and (8) Mother and Grandmother. Historian Takeda
Kiyoko summarizes the central points of Tamura's critique of the Japanese
family system.

> Because marriage in Japan is not based on love but on the importance of
> the succession of family lineage, girls are taught from a young age that they
> are inferior to boys, their marriages are decided by their parents and thus
> afford them no opportunity for personal relations with the opposite sex,
> they go from being the property of their father to being their husband's
> property and, like the relation between an absolute monarch and his sub-
> jects, the wife is expected to be absolutely obedient to her husband. Even if
> the husband engages in immoral relations with a *geisha* or another woman,
> the wife should never resist but rather bear it patiently with a smile. Disobe-
> dience to her husband or mother-in-law immediately means divorce. The
> husband can obtain a divorce according to his own wishes, but the wife has
> no rights whatsoever. Obedience is the paramount virtue in Japan. Without
> the efforts of Christians, the Japanese will never be able to taste true love.[58]

Takeda points out that, fifty-two years later, it was ironically exactly the same
issues that Tamura had raised in *The Japanese Bride* that were once again subject to sharp criticism in the aftermath of Japan's defeat in World War II.[59]

Thus, the book represents a bold and prescient if somewhat politically
naïve critique, from the normative ethical perspective of a first-generation
Japanese Christian, of Japanese marriage customs that Tamura judged to be
oppressive and antithetical to Christian faith. In the preface, he justifies this
direct critical approach by offering his own interpretation of the above-
described situation in the 1890s. I will quote it at length.

This is the age of danger and the age of confusion with Japan. Old Japan is passing away, and new Japan is coming to the threshold. The old man's opinion is no longer respected, and the young man's word has no weight. Buddhism, Shintoism, and Confucianism have lost their power of control, and Christianity has not yet taken hold of the mass of our people. Old and new customs are mingled together, and they do not work well. Old men are content to marry in accordance with old customs, but young men wish to marry in the foreign way, making their own choice of a wife, yet without moral restraint, although they breathe the air of new thought imported from Christian countries. Young men are dissatisfied with old customs of marriage, but they cannot easily adopt a new mode. . . . This shows something of the result of the confusion of old and new, and the danger to our inner life in this transition period. You might ask, on reading my book on "The Japanese Bride," Is not there a noble virtue in woman's obedience, in such a solemnity at the wedding ceremony, and in such warm devotion of young men towards their old parents? Yes, indeed! But Japanese virtue is very pharisaical — in form, not in heart. Nine out of ten ladies in Japan obey their husbands not joyfully, but unwillingly, just like the people of an absolute monarch. Our wedding solemnity does not indicate the purity of our hearts, or the sacredness of the marriage institution. I have frankly painted our home life which foreigners never penetrate, and which most Japanese hesitate to reveal, feeling it to be a shame to open the dark side of our home life in public, and especially before the gaze of foreigners. I have tried to write with sincerity, in the spirit of loving truth, without any fear.[60]

While Tamura's rhetoric anticipates a strong reaction from some readers, he had no idea that his little book, ostensibly written "with sincerity, in the spirit of loving truth, without any fear," would create such a huge stir, not only outside but inside the Japanese church. For a brief period of time, Tamura became a household name.

By the fall of 1893, Tamura's book had become the subject of harsh criticism, with over two hundred Japanese newspapers covering the story. Tamura was accused of sullying Japanese virtue, and the government even outlawed the retranslation of the book back into Japanese.[61] Tamura received some death threats from irate ultranationalists which he magnanimously laughed off, but there are reports that the boarders at his *Jieikan* stood guard for him at night with bamboo sticks.

These developments worsened the predicament of the already fledgling Japanese churches. With the recollection of Uchimura's refusal to bow before the Rescript still fresh in the public's mind, Tamura's book added fuel to the growing sentiment that Christianity was clearly irreconcilable with Japan's nationalist aspirations. Japanese society had undergone a decisive change of direction between the publication of *Beikoku no Fujin* and *The Japanese Bride.*

As Tamura and others were pointing out the more amicable situation of American marriages, the Japanese family was being "reinvented" to serve nationalist ends. According the Nishikawa Yuko, in its Civil Code (1896) the Meiji Government in effect universalized the traditional samurai family, the *ie,* by granting absolute authority to the head of the household and subordinating all other family members under a strict patriarchal lineage. But the "modern" Meiji *ie* system differed in one significant way from its Tokugawa Era predecessor. Rather than placing the household heads under the authority of the local lord, village community, or trade associations as during the Tokugawa period, the Meiji *ie* was refashioned into the basic unit of the modern Japanese nation-state of which the emperor was the inviolable patriarchal head. Nishikawa writes, "Japan, indeed, was said to have a unique system called the 'family state,' as witnessed in the Imperial Rescript on Education of 1890, which defined the nation as an extended form of an *ie.*"[62]

To return to the attack on Tamura for his book, it did not take long for the winds of suspicion stirring among the public to blow across the threshold of the churches. Uemura Masahisa, Tamura's boyhood friend and emerging leader of the Japanese Presbyterians, who had himself often expressed progressive views on marriage and the family, was the first Christian leader to publish a sharp critique of Tamura and his book on August 18, 1893.[63] Next, an investigative committee of the Tokyo Presbytery of the Church of Christ in Japan (Presbyterian) presented its findings on Tamura's case at a meeting on October 5, 1893. Outlining the points that they found especially offensive, the three-person committee, all former associates of Tamura, charged him with "slandering the people" *(dohozambuzai)* and demanded he "publish, in the near future, an appropriate retraction in five magazines and newspapers in Japan and America."[64] In language that reflected almost word for word the critique of the nationalist newspapers, one of the committee members summarized the Presbytery's concerns as follows:

> The main point is that as a result of this book Mr. Tamura has slandered the 40 million people of Japan. He has damaged the integrity and defamed the honor of our imperial Japan before other nations. He has rejected the high sense of duty and obligation for the national body politic which pastors of the Japanese Christian Church must bear.[65]

Tamura flatly rejected the Presbytery's disciplinary action and defended him-self by saying that he had written out of a "spirit of love for the truth," point-ing out that he had also praised certain aspects of Japanese culture in the book.[66] After refusing Tamura's request to present further witnesses, the Pres-bytery approved the investigative committee's decision by one vote.[67]

Convinced of the rightness of his cause, Tamura appealed the Presbytery's decision to the Synod of his church. The Synod meeting was held in July 1894. After Uemura presented a statement in which he personally maligned Tamura for his unremitting, self-defensive attitude, the Synod affirmed the Presbytery's earlier decision and added an amendment mandating the ultimate punish-ment, Tamura's deposition from the ministry. The Synod's verdict read,

> The accused has behaved in a manner inappropriate for a minister. He has engaged in activities for which he has no authority, insulting the people and damaging the honor of the Japanese people before the nations. Instead of furthering the cause he is a serious obstacle to evangelism in Japan. Even though he received counsel on several occasions he completely ignored this advice, refused to reconsider his behavior in any way and offered no apol-ogy. Instead, he rejected the counsel of others and defended himself, using whatever means were available. He has brought shame upon the position of minister in an ethical religion which requires the exercise of a high degree of personal responsibility. The first Meeting of the Tokyo Presbytery issued a very mild reprimand, requiring as punishment only that the author pub-lish a correction in the appropriate magazines and newspapers. But he re-fused to accept even this. On the basis of the ample evidence which is avail-able in the defendant's book itself, in the records of the Tokyo Presbytery, in the statements of both the plaintiff and the defendant before this session of the Synod, in the letter from the American, Mr. Phillips, and in an abun-dance of others facts, this meeting of the Synod amends the decision of the First Tokyo Presbytery. Mr. Tamura Naomi is not fit to serve as a minister. He is dismissed from his position as a minister.[68]

In his autobiography, Tamura described the Synod's action as "murder at the hands of the Yokohama Band."[69] Many of the missionaries present at the synod meeting were outraged and one yelled out, "Murder by a religious court!" *(Shukyo hotei no satsujin)*. Later, the Council of Cooperating Missions issued the following carefully worded protest:

> The Council of Cooperating Missions has heard with profound regret the decision of the Diakwai of the Church of Christ in Japan deposing Rev.

> N. Tamura from the ministry. The reasons for the same are, that, while it must be admitted that there are statements and opinions presented in *The Japanese Bride*, which are open to criticism because of their lack of good taste and their unfairness, yet these statements and opinions have no relevance to any point of doctrine or government in the standards of the Church, nor, in the opinions of the members of this Council, can the writings of them be construed as a moral offense. Therefore, without expressing an opinion as to any alleged acts or statements of the Rev. N. Tamura, outside the formal charges preferred in the Diakwai, the sentence of deposition — the extreme penalty for the gravest offenses — is regarded as excessive, and as contrary to the spirit of love and justice.[70]

After the Synod's decision, Tamura and his congregation withdrew from the Japanese Presbyterians until rejoining them after Uemura's death in 1930. Tamura never retracted and continued pastoring the same church until his death in 1934.

It is not an easy task to sort out the surface and depth dimensions of this case. Why were Japanese church leaders, many of whom were themselves "progressivist" in their views of women,[71] so quick to join the secular chorus of critics of Tamura and his book? Uemura himself had been a "strong advocate of family reform," and one of his daughters was one of the first women ordained in the Presbyterian-Reformed tradition anywhere.[72] Was it Tamura's reputedly strong and individualistic personality that had incited the extreme reaction by his church? Indeed, Tamura's stubbornness flew in the face of the "community-first" relational loyalty that was assumed within the Confucian *ethos* of Meiji Japan. Or, given the lingering rivalry between the earliest Presbyterian-Reformed factions (Tamura's Tsukiji Band vs. Uemura's Yokohama Band) and the fact that the Church of Christ in Japan (Presbyterian) had just been formed in 1890, was the book seized as a means for asserting the ecclesial dominance of Uemura's Yokohama Band? Furuya and Ohki conclude that, beyond these complex intrinsic issues, extrinsic political pressure was probably the greatest factor leading up to Tamura's deposition.

> The greatest reason that this issue escalated to the level of an ecclesial trial was the self-preserving, opportunistic attitude of the church toward ultranationalism.[73]

Similarly claiming that the church made Tamura into a "fall guy" to assuage the wrath of the virulent nationalist critics of Christianity, Takeda says,

Rather than itself becoming the victim of the increasingly virulent emperor-centered nationalistic ideology, the recently founded Japanese church went too far in strategically trying to protect itself by daring to sacrifice one of its own, with the result that it is possible to conclude the young church was a "tactician."[74]

For some time after this tragic incident, Tamura withdrew from public life and concentrated on his pastoral responsibilities at Sukiyabashi Church, his work with the students of the *Jieikan,* his reading, and gardening. Tamura's wife Ei later reported that Uchimura, the hapless victim of the *Lese Majesty Incident,* was the only Japanese who visited Tamura during this exceedingly difficult time of exile.[75] They remained friends for life, and Uchimura himself said that Tamura was the only one who could really understand and comfort him because he, too, had been labeled as a traitor.[76]

In spite of this period of "exile" following *The Japanese Bride* incident, Furuya and Ohki mistakenly conclude that Tamura, in contrast to his Yokohama Band rivals Uemura and Ibuka, "became a forgotten pastor."[77] On the contrary, not only did the Sukiyabashi Church continue to grow under Tamura's leadership, three years after the incident he joined with other Christians in the public protest against the inhumane labor conditions at the Ashio Coal Mines. Tamura also participated in the mass evangelism campaign launched by the Evangelical Federation in 1900 and,[78] more important, Tamura soon became the leading Japanese interpreter and proponent of the religious education movement. Actually, it was his reading of the North American literature on the psychology of religion and the emergent religious education movement that rekindled Tamura's aspirations for the Christian transformation of Japanese society. For his choice of methods, Tamura turned from adult evangelism to the nurture of children, and from the direct, prophetic confrontation of his earlier work to a commitment to the long-term and indirect process of religious education.

Before turning to Tamura's practical theological turn from evangelism to religious education, I want to consider this early period of Protestant missionary transmission in conversation with Hunsberger's tripartite model which I introduced in Chapter Two. While I will comment separately on each of Hunsberger's three axes for the sake of analysis, it is important to also remember that all three axes function at the synthetic level since they intersect each other at crucial points.

Gospel and Culture Tensions

While I have not focused in depth on the initial encounter of the Japanese with the North American and European missionaries, it is clear even from the above story that this encounter produced some inevitable tension between the foreign transmission and native reception of the gospel.[79] Uchimura Kanzo, who later went on to found the indigenous Non-Church Movement, exemplifies perhaps better than anyone the pendulous spiritual, intellectual, and emotional disquiet the new converts experienced between their new loyalty to the "foreign" faith and their old loyalty to Japan.[80] Indeed, Takeda says that all of the Meiji-era Christians, including Tamura, were nationalists with a strong sense of Japanese identity and pride in their cultural identity.[81] This made for a creative theological tension, as the foreign faith was expressed through a variety of tacit native conceptualities, perhaps most prominently *Bushido,* the Confucian ethical code of the warrior class (samurai).[82] Of this dialectic between challenge and embodiment, Hunsberger says "Embodiment without challenge would lead to syncretism; challenge without embodiment would be irrelevant."[83] If we depict this tension in early Meiji Japan as a continuum between what Walls calls the indigenizing principle and the pilgrim principle, three general trajectories (not a typology) present themselves.

On one end of the continuum were those who tended toward a "nationalistic syncretism." Representative of this pattern was Congregational Church leader Ebina Danjo's "nationalistic Christianity." According to Dohi, Ebina dangerously "constructed his theology around personal religious experience."[84] For example, he believed that Shintoism and Christianity could be fully reconciled. Schwantes wryly comments how, under the sway of the ultranationalism of the 1890s, Ebina "made the comforting discovery that the neo-Shinto doctrines . . . were identical with Christianity and that Japan had been 'God's country' all through history."[85]

The second pattern, exemplified by the "Japanese Progressive Evangelicalism" *(Fukuinshugi)* of Tamura's main accuser Uemura Masahisa, represents what Hunsberger calls the "challenging relevance" of the gospel in its encounter with a local culture. For example, while showing respect for his native *Bushido,* Uemura was also able to achieve and maintain a significant critical distance in what he called a "baptized *Bushido.*"[86]

> We ought not to reject *Bushido* indiscriminately. Just as the cherry flower is the queen of all flowers, so is the *samurai* master of all men. We may rightly be proud of our being descendents of *samurai*. Nevertheless, we have to acknowledge a number of shortcomings and faults in the code of

the *samurai*. Our prayer is that the spirit of the *samurai* with all its praise-worthy strong points may be grafted to that of the cross through our faith in the Lord of all creatures, the Saviour of the world.[87]

Uemura generally tried to maintain a creative tension, which preserved elements of continuity and discontinuity, between his new faith and the old culture. As a positive example of this approach, while reading Pawlette's *The Whole Duty of Man*, Uemura reportedly discovered some felicitous analogues between the practical religious *ethos* of the English Puritans and his native Confucian tradition that likely contributed to his theology of *kokorozashi*.[88]

The third pattern, embodied by the early Tamura of *The Japanese Bride* incident, unfortunately inclined toward "ideological irrelevance." Given the sociocultural and political realities of the 1890s, Tamura's prophetic critique of Japanese customs clearly went too far in the direction of discontinuity with and negation of the old culture. While the critique surely was correct in terms of its biblical, theological, and philosophical grounding, the fact that it did not contribute to the improvement of the actual situation of Japanese women suggests that the young Tamura seriously misread his own missional context. In his zeal, Tamura naïvely imagined that the North American *habitus* of truth-telling could supplant the Japanese *habitus* of loyalty in a single stroke of his pen. *The Japanese Bride* incident testifies to the fact that the cross-cultural transmission of evangelical capital does not go as effortlessly as the importation of material goods. While it may have created a huge stir initially and nearly cost Tamura his life, his little book was soon forgotten.

Gospel and Church Tensions

In terms of the ideal of a reciprocal, hermeneutical relationship between the gospel and the churches, which Hunsberger calls a "fruit of conversion,"[89] the early Japanese Protestants were originally no more than an informal federation of rival "bands," led by charismatic figures, that could hardly be called an established church. The new converts were only beginning to assert their independence from the missions. For example, since Tamura's church had been founded only three years prior to his deposition from ministry, they had little experience in engaging in serious contextual dialogue with scripture, although it should be pointed out that Uemura, who led the attack against Tamura in 1893 and 1894, had publicly come out in support of Uchimura following the *Lese Majesty Incident* in 1891. While it is tempting to lay the entire blame for Tamura's deposition at the feet of the church for their capitulation

PRACTICAL THEOLOGY AND THE ONE BODY OF CHRIST

to contemporary sociopolitical pressures, Tamura himself must bear some of the responsibility.

While he may have wished that his book would encourage the church to engage in a more direct dialogue with scriptural norms and North American views on women and the family, the form of his presentation shows that he failed to understand and interpret the actual context in which his church found itself. Given the dizzying, emotional conflagration of external and internal pressures and loyalties, the church felt they had to wash their hands of Tamura's English book since it had been thoroughly condemned by the public for parading what were perceived as embarrassing details about Japanese culture before foreigners with a suspected predilection for oriental voyeurism. If he had really wanted the Japanese church to champion the cause of women by fighting for their social and political liberation, he could have been more circumspect in the means he chose for publishing his critique.

For their part, the church's rash handling of Tamura's case shows that no consideration whatsoever was given to what the biblical witness or contemporary cultural trends might suggest in the prosecution of such disciplinary cases. Aside from the *ad hominem* accusation of the Synod that Tamura was "a serious obstacle to evangelism in Japan," there is not even the slightest suggestion in the disciplinary actions of the Tokyo Presbytery or the Japan Synod[90] that scriptural or theological norms had entered into their deliberations. Thus, at least on the surface, the documentary evidence shows that the church deposed Tamura for reasons independent of the norms of the gospel. The witness of the Japanese church suffered greatly in its rash handling of Tamura's case. A consideration of some of the complexities behind this problem takes us into the longer discussion of the third axis.

Culture and Church Tensions

Between the 1860s and 1890s, the "missionary dialogue" between the church and culture went from an initial stage of mutual fascination and openness to an emotionally charged era of mutual suspicion and closedness. While I do not want to completely reduce the lack of the young church's critical engagement with the gospel to contemporary political circumstances, it is important to recall the anti-Christian delirium that followed upon Uchimura's failure to show respect for the emperor in 1891. The major factor that contributed to the growing marginalization of Christianity within Japan was the young nation's hasty search for a unifying "modern" spiritual identity. The above-mentioned defense of Uchimura's patriotism as embodying the requisite hatred of the foreign missionaries shows that Japanese Christians were hard pressed to demonstrate their loyalty to Japan by publicly asserting their independence from the missionaries.

Given this extrinsic pressure to distinguish himself from the foreigners, Uchimura's refusal to bow is probably more appropriately interpreted as a private issue of conscience rather than as a public gesture of solidarity with the faith of the universal church. Indeed, with the confusing competition between orthodox and liberal perspectives on what really constituted the essence of Christianity, it was a daunting task for the first generation of Japanese Christians to sort out what they could and could not accept of the gospel and ecclesial traditions transmitted by the missionaries.

Two enduring trajectories in Japanese Protestantism may be traced back to these tensions between the native and missionary churches. The first is Uemura's Progressive Evangelicalism *(Fukuinshugi)* which, as I have already pointed out, strove for a balance between continuity and discontinuity with Western ecclesial and theological traditions.[91] The second major trajectory is Uchimura's indigenous Non-Church Movement *(Mukyokai)*, which arose as the missionaries' denominationalism came to be viewed as an insurmountable stumbling block. Distinguishing his non-church from what he saw as mere human inventions that had supplanted the biblical *sola fides*, Uchimura wrote,

> In the so-called church, there are bishops, elders, theologians, constitutions, and creeds. It is a kind of government or political party, which tries to expand its power and save the people, not by faith, but by public opinion. Though it is called the Church, it is not the Church built by Christ. In contrast to this kind of Church, we openly insist on the Non-Church. (*The Study of the Bible*, 1921, No. 11)[92]

While Uchimura's theology was rather orthodox and evangelical, his non-church focused on devotional, academic study of the Bible and rejected all traditional ecclesial forms, including the sacraments of baptism and the Lord's Supper and an ordained clergy.[93]

In addition to the internal pressure of rising ultranationalism, another factor that exacerbated the growing tension between the church and Japanese culture was the reactionary attitude of some of the missionaries toward the insights of contemporary science. For example, speaking on "The Training Needed for Native Pastors and Evangelists" at the Osaka Missionary Conference in 1883, the Rev. J. D. Davis strongly opposed the investigations of modern science to what he called the "fundamental truths of salvation," and considered the former to be essentially inconsequential in the training of

Japanese ministers. While he was keenly aware of the deep fascination that educated Japanese had for "Western, modern, and materialistic ideas," Davis naïvely asserts that contemporary scientific theories

> are as changing and various as a kaleidoscope; that nine-tenths of those on the surface now will be out of date in five or ten years, while a new set will have taken their places.[94]

Thus, some of the evangelical missionaries underestimated both the power and lure of scientific positivism and the serious intellectual *habitus* and ambitions of the Japanese converts who were heirs of a Confucian tradition that stressed the meticulous study of writings perceived as authoritative within a particular domain of knowledge. In 1926, as the first generation of Japanese converts was beginning to pass away, August Karl Reischauer self-consciously reflects on their intellectual virtues.

> Japanese Christianity is an educated Christianity. . . . No important book appears in Europe and American which does not soon find its way to the library of some Japanese minister. One never ceases to marvel at the way these ministers, with their small salaries, manage to purchase the best books. The average missionary and the average pastor in the West is not as well read as these men are.[95]

One well-known example of how the missionaries failed to acknowledge the intellectual freedom and independence of the new converts occurred in 1903 when Uemura introduced William Newton Clarke's *An Outline of Christian Theology* to his students at Meiji Gakuin. The missionaries strongly opposed Uemura's use of a textbook that they thought reflected a liberal view of scripture. This dispute with the missionaries led Uemura to found the *Tokyo Shingakusha,* the first independent Japanese seminary and predecessor of Tokyo Union Theological Seminary, which, with about one hundred and fifty students, continues as the largest Christian seminary in Japan today. In the prospectus for the new seminary, Uemura wrote, "Japan needs a Christianity that will be independent of foreign aid and that will have the determination to get on by itself, relying on nothing but Christ and His Spirit."[96]

As a result of such conflicts with missionaries who felt that the new science threatened the old faith, Japanese church leaders came to depend less and less on the direct influence of the missionaries and more and more on the insights they could glean from the most highly regarded Western texts. This "textual dependency" was a general intellectual trend of the times that may have also, in part, been exacerbated by the subtle anti-Western sentiment expressed by the phrase "Japanese Spirit-Western Learning" *(Wakon-Yosai)*.[97] From the point of view of these more studious Japanese church leaders, the missionaries appeared to be anti-intellectual and even sometimes mercenary in their zeal to win large numbers of converts regardless of the costs to Japanese culture.

Expressing such suspicions about the real motives of the North American missionaries, in 1926 Uchimura wrote these often-quoted words:

> Americans themselves know all too well that their genius is not in religion. . . . Americans are great people. . . . They are great in building cities and railroads, and are great inventors . . . are great adepts in the art of enjoying life to the utmost . . . are great in Democracy. The people is their king and emperor; yea, even their God. . . . Needless to say, they are great in money. . . . They first make money before they undertake any serious work. . . . To start and carry on any work without money is in the eyes of Americans madness. . . . Americans are great in all these things and much else; but *not in Religion,* as they themselves very well know. . . . Americans must *count religion* in order to show its value. . . . To them big churches are successful churches. To win the greatest number of converts with the least expense is their constant endeavor. Statistics is their way of showing success or failure in their religion as in their commerce and politics. Numbers, numbers, numbers, oh, how they value numbers! Americans are essentially children of this world; that they serve as teachers of religion is . . . an anomaly. . . . Indeed, religion is the last thing an average American can teach. Americans are among the least religious among all civilized peoples. . . . Mankind goes down to America to learn how to live the earthly life; but to live the heavenly life, they go to some other people. It is no special fault of Americans to be this-worldly; it is their national characteristic, and they in their self-knowledge ought to serve mankind in other fields than religion.[98]

While the declaration of independence from the missionaries was, at least in part, both positive and necessary, it also inadvertently led to the Japanese church's overdependence on foreign books that introduced the latest theological currents forged within the distant and radically different sociocultural and ecclesial contexts of modern Europe and North America (mostly Europe). This "turn to the foreign text" unfortunately occurred before the first generation of Japanese converts could adequately grasp and sort out the rich diversity of the faith traditions represented by the missionaries.

I want to claim that, inasmuch as the transmission of the gospel calls for both continuity and discontinuity between the faith of the transmitters (and the churches who sent them) and the faith of the receivers, this personal dimension of gospel transmission was undermined by the devastating social, cultural, and political pressures on the early Japanese church and its leaders. In *The School of Faith*, a book examining the catechesis of the reformed tradition, T. F. Torrance offers a strong theological rationale for the importance of the personal communication of the gospel. In light of the present discussion, I think Torrance's perspective sheds some light on why Protestant Christianity has still not penetrated Japanese culture. I will quote him at length.

> Kierkegaard has also reminded us that in the Incarnation the Absolute Fact has become a historical Fact, so that knowledge of it must be analogous to its historical nature. The Truth with which we are concerned is identical with the historical Jesus Christ, and therefore it is a Truth that can be communicated only historically (that is not to deny that it must be communicated spiritually). The Truth is a historical Person, and must be communicated personally and historically. That is to say, the Truth must be communicated to us by other persons in time. It is not something that we can tell to ourselves, so to which we can relate ourselves timelessly. The truth comes to us and addresses us in history, using personal and temporal means, so that in order to learn the Truth we must allow others to tell it to us and to instruct us. Thus we cannot tell ourselves that we are forgiven. This has to be announced to us, for that belongs to the essentially personal and historical nature of this Truth.[99]

In both streams of Progressive Evangelicalism and the Non-Church Movement, the turn away from the personal transmission of the missionaries in favor of the impersonal transmission of academic texts decisively shaped the subsequent character of Japanese Protestantism. Long before Barth's dialectical theology arrested the attention of Japanese theologians, the extrinsic pressures on these ex-samurai Christian leaders to distance themselves from the missionaries, combined with their native predilection for the careful study of classical texts, produced a highly abstract form of Protestantism that is still inaccessible to most Japanese today.[100] After the deaths of the first generation, who still personally embodied and wrestled with Japan's premodern intellectual traditions and *habitus,* Japanese Protestant theology became an increasingly abstract academic rather than ecclesial enterprise, focusing not on the actual tensions between the gospel, the Japanese church, and its particular social, political, and cultural location, but on the translation and study of the latest and most highly regarded Western texts.

To complicate matters even more, at the very time that this shift from a personal, concrete transmission of the gospel to an impersonal, abstract textual transmission of authoritative Western theological texts was taking place, the personal and familial morality of all Japanese citizens, Christians and non-Christians alike, was being carefully nurtured, as I have already mentioned above, within the monolithic modern-premodern synthesis of State Shintoism. It is not at all surprising that, given this particular Japanese experience of the "public fact-private value" dualism of modernity, the academic/intellectual dimensions and moral-religious dimensions of life became increasingly dissociated.

The German philosopher Karl Löwith, who taught in Japan from 1936 to 1941, reflected on the stark epistemological dichotomy he had observed.

> The way in which Japanese, for the most part, accept European thought seems doubtful to us, insofar as we cannot regard it as genuine assimilation. The students certainly study our European books with dedication, and thanks to their intelligence, they understand them; but they fail to draw any consequences from them for their own Japanese identity. They do not make distinctions or comparisons between European terms, such as will, freedom, and spirit, and corresponding concepts in their own life, thought and speech, or where they differ from them. . . . They live on two stories, as it were: a lower, fundamental one, in which they feel and think in the Japanese manner, and an upper one, in which they line up with European knowledge from Plato to Heidegger, and the European teacher wonders: Where is the staircase, to take them from the one to the other?[101]

As a legacy of the early Protestant privileging of academic Christian texts, Löwith's criticism could be leveled at many Japanese theologians today who are capable of debating fine conceptual nuances but refuse to treat the really pressing practical theological problems threatening the survival of their churches.[102]

This long discussion brings us full circle back to Tamura's 1928 criticism of the unnatural antipathy he decried between the education of the head and the religious nurture of the heart. From early on, he was intuitively vexed by the damaging divorce between theoretical and practical forms of knowledge. He was also fully convinced that the religious education movement, which wedded Darwin's evolutionary paradigm to a non-dogmatic, personalistic, and child-centered understanding of Christian faith, offered the positive means for overcoming the modernist theory-practice, fact-value rift that had taken a particularly virulent form in his beloved Japan. While Tamura's work did not engender a third alternative to the movements inaugurated by Uemura and Uchimura, his lifelong personal commitment to missional and ecumenical issues still presents a relevant challenge to Japanese Protestants today.

I will now turn in Chapter Four to Tamura's practical theological conversion from evangelism to religious education.

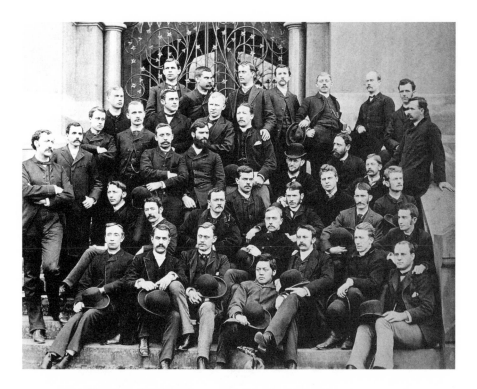

Tamura's graduating class from Princeton Theological Seminary (1886); Tamura is at the center of the front row

Wife dressing husband, from *The Japanese Bride* (1893)

Cartoon attacking Tamura from *The Japanese Bride* **(1893)**

Tamura at the age of 49, from the frontispiece of *Twentieth Century Sunday School* (1907)

**Ruth and the gleaners, from *Sunday School Lessons Graded Series*
(1912, 4th edition)**

Jesus calming the sea, from *Sunday School Lessons Graded Series*
(1912, 4th edition)

Tamura at the age of 66, from the frontispiece of *Memoirs of Fifty Years of Faith*

**A painting of Tamura at the age of 76, by a church member (1934);
it was displayed at Tamura's funeral**

CHAPTER FOUR

From Evangelism
to Religious Education

Reporting on the situation of Japan's Sunday Schools at the World's Fifth
Sunday School Convention in Rome, 1907, Dr. Frank Brown, a leader of the
World Sunday School Association (WSSA) said that Tamura Naomi was
"probably the most forceful Sunday-school man in Japan, thoroughly versed
in up-to-date Sunday-school bibliography."[1] Brown had visited Japan in 1906
at the bequest of H. J. Heinz to encourage Japan's emerging Sunday School
Association (*Nippon Nichiyogakko Kyokai*/NSSA, officially founded in 1907).
Tamura was a founding member of the NSSA and the first chair of its literature committee.[2] At the World's Sixth Sunday School Convention held in
Washington, D.C., in 1910, Tamura himself delivered an enthusiastic report
on the situation in Japan titled "The Victories of Christianity in Japan."[3] In
that report, he boldly asserted,

> We have tried in many ways to Christianize Japan in the past twenty-five
> years, but we have found by experience that the surest and quickest way to
> do so is by educating the children and leading them to Christ in their ten-
> der years.[4]

In the preface to *The Child the Center of Christianity* (1926), Tamura recounts how, while he had spent his first twenty-five years as a pastor
"preaching the Gospel to grown folk only," he had spent the past twenty-five
years "aiming to build up the church from the children."[5] He accurately portrays this approach as "a new departure in Christian work in Japan" and adds
the following rationale for his shift from adult-centered to child-centered
ministry.

> Psychologically Japanese children are very different from American children. Our children from birth breathe a Buddhistic atmosphere while American children are grown in a Christian environment. The result is that adult Japanese who hear the gospel are drawn to Christianity and liable later to fall back to the faith of their childhood and are lost to the church. My experience convinces me that Christian training from childhood is the only satisfactory and enduring method. Yet it requires painstaking work for several years before we see the blessed results. The Christian church built by this method in Japan will be more substantial and enduring and of a higher spiritual type.[6]

From the time of this "conversion" in 1900 to religious education until his death in 1934, Tamura wrote numerous books and articles on religious education and was active as one of most prominent leaders in the field. In an article written to commemorate the fiftieth anniversary of Tamura's death, Miura Tadashi variously calls him the "Comenius of Japanese Sunday School theory," "the discoverer of children," and the "liberator of children."[7]

After returning to Japan from his studies in the United States in 1886, Tamura had initially followed the mass evangelistic methods he had learned there,[8] and reports that, at the time, he was even called "the Moody of Japan."[9] While expressing gratitude for the "revival fire," which once resulted, according to Tamura, in "over 100 converts on a single Sunday," he also wondered why the fire never seemed to last long.[10] Such painful pastoral observations of raised and betrayed expectations led him to what he later called the "great revolution" in his life. While he never condemned revivalism *per se* and was willing to concede its relative successes in the United States, he concluded that this approach was decidedly inappropriate for the missional context of Meiji Japan. According to Tamura's own account, his turn from the conversion of adults to the religious education of children and youth took place during 1900 after he had completed a three-month-long evangelistic campaign during which he preached every day and sometimes two or three times a day.[11]

Looking back at his "great revolution" after a quarter century, Tamura recounted in greater detail his reasons for rejecting adult evangelism in favor of the religious education of children as the most effective means for building up the Japanese Protestant churches. Since these reflections are a wonderful example of local (missional) and intercultural (ecumenical) practical theological thinking, I present them in terms of Richard Osmer's "consensus model," which encompasses the following four common tasks of practical theology: descriptive-empirical, interpretive, norms of practice, and rules of art.[12]

(1) Firstly, Tamura observed a regular pattern of post-revival defections from the church and attributed this pattern to the overwhelming strength of Japan's non-Christian sociocultural *habitus*. He says,

> These new (adult) Christians did not have a Christian sentiment and complex back of them to help them to stand. They naturally drifted back to their old life.[13]

This statement links what Osmer calls the "descriptive-empirical" and "interpretive" tasks of practical theology.[14] Elsewhere Tamura wonders about the faith of these adult converts, asking "While they may have the name of Christian and are members of the church, isn't their faith as Buddhistic as it ever was?"[15] This contextual observation and argument provided strong rhetorical grounds for Tamura and other Japanese religious educators to advocate for sweeping church reforms that concentrated on children.

(2) Next, Tamura recalls his puzzlement over the marked increase in sexual sin that followed the revivals in which he had participated.

> Following every great revival we have felt untold agony because many of our respectable friends have fallen into the sin of adultery. It took me a long time to discover the cause, but in my study of the psychology of revivals I have decided this is a universal disease.[16]

The free expression of emotion in public that was encouraged by revivalistic methods was indeed a bizarre anomaly within the reserved Confucian-based public *ethos* of Meiji Japan, and Tamura judiciously observed that such an extreme subversion of Japanese *habitus* easily led to other rule-breaking behaviors.

In addition to the "descriptive-empirical" and "interpretive" tasks obviously at work here, Tamura's criticism of the *emotiocentric,* evangelistic practices comes out of the "norms of practice" he developed from reading scripture in light of the psychology of religion literature. On the one hand, one is reminded of the apostle Paul's pastoral instructions to the church at Corinth that suggest, if not direct causality, at least an indirect relation between free-wheeling religious ecstasy and moral disorder in the community.[17] In terms of the psychology of religion research, Tamura was most likely reading George Coe's *The Spiritual Life* at the time of his conversion to religious education.[18] In that early work, Coe builds on the work of G. Stanley Hall and E. D. Starbuck by utilizing empirical methods to analyze and interpret the meaning of religious experience.[19] His conclusions cast doubt on the spiritual effectiveness of the methods of revivalism. In a passage titled "Employment of Suggestion in Revival Meeting," Coe reveals that his own theological norm for evaluating the authenticity of religious experiences is the individual's subsequent moral conduct.

> It does not follow that conversions thus brought about (by revival techniques) are worthless. The worth of the experience depends, not upon the presence or absence of suggestion, but upon whether it includes a decision and a renewal that reach deep into the springs of conduct. The form of John Wesley's conversion was perhaps determined by suggestion, but we know, from both his earlier and later life, that his moral nature was now stirred to the depths. Suggestion, then, may lend shining garments to the change that takes place whenever the decisive determination of the will occurs; or when moral awakening is superficial, suggestion may delude into the belief that a given change is more profound than it really is. In the latter case we may look for evanescence like that of the morning dew. The danger, then, is that what is a product of mere suggestion should be mistaken for special evidence of the presence of God or of a renewal of character.[20]

Coe's strong emphasis on active volition and morality likely appealed to Tamura, who had been nurtured within the Confucian *ethos* of *kokorozashi*.

(3) These biblical and scientific "norms of practice" led to Tamura's phronetic judgment about the inappropriateness of revivalism in the Japanese context.

> Mr. Moody was unacquainted with the New Psychology. Yet he wonderfully controlled his great audiences by the psychological law of suggestion. I have arrived at the conclusion that in leading so many souls to Christ at one time, the power of the Holy Spirit is less potent than the power of suggestion.[21]

In his reflections on fifty years as a pastor, Tamura refers again to what he perceived as the dangers of mass psychology operative in revivalistic methods of evangelism. While not wanting to lose the longing for revival and even reminding pastors to pray daily for the kind of revival that is "possible only by the power of God," Tamura bemoans the fact that the true meaning of "revival" had been lost by reducing it to the kind of dramatic results we read about in Acts 2 when three thousand converts were added after Peter's Pentecost sermon. Again, while conceding the success of revivalistic methods in the

United States, he is highly critical of Japanese pastors and evangelists who naïvely imitate American models, "even to the point of going to the United States to make a study of Billy Sunday."[22]

> We know today from the progress in the research on mass psychology that the psychological condition of a group is very dangerous. Spiritual attention to each individual is a healthier method of saving their spirit. . . . "Revival fever" seems to have become a commercial enterprise. When a revival centered in human agency occurs, true revival becomes a laughing stock. The church pastor is like one who is left to clean up after a typhoon, and those pastors who can't clean things up are considered to be incompetent. I find this situation problematic.[23]

(4) Finally, without rejecting the positive role of emotion in religious experience, he warns of the perils of *emotiocentric* revivalism and intuitively suggests some preliminary, general practical theological "rules of art" to guide the Japanese church in distinguishing authentic and inauthentic religious experiences.

> There is a danger in drawing large crowds together and stirring up their emotions to a high pitch. In some cases it has led to insanity. There is a great difference in the psychology of an individual and of a crowd. The crowd is emotional and reason is pushed into the background. There is no question in my mind but that wholesale evangelism is harmful. A true, genuine religious experience should not be one-sided. It should capture the whole mind, intellect, emotion, and will. We can never build up a solid church in Japan by revival methods.[24]

Thus, it is clear that Tamura turned to religious education because he believed it offered the Japanese church a healthier, holistic approach that integrated the rational, affective, and volitional dimensions of human agency. Again, the strong influence of the early Coe is conspicuous here. Tamura marked the following passage in his copy of *The Spiritual Life.*

> Now, it is necessary to enter a loud *caveat* lest all this should be taken to be a denunciation of the cultivation of religious feeling. On the contrary, to seek to experience religious emotion, or rather, to put oneself in the way of experiencing it, is as reasonable as any other religious aspiration. To take feeling out of religion would be as absurd as to take parental or conjugal fondness out of the family. Yet it is not possible to maintain the

family solely, or even chiefly, by reliance upon feeling. What we protest against is one-sidedness; what we plead for is symmetry. Religion ought to rest upon and call into exercise all the faculties of the mind, and no superior sanctity should be ascribed to persons whose temperamental makeup is sentimental rather than choleric.[25]

Just as Coe's early empirical research on the psychological dynamics of conversion was his "practical theological" response to what he saw as the negative consequences of conversionism in the churches of North America,[26] Tamura's shift from adult evangelism to the religious education of children was his practical theological response to the situation of the Japanese church which, on the one hand, had inherited the conversionist emphasis from the missionaries but, on the other hand, was located in a very different social, cultural, and political milieu.

Thus, while drawing heavily on the literature of the North American movement, Tamura was well aware that the situation of the North American and Japanese churches was vastly different. He knew this difference firsthand from his experience of public humiliation at the hands of the Japanese church. As his comments about the lack of "Christian sentiment and complex" in Japan show, he knew that the Japanese church existed in a radically different socioreligious environment. Moreover, he knew the demographics. For example, at the time of his turn to religious education in 1900, there were only 416 Protestant churches in Japan, as compared with 864 Sunday Schools, and 43,273 church members, as compared with 33,039 Sunday School pupils.[27] Further, he knew that many Japanese churches continued to be dependent on the personnel and financial support of the missionaries and their denominations.[28]

Thus, in spite of significant numerical growth from the time when the missionaries arrived,[29] the Japanese Protestant churches at the turn of the twentieth century represented a tiny, often dependent, and for the complex sociopolitical reasons described above, beleaguered minority. Reischauer dramatically compared the situation of the early Japanese Protestant church to the early churches in the ancient Greco-Roman world.

Like the early church in the first century, this little Japanese Church could hardly think of itself other than as a small company united in Christ for mutual comfort and exhortation in the midst of an evil and hostile world. These Christians could look forward to winning a few others one by one to enter their fellowship, knowing, however, full well that only a few daring souls would be willing to pay the price. To think of Christianizing Japanese society as a whole, or enlisting the nation as such in a Christian program, was quite out of the question.[30]

In spite of these realities, Tamura, like many of the first-generation converts who were grounded in the Confucian ideal of selfless patriotic service *(messhi-hoko)*,[31] continued to believe that a robust Christian church would eventually contribute greatly to the social and cultural transformation of modern Japan. While other Japanese Christian leaders, such as Tamura's old friend-turned-nemesis Uemura, concentrated more on preaching and writing ministries as the best means for building up the churches, Tamura decided that a well-rounded and thorough pedagogical program was the most appropriate methodology for Japan's "pre-Constantinian"[32] missional situation. Even though the numbers represent a tiny fraction of Japan's population at the time,[33] Tamura had some reason for being optimistic. For example, at the Washington convention in 1910, he reported that there were "more than one hundred thousand Sunday-school scholars in Japan," representing a threefold increase in only ten years![34]

While evangelistic Sunday Schools had been part and parcel of the missionary church-planting strategy in Japan from the very outset,[35] Tamura had kept abreast of the latest developments in the United States that culminated in the founding of the Religious Research Association (REA) in 1903. He took his theoretical and practical direction from this new, emerging educational approach that represented a radical break with the old conversionistic paradigm associated with evangelical revivalism.[36] Convinced that the religious education movement had disclosed effective scientific means for the transformation of Japan into a modern Christian nation, Tamura zealously set out to apply the recent findings in education, the psychology of religion, evolution, heredity, and child development to the missional situation of the Japanese churches.

The new Tamura typifies Schleiermacher's classical description of the modern practical theologian as one "in whom an ecclesial interest and a scientific spirit are united."[37] Considering the pressure on Japanese Christians to demonstrate how their new faith — not the missionaries' faith! — could positively serve their country, it is not insignificant that the organic, developmental, whole-person approach of religious education represented a radical alternative to the dramatic, emotiocentric, conversionistic methods of the missionaries. The evolutionary paradigm of progressivism was also very much in harmony with the Japanese aesthetic sense of the progressive cycles of nature. Further, Tamura's passion for a holistic integration and balance of reason, emotion, and willful action likely arose from its resonance with the Confucian doctrine of the mean.[38]

In terms of Lamin Sanneh's description of missionary translation of the gospel as a process that embraces the complementary movements of relativization and destigmatization, Japanese converts like Tamura needed to relativize the missionary roots of their new faith while destigmatizing and adopting Japanese culture "as a natural extension of the life of the new religion."[39] In terms of the historical cross-currents within which this transmissional process occurred, Tamura utilized a "Constantinian-Cartesian" methodology to address a decidedly "pre-Constantinian" situation.[40]

Next I will consider Tamura's practical proposal in greater detail.

A Vision for the Christian Transformation of Japan

Following his "conversion," Tamura wasted no time in launching his crusade to introduce the new paradigm of religious education in Japan. The following long sample from the preface to his programmatic guide titled the *Twentieth-Century Sunday School* (March, 1907) shows how thoroughly Tamura had imbibed the optimistic spirit of the new North American movement and literature.

> During the last twenty-five years, the academic study of children has witnessed an amazing and rapid progress. As a result, a serious revolution has come to the teaching methods of the Sunday Schools. Up until now, neither the administration nor the teaching methods of the Sunday School were based on the great principles of education. However, the administration and the teaching methods of the Sunday Schools in the twentieth century must take their direction from pedagogical and psychological principles. As its name reveals, the Sunday School is a type of school. It is not a place for evangelism but a place for carrying out education. If the proper education is not provided in infancy, it is not possible to quickly provide education for pre-schoolers. If the proper education is not provided in childhood, it is not possible to quickly provide education for adolescents. A perfect education begins while the baby is still in the mother's womb. This age becomes the first step in the development of the body, mind, and spirit of the child. If there is no shortcut in education, neither is there any skipping of stages. One must proceed one step at a time. In summary, education is that which can indicate the order of development. As a result, religious education must not fail in this process.[41]

Tamura saw the new movement, which drew heavily on academic research in pedagogy and developmental psychology, as a more scientific and thus more relevant response to modernity. Also, since religious education represented a sharp contrast to the missionaries' methods, Tamura could employ the new paradigm both to declare his independence from the missionaries and to show how a modernized Christian faith might make a positive contribution to Japan's national aspirations.

As further evidence of Tamura's wholesale commitment to the child-centered, developmental perspective of progressive education, the same year he wrote the *Twentieth-Century Sunday School,* he also published another little book titled *The Rights of Children.*[42] Although Kagawa Toyohiko is often credited for being the first Japanese Christian to advocate for children's rights, Tamura's book was one of the first of its kind to appear in Japanese and is a probable inspiration for Kagawa's later views.[43] As *The Japanese Bride* should be read as a passionate Christian *apologia* aimed at overthrowing traditional Japanese marriage customs in favor of a more modern, egalitarian arrangement, the somewhat less confrontational yet equally passionate and prophetic *Rights of Children* rejects the common Japanese view of children as the possession of their parents in favor of the modern Christian view that understood children as a gift of God to be loved, respected, and educated.

> Hasn't God created parents for the sake of loving their children? Don't children have the right to be loved by their parents? Parents who do not love or educate their children rob them of their rights. . . . It is a great error to think of children as their parents' possession. Parents are simply the protectors of their children.[44]

Drawing on Jesus' teaching in the gospels and modern educational philosophy (especially Friedrich Froebel), pedagogy, and psychology, *The Rights of Children* aimed to educate Japanese parents and teachers about the emotional, intellectual, and social needs of their children and pupils. In the preface to the second edition (1911), Tamura writes,

> If we wish to fundamentally improve Japanese society, it is a far better plan to soundly educate children who are not yet immersed in evil than to try to heal sick, tuberculin adults.[45]

This comment clearly shows that Tamura saw his advocacy for the rights of all children in tandem with his programmatic turn to child-centered religious education in the church. Almost twenty years later, Tamura looked back on the controversy that followed the publication of *The Rights of Children.*

People were much alarmed at such an unusual suggestion, — the rights of a child. As if a child had any rights! Naturally they feared that if such a book were published and children should read it, it would do great harm. Those who treat children like playthings or as subjects of absolute monarchy were greatly disturbed.[46]

In his context, Tamura's dauntless Christian advocacy for children's rights amounted to a radical attack on the government-sponsored educational top-down policy and the government-sanctioned patriarchal family *(ie)* structure.[47]

At this juncture it is appropriate to consider in more detail the continuities and discontinuities between the Tamura who had written *The Japanese Bride* and the Tamura who advocated for children's rights and almost single-handedly launched Japan's religious education movement. While the focus of his social critique changed from the situation of women under the servile conditions of the old feudal order to the plight of Japanese children within the new conditions of a modern, industrialized Japan, it is clear that Tamura never wavered in his strong commitment to the Christian reform of his beloved country. In both *The Japanese Bride* (1893) and *The Rights of Children* (1907), he contemplated nothing less than the radical transformation of Japanese society according to his normative understanding of Christian ethics.

However, beyond this continuity in ultimate purpose, an unequivocal shift in methodology occurred between the time of the publication of the earlier and latter social tracts. In *The Japanese Bride*, the younger Tamura, his head still full of personal impressions of nineteenth-century American family life, had attempted a strong critique of the Japanese marital *habitus* of patriarchal consanguinity. As I have already shown, the timing of that English publication could not have been worse. With the growing nationalism centered in the reinvented modern *mythos* of imperial inviolability, the barely organized Protestant churches were virtually compelled to take a defensive posture. Just when a careful, conciliatory Japanese Christian *apologia* for marital conjugality and equality was called for, Tamura's passionate tract was perceived as a judgmental confrontation bordering on treason. In spite of the validity of many of the book's truth claims, the English form of the presentation ignited the severe reaction of the Japanese public and even Tamura's fellow Protestants. To the church suffering under the pressures of rising nationalism, *The Japanese Bride* read like a heavy-handed, universal ethical judgment devoid of local wisdom, a trumpet of judgment without love, truth-telling without loyalty, pathos without logos. *The Japanese Bride* also may show how Tamura himself was thoroughly under the sway of the *emotiocentric* methods of evangelism he had inherited from the missionaries and learned during his student days in the United States. Thus, the problem with Tamura's early work was not only that he seriously misread the situation, but that he offered no constructive, rational practical theological "rules of art" to help guide Japanese Christian practice away from the old traditions of the ancient regime toward the alternative *habitus* of egalitarian conjugality.

He was careful not to repeat the same mistake after coming out seven years later (in 1900) as a leading advocate for child-centered Christian education. As evidence of the radical change in his methods, Tamura published the *Twentieth-Century Sunday School* (March 1907) six months prior to his publication of *The Rights of Children* (September 1907). Instead of beginning with a polemic against the Japanese view of children from the ideological perspective of Christian ethics, this time Tamura first published his constructive "rules of art" for the Sunday School in preparation for his pioneering tract on children's rights.[48] His agonizing experience of ostracism and accumulative experience as a pastor had given birth to this more constructive, reasoned, apologetic approach. Tamura had come of age as a missional-ecumenical practical theologian who, while engaging in conversation with North American scholarship, remained carefully focused on the situation of the Japanese churches.

With these two publications in 1907, it was clear that Tamura's concern had turned from simply attacking the old orders of Japanese society. He now focused on the vulnerable predicament of Japanese children within the new situation of a modern, industrialized, technological society. Though the question of children's rights was an important issue facing church and society, Tamura was resolutely convinced that only the church or, more specifically, only a church thoroughly committed to religious education would be able to improve the social conditions and status of all Japanese children. Thus, he linked ecclesial and social issues directly by reimagining the Sunday School as the divinely ordained means for publicly promoting the rights of all Japanese children.

He was convinced that a Sunday School based on the progressive pedagogy would transform Japan into a healthy modern nation-state. In the preface to the second edition of the *Twentieth-Century Sunday School* (1913), he wrote,

> Above all else, the religious education of children is indispensable for producing whole citizens. Citizens who have not received religious education are imperfect citizens. Since the way to heal imperfect citizens is to reform the Sunday School, the Christian churches of our country have a great responsibility to attend to the religious education of children.[49]

In terms of the tiny church's witness within the non-Christian sociocultural context of Meiji Japan, Tamura believed that Christ's love for all children could be communicated and authenticated by the church's practical commitment to religious education. While he remained focused on the church's witness, it is clear that the "post-conversion" Tamura saw the ecclesial practice of religious education and the public advocacy on behalf of all Japanese children as forms of Christian service. In Tamura's new view, *ecclesia* was not conceived of as an alternative *polis* called to bear proleptic, prophetic witness to the free and sovereign in-breaking of Christ's eschatological kingdom, but was defined as the institutional foundation for a healthy modern nation-state.

This strategy that conceives of Christian witness in terms of its unique and positive contribution to the modern nation-state is evidence that Tamura drew deeply from the socially oriented theology behind the North American religious education movement. Within that optimistic context, Coe could boldly proclaim in *A Social Theory of Religious Education* that "the redemptive mission of Christ is nothing less than that of transforming the social order itself into a brotherhood or family of God."[50] Further, Coe says the aim of Christian education is the "Growth of the young toward and into mature and efficient devotion to the democracy of God, and happy self-realization therein."[51] This definition effortlessly ties Coe's theological ideals to three specifically North American axiological norms: (1) "efficient devotion" (pragmatic norm); (2) "democracy of God" (sociopolitical recasting of a theological norm); and (3) "happy self-realization" (personal norm).

On the other hand, while his own writings are in no way lacking in the progressive social gospel's rhetorical optimism, Tamura could not simply mimic Coe within the non-Christian missional context of Japan. For example, considering the fact that he drew so often from Coe's work, it is singularly revealing that Tamura never even mentions the "democracy of God." Even in retrospect, Coe said that the "issue of democracy" was the heart of the North American religious education movement.[52] While this key concept, which was derived from Coe's Christian appropriation of Dewey's democratic experientialism, may have made perfectly good sense in the United States, it was just too far removed from the sociopolitical realities of Tamura's Japan to be redeemable. To speak in Meiji Japan of the biblical kingdom of God in terms of this modern American dynamic equivalent would have thoroughly undermined Tamura's new, more cautious constructive approach. While this discussion raises important questions about Coe's recasting of a biblical concept in unmistakably American terms, it is also another clear indication of Tamura's maturing practical theological sensitivity to the gospel-culture tensions in his own context. As an even more ironic example of the contrast between the development of the REM in the United States and Japan, while Coe and his followers advocated a generic theory of religious education within the North American context of Protestant hegemony, Tamura was convinced, within the missional context of Japanese religious pluralism, that *Christian* religious education alone, and not some generic approach to religious education, had the power to transform Japan.[53]

Tamura was personally and painfully cognizant of the omnipresent potential for disastrous collisions between the gospel and his country's fiercely nationalistic *ethos*. While strongly advocating the general principles of religious education as the means for transforming Japanese society and culture, Tamura carefully restated the ultimate goals of religious education in missionally contextualized terms. In place of Coe's modern American virtues of "efficiency," "democracy," and "self-realization," Tamura stated repeatedly that the goal of religious education in Japan was the "education of Christianized, good citizens."[54] In this context, the Japanese word for "good citizens" *(zenryo)* connotes law-abiding citizens with an upright and mild disposition. While Coe aimed at the education of individuals committed to the "progressive reconstruction of society,"[55] Tamura portrayed his goal in terms of more conservative virtues that would contribute to the building up of this first modern Asian nation-state. Given the Japanese public's continuing suspicions of Christianity's animosity toward the imperial *ethos* of modern Japan, it is not difficult to imagine how Tamura's goal would be much easier for his compatriots to hear than some alien American paean to the "democracy of God" or the "progressive reconstruction of society."

Keeping in mind the sociological, political, and cultural factors I have been considering, I want to now turn briefly to Tamura's personal spiritual formation as a practical theologian and religious educator. Undoubtedly, Tamura's bitter experience of "exile" as a result of *The Japanese Bride* was behind his move from a gospel-culture position that stressed a passionate, prophetic confrontation to a more nuanced position that, without sacrificing passion, also emphasized a more reasoned, gradualist contribution to society. This new missional strategy was clearly a consequence of the period of personal spiritual testing *(tentatio)*[56] that Tamura had endured as part of his formation as a practical theologian.

Because of *The Japanese Bride* incident, Tamura and his independent Sukiyabashi Church had become a marginalized minority that was even further disassociated from the already marginalized minority Japanese churches. This precarious psychocultural and spiritual condition of "liminal marginality" or "exile" needs to be further explored. In a culture that anchors and circumscribes personal identity within what Nakamura Hajime calls some "limited social nexus,"[57] and prizes loyalty to that nexus far above truth-telling, it is quite remarkable that Tamura not only survived the public humiliation he suffered at the hands of his former companions in the Church of Christ in Japan (Presbyterian) but that he continued to make a significant, though quieter contribution to the building up of the Japanese churches. Nakamura helps us grasp how Tamura's refusal to repudiate *The Japanese Bride* flew in the face of the Confucian ideal of selfless service *(messhi-hoko)* that prevailed in Meiji Japan.

> Later the highest virtue was considered to be sacrifice of the self for the sake of the sovereign, the family (especially the parents), or the community. This feudal mentality assumed an extreme form after the Meiji era when it came to be expressed in the form of sacrifice of one's life for the sake of the emperor. . . . In contrast to this we find only a few cases in which sacrifices of life were made by the Japanese for the sake of something universal, something that transcends a particular human nexus, such as academic truth or the arts. And if we exclude from this the persecution of the True Pure Land sect, the Hokke sect, and Christianity, cases of dying for religious faith are exceptional phenomena. Sacrifice of all for the sake of truth, when it went contrary to the intentions of the ruler, was even regarded as evil.[58]

Considering the intense psychocultural pressure that was placed upon him by the leaders of his own circle of belonging, Tamura's refusal to retract his writing should be seen either as a suicidal masochism or a Luther-like heroism. Stubbornly spurning the *habitus* of the cultural nexus that had nurtured him, Tamura was banished to a Judas-like liminality. In effect, he became a "no-self" who had lost his "standing place" *(tachiba).*[59]

Tamura later characterized his entire life as a "picture scroll of misunderstanding and persecution."[60] However, in spite of this suffering and experience of a loss of self, he later paradoxically characterized the solitary years following his deposition from ministry as a time of great spiritual growth and blessing.

> As a result of this persecution, I gained many friends at home and abroad. I have been greatly encouraged by their sympathetic letters. . . . Without this persecution, my work may not have succeeded. While my enemies wished to kill me, they have actually given me life. I was able to taste the sacred words of Christ, "Bless those who curse you."[61]

I want to briefly consider Tamura's situation in terms of Loder's transformational or Chalcedonian model. In Chapter One, I described how this model provides a post-critical, Christocentric practical theological approach for discerning the possible trajectories of human and divine agency that may be operative in epistemic events. It is quite possible, on the one hand, to attribute Tamura's experience of life out of death to unconscious psychological mechanisms such as reaction formation. The fact that he had been adopted when he was just entering adolescence surely had some lasting effect on his subsequent development. His birth family had fallen into hard times financially and, through the mediation of his classical Chinese teacher, he was adopted by the well-to-do Tamura family in Kyoto. In his autobiography, he soberly yet poignantly records this traumatic experience by saying, "In 1868, when I was eleven, I said good-bye to my two brothers and two sisters, left the Asaba family and was adopted by the Tamura family."[62]

On the other hand, the fact that Tamura was able to positively reframe his public humiliation, ostracism, and loss of self may also be interpreted as a Spirit-mediated, personal appropriation of the biblical words of Jesus. Tamura's bold determination to stand firm against the full weight of his culture — the very womb of his identity! — seems to have been compellingly bolstered by the "mediating discontinuity" of Jesus' words to "Bless those who curse you."[63] However one interprets this intersection of psychological and theological dynamics, the fact remains that the formerly impetuous Tamura of *The Japanese Bride* did not throw in the towel. Instead, he fully committed himself to both the immediate objectives and ultimate goals of religious education. His acknowledgment that the Christian transformation of Japanese society would take more than one hundred years to achieve shows that an older, more generative Tamura was content to contribute toward a future he would never personally witness.[64]

Here we may wonder how Tamura's personal, missional-experience of *tentatio* differed from the experience of the North American theorists who were his print-mediated, ecumenical conversation partners. Given the unquestioned hegemony of Protestantism in the United States at the turn of the twentieth century, no comparable cruciform witness had to be made by religious education theorists there. There the danger lay in a very different direction, in assuming a too cozy continuity between the spheres of society and church, or in New Testament terms, the kingdoms of Caesar and Christ.

As Stanley Hauerwas has shown in his provocative rereading of twentieth-century U.S. intellectual history, the sociocultural, political, and religious assumptions of U.S. church and secular opinion leaders were often indistinguishable up until the 1960s.[65] Focusing on Reinhold Niebuhr's often unacknowledged but substantial debt to William James, Hauerwas says,

> Under Niebuhr's influence, theology — particularly in America — became ethics, and ethics became the investigation of the conditions necessary to make a liberal social order work.[66]

This comment might also be made in regard to Coe and the influence of his "democracy of God" on religious education theory in North America. Coe, who had also been strongly influenced by James,[67] is another unambiguous exemplar of the naïve faith in an easy trafficking between theological conceptualities and sociopolitical realities in North American thinking in the early twentieth century.

Even given the continued popularity of the worldwide missionary movement in the North American churches at the time, the increasing body of intercultural scholarship that the movement produced,[68] and the emergence of the new discipline of cultural anthropology, it never seemed to dawn on Coe that reframing biblical concepts such as the "kingdom of God" in terms of the "democracy of God" might be highly problematic in non-Western sociocultural and political spheres of the *ecumene* like Japan. The fact that Coe could say, in using that term, that he did not intend to "substitute a new social principle for that which Jesus taught but because the idea of democracy is essential to full appreciation of his teaching,"[69] shows, at the very least, his belief that the Christian God and scripture endorsed certain American political ideals and orders over other cultural alternatives.

While, in fairness to Coe, it should be remembered that he was writing for a North American audience under the sway of the non-Trinitarian, immanental norms of the social gospel movement (the "Fatherhood of God" and the "brotherhood of man"), certainly the subsequent history of the twentieth century revealed that he placed way too much confidence in the potential of modern people to achieve the divine ideal.

> Moreover, if brotherly love is, as our religion has always taught, the carrying out of the Father's loving will in human relations, how can the Father himself be willing to be an autocrat, an aristocrat, or a plutocrat? Must not Christians think of God as being within human society in the democratic manner of working, helping, sacrificing, persuading, cooperating, achieving? "My Father worketh even until now, and I work." Divine love, it appears, cannot realize itself anywhere but in a genuinely industrial democracy.[70]

Coe and his peers saw signs of divine agency in American politics but over-looked the specifically cruciform shape of Christian experience of God.[71] Be-yond the problematic assumption here of universalism that is so common-place in modern Western theorizing, the organic, developmental, evolutionary paradigm that supported the unbounded optimism of early religious educa-tion theory precluded the possibility of offering any positive theological ac-count for *tentatio* such as that experienced by Tamura.

To reiterate, in addition to the enduring goal of Christian social trans-formation and the new methodological strategy that placed practical theol-ogy and Christian social ethics in service to the nation-state, Tamura's shift from conversionism to developmentalism was also a fruit of his psycho-spiritual experience of marginalization and his ecumenical engagement with the literature and people associated with the North American religious edu-cation movement. *The Japanese Bride* had been written in his late twenties, soon after his return from four and one-half years in the United States, while the *Twentieth-Century Sunday School* and *The Rights of Children* had been written in his late thirties. The latter books were the fruit of his reflections on almost twenty years of pastoral ministry. Behind this new direction was Tamura's emerging conviction of the organic, developmental continuity be-tween the instinctual (biological), psychological, and social dimensions of re-ligious life. He had learned this new theoretical understanding from his grad-uate studies in psychology with James McCosh at Princeton University as well as his reading of Bushnell, Hall, James, Starbuck, Coe, and others. After the next biographical section that surveys some of the successes and struggles that attended the next phase of Tamura's work, I will return in more detail to the question of how he understood and interpreted religious educational the-ories and practices in his mature work.

The Graded Lessons and the Testing of Tamura's Vision

As I have already mentioned, Tamura was instrumental during the initial pe-riod of growth of the Japanese Sunday School movement. Even before the offi-cial founding of the NSSA, he had already launched what was to become a pro-lific writing and editing career.[72] In addition to *The Rights of Children* and the *Twentieth-Century Sunday School,* between 1906 and 1913 he founded two weekly Sunday School publications, the "Friend of the Child" for use with chil-dren and "The Home" for family use, and edited a complete thirteen-year cycle of graded lessons for the Sunday School.[73] He remembered those six years of intensive labor on the graded lessons as one of the happiest times of his life.[74]

Tamura's graded lessons were a huge leap forward in terms of providing Japanese Sunday School children with culturally appropriate materials in their own language. Previously, teachers had to use, adapt, or translate English materials provided by the missions, but now each child received his or her own copy of this original Japanese textbook. I will comment briefly on the first-year primary course to indicate the level of thought and care that Tamura had poured into these new materials.

This first textbook in the series covers the following eight thematic units: (1) At Home; (2) The God Who Made Everything; (3) God's Protective Care; (4) Thanking God; (5) God's Best Gift; (6) Learning About the Child Jesus; (7) What Jesus' Resurrection Did; and (8) God Is Near His Children, Always Helping Them.[75] Each unit is broken up into a number of lessons, making a total of fifty-two weekly lessons. The first four units covering the Old Testament are allotted fourteen weeks, while the final four units covering the New Testament are allotted the remaining thirty-eight weeks. The Old Testament section covers creation, Elijah, Moses, and the worship of God, while the New Testament focuses almost exclusively on the life of Jesus. The transition lesson from Old to New Testament (lesson 15) focuses on the Garden of Eden, Adam and Eve's (and our) refusal to listen to God, and God's gift of the "good Jesus." Each lesson begins with a woodblock print portraying a scene from everyday Japanese family life, the Bible, or some creative combination of the two; i.e., a picture of a Japanese mother and father bowing at the feet of the risen Christ (lesson 50). Each lesson is presented through a story or a conversation between a Sunday School teacher and children and concludes with a biblical adage. The initial popularity of the series is seen in the fact that the books had already gone through four editions between 1908 and 1912.

Encountering Missionary Opposition

Following the years of frenzied activity as the chair of NSSA's literature committee and publication of his graded lessons, Tamura's comprehensive vision for reforming the Sunday Schools started to meet with serious opposition, especially from a group of missionaries who were opposed to the recent modern developments in religious education theory and practice.[76] I will recount this story in some detail since it discloses the complexity of the intercultural and ideological tensions that Tamura experienced as a missional-ecumenical practical theologian. These tensions between his cultural, intellectual, and faith convictions touched the core of Tamura's identity as a first-generation Japanese Christian.

Analogous to the epochal shift experienced by Luther and the first generation of Protestant reformers in Europe, Tamura and the first generation of Japanese Protestants had been simultaneously nurtured in a well-defined but disappearing premodern Japan and a new, emerging, yet ill-defined modern Japan. In sharp contrast to the reformation, however, Protestant faith and modernity had burst upon the Japanese scene as an invasive apocalyptic *kairos* and not as the outcome of any protracted internal development. In terms of practical theological theory, with no interdisciplinary model for negotiating the relationship between the competing discourses of traditional Japanese identity, nineteenth-century evangelical faith, and modern science, Tamura had to struggle intuitively to square his personal reception of the missionary transmission of the gospel and his growing intellectual convictions about the power of religious education for building the Japanese church and nation with his need to demonstrate his love of Japan by declaring his independence from the foreign missionaries. Given his openness to a more modern approach to Christian faith, it is little surprise that he eventually ran into conflict with some of the missionaries.

During the initial Kamakura discussions on the NSSA in 1906 with Brown, some other Japanese pastors, and missionaries, Tamura had insisted that only Japanese should be allowed as official members of the NSSA. When the missionaries strongly objected to this restriction on membership, Tamura threatened to walk out of the consultation. According to Tamura, missionaries were dominating the Sunday School Associations in Korea, China, India, and the Philippines. After some tense discussion, Brown pleaded with the missionaries in favor of Tamura's proposal, and it was then written into the original constitution of the NSSA.[77] Later he recalled,

> When it came to ecclesial matters or the launching of any new projects, I had taken a firm stand on the Japanese principle. As a result of this principle, I made enemies, met with persecution, and suffered great pains.[78]

Thus, he expressed great pride in the original decision of the NSSA to be administered according to what he called "the Japan principle."

However, as Tamura's editorial work on his graded lessons proceeded, the criticism from some of the missionaries also grew. In the following quote from his autobiography, Tamura interprets this escalating tension with the missionaries.

> The main point of their criticism was that the Sunday Schools of the Japanese churches had yet not developed to a level where they could effectively

utilize the new graded lessons. Further, they complained that the editing had been single-handedly carried out by one Mr. Tamura and that not a single missionary had been invited to participate. From my point of view, it was not only that there was not a single foreign missionary who had academically studied the Sunday School or who had the brains to apply such research to the huge project of creating texts for Japan's Sunday Schools, but it was also true that there were only a handful of Japanese pastors who had sufficient knowledge for such an undertaking. With a heart-felt determination to do what I felt I needed to do regardless of the opposition, I completed the editing of the thirteen year cycle of graded lessons.[79]

This reflection clearly reveals Tamura's personal sense of being uniquely equipped and called to complete this task on behalf of the Japanese churches. In terms of his own practical theological "norms of practice," it also shows that Tamura, in contrast to some of the missionaries, was open to utilizing the resources of modern culture for the Japanese church's educational ministry.

These tensions with the missionaries eventually led to Tamura's decision to resign from the NSSA. As Heinz continued to make good on his yearly support for the NSSA, more and more pressure was placed on the Japanese board to appoint a missionary as a foreign secretary to serve alongside the Japanese secretary. In spite of these pressures, Tamura remained resolute in his commitment to the "Japanese principle" and made it clear that his continuing membership was contingent upon keeping to the committee's original decision. Wanting to avoid what he called a "two-headed secretariat," he was especially concerned that a missionary on the NSSA would influence decisions about the allocation of the unrestricted annual gift of $1,000 from Heinz. While he was well aware of the continued dependence of many Japanese churches on the largess of U.S. Christians, he still felt that the Japanese committee was under no obligation to bow to missionary pressure. Having worked hard over the years to develop a positive personal relationship with the U.S.-based leadership of the WSSA, Tamura worried that the missionaries would treat the Japanese as inferiors if they were allowed into the NSSA leadership. He bitterly laments that he did not get any support when he reiterated these concerns to the all-Japanese board.

When I presented my case with tears at the NSSA's board of directors meeting, not a single person responded. This led to their regrettable decision to appoint a missionary as foreign secretary general.[80]

Tamura resigned immediately following this decision.

Tamura reports that the decision to go with the laughable "two-headed secretariat" quickly led to the dominance of the NSSA by the missionaries, just as he had feared. For example, when Heinz died and willed millions of dollars for the work of the world's Sunday Schools, the Japanese NSSA received nothing. According to Tamura, the missionaries received a substantial sum that they used to build their own office and hire a clerk. He bitterly taunts, "Didn't they lord it over the Japanese committee?"[81]

In the meantime, things went from bad to worse for Tamura's graded lessons. In 1916, the NSSA met in Nagoya and, under the influence of the opinions of Methodist missionary David S. Spencer and some other missionaries, a proposal was put forth claiming that Tamura's popular graded lessons were inappropriate. The proposal went on to suggest that Japanese and missionary representatives from each denomination should form a new committee and undertake the task of creating more appropriate texts for Japan's Sunday Schools. Tamura bitterly recalls the NSSA's decision to adopt this proposal without any dissension. "The thirteen year cycle of graded lessons on which I had fervently spent six years of hard toil and labor were officially labeled 'unsuitable texts'!"[82] While Tamura freely admitted that his texts were imperfect and had already inaugurated a committee to revise them, he felt that this missionary-led attack on his work was not only rude but pedagogically misguided.

However, as another sign of his unfailing commitment to his project, instead of immediately attacking the NSSA decision, Tamura decided to wait until the committee came out with their own "more appropriate" lessons. In 1919, when Methodist publisher Kyobunkan published the new NSSA texts, Tamura says he stayed awake for two or three nights, carefully reading and examining their work. Since it clearly reveals Tamura's passion for the religious-education approach to the writing of children's Sunday School texts, I will quote his three-part critique at length.

> I was truly shocked. First of all, though the cover advertised these books as textbooks, they were actually lesson plans. The editors could not even distinguish between textbooks and lesson plans! Doesn't this plainly reveal the lack of any settled pedagogical principle? Secondly, while the cover says these texts were edited, they are actually translations. . . . Thirdly, there are too many errors in the translation to count. It is obvious at one glance that the translation was done by people who cannot read English. . . . As an extreme example, the text says that Joseph and Mary went to the town of Bethlehem to pay their taxes! Isn't it an insult for these books to be published as the combined effort of the Japanese

churches and for the publishers to boldly claim that the texts I edited were unsuitable? Do these books really have any value for use in Japan's Sunday Schools? Moreover, shouldn't they cut off their work with the four or five they have completed rather than wasting eight more years? I cannot help but be deeply saddened by their irresponsibility. Doesn't Spencer and his band of missionaries have any sense of pride?[83]

Especially considering that Tamura's lessons and the new lessons were both written under the auspices of the NSSA and published by Kyobunkan, this response needs to be read more as a comparison with Tamura's own graded lessons than as a critical analysis of the new material. The exclamations and string of rhetorical questions communicate how personally distressed Tamura was about being upstaged by the missionary-dominated NSSA. While this temporary setback did not spell the end of Japan's religious education movement, it did serve to outline in bold relief the contrasts between the older, evangelical approach and Tamura's newer, child-centered progressive approach.

In spite of these sharp philosophical and political conflicts with the missionaries, Tamura always remained on good terms with Brown and the other Americans in the home office of the WSSA. Perhaps it was because of his friendly relationship with members of the WSSA that the missionaries, who had a very different agenda for Japan's Sunday Schools, viewed Tamura and his progressive approach as a threat. According to Tamura, after the missionaries pressed the WSSA to approve the NSSA decision to appoint a missionary as foreign secretary, Frank Brown sent his deep regrets over losing Tamura in a personal letter that read, "What gain could there possibly be in getting a foreign secretary if we lose you?"[84]

World's Sunday School Convention Held in Tokyo

One year after the new, missionary-inspired NSSA lessons were published, the Eighth World's Sunday School Convention was convened in Tokyo from October 5 to 14, 1920. The original idea for holding the meeting in Japan had been suggested by one of the secretaries at the Second World's Sunday School Convention held in St. Louis in 1893.[85] In order to account for the surprising choice of faraway Tokyo as the venue for the WSSA convention, we have to look beyond the statistically significant growth of the Japanese Sunday School movement. Behind this seemingly insignificant decision is the story of a striking new confluence of global religious, political, and economic factors that needs some explanation and comment.

In the early 1890s, there had been an almost delirious optimism about the imminent Christianization of Japan among church leaders in the United States. This buoyancy was surely grounded in the early enthusiastic missionary reports "from the field." For example, at the "Third Gathering of Christian Laity" that had been held in Tokyo in 1883, a joint statement was issued that proclaimed, "Our nation will become Christian in fifteen years."[86]

Andrew Walls mentions in passing another example of this optimistic Zeitgeist in the first Students' Lectures on Mission, delivered in 1893 at Princeton Theological Seminary by missionary James Dennis.

> Dennis's analysis of the world situation both in terms of church growth and the beneficent social results of that growth is almost unfailingly upbeat. The analysis begins with Japan, where political, social, commercial, educational, literary and religious change had occurred since Commodore Perry opened the country to foreign influence "on a scale unprecedented in the history of any other nation" (p. 66). Japan — already influencing China in helpful directions — was the key to the Orient. If the church of Christ would seize the present opportunity, Japan would be the "grandest trophy of modern missions" (p. 71).[87]

In fact, as I have already mentioned, the missional situation of the Japanese churches was becoming increasingly tense due to the rise of nationalism in the late 1880s and early 1890s. Ironically, in the very same year (1893), while optimistic U.S. Sunday School leaders and missionaries like Dennis were projecting the triumph of the gospel in a rapidly industrializing Japan, Tamura was defrocked for refusing to recant *The Japanese Bride.* The chasm between the missionary hopes and the Japanese realities could not have been wider. In 1893 Tamura could never have imagined, even in his wildest dreams, that any international Christian meeting would be convened in Tokyo during his own lifetime.

The chair of the WSSA committee was none other than Tamura's old friend and supporter, Dr. Frank Brown. Coming on the heels of the horror of World War I, this meeting was an impressive symbolic expression of the increasingly friendly relations between the churches, businesses, and governments of Japan and the victors of the recent war, the United States and Great Britain. With the financial backing of U.S. businessmen H. J. Heinz and J. Wannamaker, the North American churches, Japanese business leaders and churches, and even Japan's imperial household agency, about 1,800 people from thirty-two foreign countries assembled in Tokyo for the meeting. To date, it was the largest gathering of foreigners ever assembled in Japan!

The official report, titled *The Sunday School and World Progress*, reads like an *apologia* for exactly the kind of North American, Christian, capitalist, industrial democracy for which the early Coe had been advocating. The opening chapter, titled "How New Japan Was Born," romantically depicts the providential synergy of military, commercial, and religious means that brought about an "entrance of civilization" to Japan that "would transform the people and the country."[88] The missionary and Sunday School movements are unembarrassingly depicted as indispensable means for advancing the interests of the modern nation-state. One statement that attempts to combine the competing evangelical and progressive approaches to the Sunday School says, "It was believed, too, that the Convention could demonstrate the Sunday School as the best method of winning the world for Christ and the best plan by which the individual, home, community, and national character must be secured."[89] The report also quotes former Prime Minister Marquis Shigenobu Okuma's explanation of the reasons for the enthusiastic support of Japanese "government and business circles."

> In these days of social and industrial reconstruction, the enforcement of the day of rest has intimate relations to the question of morals of the workers. As the number of days of rest increases, so must we pay more attention to resist the tendency of indolence and moral deterioration. Therefore I expect a good deal of the Sunday Schools and the Christian churches for the work of the social uplift in these days of modern industrialism.[90]

Interpreting the Sunday School movement as a positive, utilitarian moral response to industrialism, it is not surprising that so many non-Christian representatives of the Japanese government, business world, and even the imperial household expressed their enthusiastic support. The emperor himself is reported to have given 50,000 yen toward the convention hall.[91] The Japanese Patron's Association included nobility, politicians, businessmen, a handful of Japanese Christian leaders, and one missionary.

One has to look hard in the upbeat report to discover even the slightest hint of any consciousness of tensions between the ambitions of the churches, nascent global capitalism, and the modern nation-state. The meeting looks very different, however, when considered from the regional perspective of East Asia. Since Japan had recently "annexed" Korea (1910) and had experienced increasing tensions with China since the Sino-Japanese War (1894-1895),[92] it is not surprising that the only hint of any tension between the domains of Christ and Caesar came in the form of official opposition to the Tokyo meetings by some Korean Christians and Chinese Sunday School lead-ers.[93] While the official report does not explicitly mention this protest, it does recount one revealing encounter between a certain Mr. H. Nagao, the minis-ter and board of directors of the Japanese Imperial Railways, and an Ameri-can missionary woman that sheds light on the reasons for the Chinese and Korean opposition to the meeting. Referring to a speech he had recently de-livered at the YMCA in Hankow, Nagao says,

> In the course of my speech I touched upon the Sino-Japanese relations, saying: "Understanding is everything. It is essential for the people of the two countries that they should have mutual understanding." After my speech an old American lady came to greet me, and said: "You said, 'Un-derstanding is everything.' But I do not believe that understanding is ev-erything. I have spent forty years in China, and I have given my constant love to the Chinese people. Why does not strong Japan give her love to the weak and helpless China? You should not stop at understanding only." When she gave me this advice with earnestness, and shook my hand, I saw tears were running from her eyes. Never before have I been so deeply im-pressed as I was then by her Christian spirit of love. From that time on, whenever I talked on the Sino-Japanese relations, I changed my slogan of "Understanding is everything" to "Love is everything."[94]

Given the part that the Japanese Imperial Railways would play in the subse-quent history of Sino-Japanese relations,[95] Nagao's account of his moving en-counter with the pious missionary lady seems disgracefully naïve if not scan-dalous. While the report recounts this story as an example of the positive influence that Christian missions can have on worldly affairs and ambitions, it also ironically illustrates how a facile and ambiguous convergence of ecclesial, entrepreneurial, and governmental interests, such as those that came together at the Tokyo convention, may actually engender a fanatical and dan-gerous optimism. Those who were beyond the margins of this marriage of missionary, money, and national interests would surely be the most sensitive to the potential hazards of such arrangements. This helps explain the absence of a single native Chinese among the seventeen-member missionary delega-tion from China or the presence of only four native Koreans among the forty-seven-member missionary delegation from Korea.[96] The report, which fails to mention the official protest of the Chinese and Koreans, still testifies, by their tiny numbers, that Japan's closest neighbors voted with their feet.

In a bizarre development, the convention began in tragedy when the newly constructed convention hall burned down just three hours before the opening ceremony due to an electrical fire. A huge choir was in the midst of their practice when the fire broke out in the hall, but everyone managed to escape without serious injury. According to Tamura's eye-witness report, the wooden building was gone in fifteen minutes.[97] While confessing his puzzlement over the disaster, he also said that God surely had some deeper purpose in mind because the fire helped those who were truly committed to the Sunday School to clarify what this meeting was all about.

> While the financially powerless Japanese Sunday Schools had received the backing of many people who knew nothing of the true purpose of the Sunday School, it was unclear if the Sunday School or the Patron's Association was really the main focus of the meeting. Given this confusing ambiguity, the idea of holding that huge meeting in Tokyo was probably a mistake from the beginning. However, from the Christian perspective, the absurd beginning of the meeting with the convention hall fire gave us a unique chance to make our case.[98]

As a result of the quick negotiations of the well-connected Japanese executive committee, a decision was made to utilize the magnificent Imperial Theatre for the meetings which would begin the next day.[99] However, as a result of Tamura's personal efforts, the opening ceremony of the convention actually took place at the YMCA. Tamura said, "After God removed our Convention Hall, I had a deep realization that it was God's will that the only remaining Japanese Christian building, the YMCA Hall, should be used for the meeting."[100] While the convention had been scheduled to begin at 7 P.M., it actually got underway at 7:30 P.M. on the day of the fire.

Whereas Tamura had been involved in the initial stages of planning for this convention, the conspicuous absence of his name from the report's appendix is a sign of his lingering tensions with other Japanese Christian leaders and the NSSA-related missionaries. Tamura's companions in youth, Ibuka, Yamamoto, and Kumano, who had sat on the presbytery's investigative committee during The Japanese Bride incident, were all mentioned in the report. Kozaki Hiromichi, another early associate of Tamura's and now the president of the NSSA, was chosen to represent Japan in an address to the convention on the subject of "The Children of the Orient."[101] Even Uemura, Tamura's former friend turned nemesis, addressed the convention on the theme of "The Sufficiency of Christ for the New Day."[102] While Tamura attended the meeting and the influence of his ideas are echoed in the speeches of Kozaki and even Uemura, he was not involved in direct leadership. His absence does not mean that he had ended his involvement in the religious education movement. On the contrary, he had simply taken yet another new direction. Entering his early sixties, he had turned from active political involvement in the movement to the task of constructing a contextual critical theory. In Chapter Five, I examine his theory and some of the biblical and theological norms that inform it.

CHAPTER FIVE Tamura's Mature Work

The Principles and Practice of Religious Education

The fact that Tamura published *The Principles and Practice of Religious Education* in September 1920, just one month before the October convention in Tokyo, shows that in spite of his personal struggles with the missionaries and other Japanese Christian leaders, he continued to see himself as the dean of the religious education movement in Japan.[1] His unreferenced quote from Abraham Kuyper in the preface reveals the powerful personal conviction and sense of destiny with which Tamura wrote this book.

> I died with the writing of this book. I am not concerned whether this book is read by people today or those who come later. When I think that God is willing to wait tens of thousands of years for even one who grasps the mysterious working of divine providence, I will not utter a word of complaint if my book is not read for thousands of years.[2]

Since the first three chapters of this book represent Tamura's most comprehensive, contextual practical theological work, I will present his argument in some detail.[3]

While continuing to rely in this book on the literature of the North American religious education movement, he also sustains and indeed refines the contextual practical theological approach he had started to work out at the time of his turn to religious education.[4] From beginning to end, without losing the global ecumenical perspective, he keeps the particular missional context of Japan in mind. The preface begins,

The scientific study of religious education is a recent arrival in the academic world. Largely for that reason, this issue has still not attracted the attention of too many people in Japan. Ironically, while Buddhists and Christians take a defiant attitude toward each other, Buddhists think religious education consists simply in teaching the interpretation of the sutras while Christians similarly claim that expounding the Bible is the main function of religious education. Further, since our public educators ignore religion, religion is banished from the sphere of education, and it is dreamed that one can train healthy citizens by teaching history and ethics. Presently the voices of reform are shaking the world. Yet, more than anything else, what first needs reforming is the human person. There is surely no other means of training people as healthy citizens than religious education. As one happy result of the World War, there is a gradual awakening to this truth that is beginning to draw public attention.[5]

Given the continuing presence of Christian missionaries who often took a negative stance in regards to Japan's religious traditions,[6] this tension and misunderstanding between Buddhists and Christians is hardly surprising. As his tongue-in-cheek comment implies and we will see below, Tamura tried to positively interpret the missional situation of Japanese religious pluralism in conversation with North American progressivist thought.

His somewhat opaque critical reference to the non-religious "teaching of history and ethics" needs further explanation, since it is indicative of the ongoing tensions between Christian faith and the government's nationalistic education program. Tamura here is taking aim at the way that Japan's public schools, under the aegis of the Imperial Rescript, were approaching moral education at the time. Stuart Hoffman fills in the background on the related developments in moral education and the teaching of history during this period.

A decisive turning point is noted in the early part of the Taisho period (1912-1926) when Japan's rapid ascendancy to Great Power status was interpreted as evidence of the nation's economic, political and spiritual progress to modernity. Moral education assumed a position of preeminence among all school subjects and regimented educational indoctrination increased the power of the Emperor cult. The publication of the third state moral textbook in 1918 reflects Japan's successes in foreign wars and diplomacy (e.g. Twenty-one Demands presented to China in 1915). The *Tenno* (explicitly the recently deceased Emperor Meiji) was represented as a direct descendant of *Amaterasu Omikami* (as Goddess of the

Sun, the chief divinity of the Shinto pantheon); a "Divine Ruler." The *Tenno* was taught to have metaphysical powers and to be the source of godly virtues and powers in the Japanese state *(Bansei Ikkei-no Tenno)*. Spiritual unity doctrine focused on instilling nationalistic values exemplified by historical reinterpretation of "Once-upon-a-time" myths. History courses were renamed "National History" *(Kokushi)* and allotted increased curriculum hours. Furthermore, literature used in Japanese classes supplemented the teaching of desired values. The conformist ethic began to be infused with overt militarism.[7]

Given this ideological context, Tamura's comment on "the teaching of history and ethics" is a courageous and prescient evangelical criticism of the government's systematic program of indoctrination into the imperial cult.

Like the other leaders among the first generation of Protestants, Tamura was devoted to Japan and the emperor, but he had from early on rejected any notion of the divinity of the emperor. As an indication of how cognizant Tamura was of the need for a carefully nuanced Christian approach to Japan's modern nation-state, as early as 1890 he had published a small book titled *Christianity and Politics,* the same year that the Imperial Rescript was promulgated and a full year before Uchimura's fateful refusal to bow had provoked the nationalist attack on Christianity! There he describes Christian teaching as "containing the great power to stand behind political society in order to insure that the policies of the government do not move in a wrong direction."[8] Later, he clarifies why Christians must respect the emperor while refusing to worship him as God.

> Christianity teaches that there is only one God and that there is absolutely no other God besides the God who made the universe in the beginning. Though the emperor has a high position and is to be greatly respected, yet because he is a person just like us, to worship the human emperor as God is a great sin toward God. Thus, the respect that Christians pay the emperor is not because he is God.[9]

Tamura's position might be called qualified Christian patriotism. To return to the preface of *The Theory and Practice of Religious Education,* Tamura clearly states that the "teaching of history and ethics," even if formulated in a pseudo-religious mythical modality, can never substitute for the positive place of true religion in education. I will return to Tamura's criticism of the government's approach in more detail below.

The first chapter, titled "The Psychological Foundations of Religion," begins with the buoyant assertion that scientific evolutionism is not an enemy but a friend of religion. Here he is indirectly addressing the interdisciplinary issue by assailing the conclusions of above-mentioned naturalist Edward Morse, who had introduced Darwin's theory of evolution, and others who had confidently asserted that the findings of modern science seriously undermined the Christian faith. Tamura confesses that, since he himself was a young Christian when Morse delivered his famous lectures in Tokyo in 1877, he had originally feared that Morse and others might be right. He acknowledges that in 1920 there were still many Japanese intellectuals who continued to believe that religion was merely a superstition that could not bear the light of modern science.

In spite of the positivist bias against religion, things had changed drastically in the academic world, according to Tamura. Quoting from Steven, he says, "When we examine the idea that the theory of evolution banishes God to some place outside of the universe, we find out that evolution actually gives God a central and safe place within the universe."[10] While such comments show that Tamura's concept of God was leaning in the direction of the immanentalism that characterized the social gospel and the religious education movement, Tamura believed that, in Christian progressivism, he had found a positive mediating synthesis between evangelical faith and scientism.

In sharp contrast to the sometimes anti-modernist missionaries, Tamura extols scientific research as the "spirit" and "glory" of the twentieth century and wants to show how Christianity itself may positively benefit from the light of science. Rather than simply claiming its basis in scripture as God's revelation, Tamura believed that Christianity must be rigorously examined as a religion among other religions. Praising the emergence of religious studies as a new academic discipline in Western universities, Tamura goes on to say that, since religion is a universal phenomenon that arises primarily from innate psychological dynamics, it needs to be elucidated with the help of empirical psychology.

He then mentions the older psychological approach that understood religion as an innate capacity and distinguished the acquisition of religious knowledge from the common acquisition of knowledge. He says that such an epistemological dualism naturally lent support to the modernist claim that religion was nothing more than superstition or a projection of human desires. However, he claims that, since recent social psychological theory has overcome this bifurcation by asserting a continuity between personal and communal religious consciousness, there is no longer any scientific basis for the claim that religious consciousness is nothing more than infantile superstition or projection. He says that just as adults have no empirical basis for calling a child's faith superstitious, so it is with the true scientist of religion.

Further, since inner religious experience precedes the construction of religious institutions, Tamura says that the reductionist view that religion is merely the convenient invention of a clerical or political class also has no scientific basis. Here again he shows his indebtedness to Coe, who similarly insists that the foundation of religion is in the heart.[11] Extending his argument, Tamura says that while some anthropologists had formerly claimed that certain archaic peoples had no religion, it was later revealed that such peoples simply did not have a highly developed religion. In other words, those anthropologists erroneously judged the simpler archaic religion by the standard of a more highly evolved religion. He quotes Coe for support of his claim that today, no anthropologist or psychologist claims that there are peoples without religion. "There is no child and no citizenry who do not believe in some religion. Those who do not believe in religion are diseased."[12]

Next, Tamura considers how religion is related to the theory of evolution. Whereas it was previously assumed that either fear or desire was the innate psychological ground for religion, it gradually became common to describe the psychological foundations for religion more holistically, in terms of reason, emotion, or volition. Tamura divides prominent modern Western thinkers into three groups who variously emphasize the intellectual (i.e., Marx, etc.), emotional (i.e., Schleiermacher, etc.), or volitional (i.e., James, etc.) dimensions of religion. He then concludes that, while this divergence reveals a lack of unity on the question of the precise psychological basis of religion, it also suggests that there is no other place beyond psychology to look for a definition of the nature of religion.

Tamura next turns to the recent emphasis on instinct theory as a more helpful way to grasp the nature of religion. He mentions Wilhelm Max Wundt's quip that "The definitions of instinct are as confusing as a museum of natural history."[13] On the other hand, he also quotes Wundt as saying, "Instinct is that which has the power to achieve a great purpose without any education."[14] He then describes two opposing views on instinct. The first group, represented by King and Ames of the Chicago school, sees religious instinct, like religious capacity, as having a certain biological function, yet is opposed to thinking of religious instinct as foundational. These pragmatic thinkers are only interested in how religious instinct functions, not in any abstract or metaphysical assertions about religious "nature." The other group, represented by McDougall, sees religion primarily in terms of the social collectivity, and therefore rejects any attempt to suggest any single instinct that adequately accounts for such a complex, communal phenomenon. Since religion is such a complicated subject, McDougall favors a view that allows for the working of multiple instincts. Without attempting to solve the theoretical differences between the functionalists and social-psychologists, Tamura states his own preference for Galloway's terms "principle of religious development" and "religion's psychological character" over "religious instinct." This preference will become clearer when we look later at how he tried to apply this theory to the Japanese missional situation.

In a move that again brings his epistemological "norms of practice" into clear focus, Tamura goes on to criticize post-Kantian modern thought for its tendency to characterize reason, emotion, and will as independent functions. His approach is very close to the critique I offered in Chapter One of Loder's use of Parsons's four-part model of human action. The claim in both cases is not to dispute the descriptive power of such categories but to question the adequacy of an analytical epistemology for describing the inherent synthetic relationality that characterizes these spheres of human knowing and action.

Intimately conversant with the competing rationalities of premodernity and modernity, Tamura is deeply vexed by this fragmented analytical approach to human reason, emotion, and volition. As a practical theologian *pathically* engaged in both ongoing missional ecclesial practice (at Sukiyabashi Church and beyond) and ecumenical dialogue (mostly via the resources of the REM), he intuitively grasps the need for religious education to overcome the analytical partitioning of the inherently integrated human spirit *(shinrei)*. Tamura utilizes the suggestive Japanese word *shinrei*, which is a compound word composed of the Chinese characters for heart *(shin)* and spirit *(rei)*. While no longer in common usage among Japanese Christians because of its association with spiritualism, this native word stresses the inherent synthesis or unity between the various dimensions of human life.[15] Thus, Tamura draws on the cultural-linguistic categories of his native land, the resources of contemporary psychology, and his personal experience of Christian faith to normatively ground his own theoretical synthesis that attempts to overcome the analytical approach.

> Recent psychology has made great progress on "the unity of the human spirit." While still speaking of the three dimensions for the sake of convenience, the crux of the new thinking is to understand the human spirit as a unity, and not as something that can be clearly divided into the functions of reason, emotion, or will. By no means are the functions of reason, emotion, and will mutually isolated functions. There is emotion in reason and reason in emotion. All three function in unison as human spirit. Thus, to posit the basis of religion in reason, emotion, or will is an example of faulty thinking that has yet to penetrate the mystery of psychology. In religion, we must deal with the whole work of the human spirit.

> Knowing God, trusting God, and keeping God's commandments neces-
> sarily involves the work of the entire human spirit.[16]

The structure and movement of Tamura's thought is an amalgam of his own cultural background, careful academic reflection, and personal religious and pastoral experience.

Tamura's attempt to posit an anthropological basis for the paradoxical relationality of the one human spirit in three modalities or the three modalities in one human spirit is reminiscent of Augustine's *vestigia trinitatis*.[17] However, unlike Augustine, Tamura unfortunately never acknowledges the theological ground or analogy for these claims and thus falls easy prey to the common criticisms of the *vestigia*.[18] In spite of his somewhat weak biblical and theological norms which I will examine in more detail at the end of this chapter, Tamura's creative practical theological deliberations nevertheless exemplify the kind of post-critical, synthetic, missional-ecumenical engagements desperately needed in this discipline today. With the criticisms I offered in Chapter One, I believe Loder's attempt to bring the relation of human spirit and Holy Spirit into conversation is exactly the direction in which we need to move.

Tamura now moves from his insistence on the unity of reason, emotion, and will to the insights of Freudian psychoanalysis. Here again, in his attempt to bring religion and psychology into conversation, we see him leaning away from analytical toward synthetic thinking. He calls the discovery of the function of the unconscious or subconscious "the greatest recent invention of psychology"[19] and says that the recent advances in this field have huge significance for psychology, education, and the religious world. He is especially concerned with the educational implications of these breakthroughs.

> Energizing the holistic functioning of the human spirit surely does not
> end with the functions of reason, emotion, and will, but must attend to
> the entire consciousness of the human spirit. The entire consciousness
> means upper and lower consciousness. In other words, normal con-
> sciousness and the subconscious. . . . As long as they exist, human beings
> can never be detached from religion.[20]

Following Coe, who asserts the universality of religion while insisting on the primacy of personal religious experience ("inner life"),[21] Tamura's psychological totalism similarly abandons all normative theological grounds for religious truth. He claims that, in the context of modernity, the only firm, "scientific" basis and support for religion is the inner, psychological experience of

the individual. This buoyant trust in psychology reflects the enthusiasm gen-
erated by Freud's magisterial description of the architecture of the human
psyche. Swayed by such positivist claims, Tamura seems to be completely un-
aware of the tendency of this view toward a theological obscurantism that
sacrifices every evangelical conviction on the altar of individual experience or
measurable phenomena.

Having confidently established that religion is rooted in the structure of
the human psyche, Tamura now returns to his broader missional apologetic
by asserting the huge responsibility of Japanese educators to nurture this universal, innate religiosity. While his ecumenical dialogue partners are mostly
the books of Coe and other distant foreigners, his missional concern is completely focused on the situation of the Japanese churches and public schools.
Given the case he has presented up to this point, he now boldly asserts his
conclusion. Since this section is one of the clearest articulations of Tamura's
core practical theological concern, I will quote it at length.

> If given the appropriate extrinsic stimuli, religion will flower of itself and
> bear fruit. Religion is truly built on a solid foundation. However it is re-
> viled or laughed to scorn, and even if it is completely cut off from society,
> religion will continue as before even if in a shadowy valley. Religion has its
> own adequate reasons! Thus, to claim that religion is superstition or the
> invention of the priestly class are shallow arguments. If religion were built
> on these kinds of weak foundations, it would be easy work to eradicate it.
> It would naturally vanish with the advance of civilization. However, the
> facts are exactly the opposite! Doesn't scientism strengthen the foundation
> of religion? Aren't the faces of those scholars who have previously opposed
> religion turning pale today? Isn't it clear that their prophecies denouncing
> religion have proven to be false? They could not in their wildest dreams
> imagine that religion was actually built on such a solid foundation. Their
> sins can still be forgiven. However, given the progress of science today, we
> can no longer forgive the sin of using science as a weapon to ignore reli-
> gion. It is a human duty to earnestly examine religion![22]

While Tamura's rhetoric may sound excessively optimistic and naïve to a
twenty-first-century reader, it is important to recall that he was addressing a
religiously pluralistic society caught between the "rock" of a deeply rooted,
premodern cultural *habitus* and the "hard place" of the increasing global hegemony of a Westerncentric modernity. As I will show in my examination of
the next chapter of *The Principles and Practice of Religious Education*,
Tamura's case for the universality of religion and the need for Japanese educa-

tors to take religion seriously was discreetly aimed at the government's educational policy of ideological indoctrination under the Imperial Rescript. While in no way abandoning the importance of the educational ministry of the churches, he was also trying to make a case for a public and critical missional-ecumenical practical theology.

The second chapter is titled "The Development of Religious Consciousness." Precisely because they both develop progressively, Tamura wisely concedes the impossibility of arriving at any fixed definitions for religion or consciousness. He says that reading the history of religions reveals the great diversity of scholarly opinion on religion. In a way that anticipates Polanyi's post-critical view of "personal knowing," Tamura attributes this diversity of views to the dispositional interest of the individual scholar. "Since intellectual scholars define religion in terms of reason, passionate scholars in terms of emotion, and activist scholars in terms of will, the number of definitions of religion is on the rise every year."[23]

Then, sounding like Nietzsche or even Foucault on the relation between self-definitions and power, he says that, in the competitive religious marketplace of Japan, Buddhists purposely chose their own definition of religion to clearly distinguish themselves from Christians. Given this combination of personal dispositional and collective ideological reasons for the multiplicity of definitions of religion, Tamura pragmatically concludes that investigating the ways that religion progressively develops and functions at various stages is likely to yield a better understanding of the phenomenon than beginning with some grand theory about essence. Taking the same pragmatic or functional view toward consciousness, he suggests looking closely at its development before making any generalities about its structure or essence. Tamura's reticence toward "grand" or "meta-narratives" sounds surprisingly contemporary because he lived and worked as a leader of a minority religious group within a religiously complex society. However, his "proto-postmodern" stance did not lead him to nihilism or absolute relativism, but was in fact part of his missional *apologia* for the Christian faith.

Tamura next describes what he calls the antithetical theories of religion proposed by the missionaries and by science. He says that the first theory, emphasizing the fallen condition of humanity, claims that religion lost its true value with the fall. The second theory, based on the theory of evolution, sees religion originating in extreme simplicity and progressing along lines analogous to an individual's psychological development. He says that while the first theory held sway for hundreds of years, it has recently been overcome by the scientific view, with the result that there is not a single scholar today who holds to the old view.

Whereas religion was previously thought to be sacred and mysterious and therefore beyond the reach of science, Tamura says that science has changed all that by the empirical study of religion. He claims that the dogmatic proposition that the Christian God is true while the gods of other religions are false is a thing of the past. On the one hand, here Tamura is making a clear break with his exclusivist missionary roots and trying to establish a scientific basis for religious tolerance within Japan's religiously pluralistic society.

> Looking from the light of science, there is no basis on which to distinguish the truth or falsity of God. Anyone would be at a loss if asked about the standard for the truth or falsity of God. That is, the only basis for truth and falsity is the principle that one sees one's own religion as superior and looks down at other religions. From a Christian's point of view, those who have a curse put on someone, bow to a *Jizo* (a Buddhist guardian deity of children), or worship the sun are called idol-worshipers or superstitious. However, those people are surely not worshiping false gods nor are they superstitious. Their beliefs are sacred. The fact that there is Shinto, Buddhism, and Christianity in Japan is not an accident. There are good reasons for the existence of each religion.[24]

Building on his earlier argument, he finds those "good reasons for the existence of each religion" first in psychology, claiming that religious beliefs are a matter of personal experience before they find rational, propositional expression in doctrine. Because of the personal psychological ground of religious experience, he concludes, "Even after many years, Shinto and Buddhism will undoubtedly continue to exists in Japan."[25] Just as he intuitively wants to see the individual as an integrated whole, he similarly embraces the whole historical, religious development of the Japanese people. Again, this more positive approach toward the Japanese religions is in stark opposition to the "displacement theology" of many of the missionaries.

At the same time, Tamura's religious tolerance cannot be mistaken for religious relativism. Taking a page out of Durkheim, he introduces the classical typology of "folk religion, national religion, and world religion."[26] Again, with the Japanese missional situation in mind, he then attempts to correlate this tripartite typology with the three developmental stages of "children's religion," "youth's religion," and "adult's religion." He outlines what he sees as the correlations between folk religion and child religion, national religion and youth religion, and world religion and adult religion. He further enlarges this developmental analogy to include a schooling metaphor, calling the three progressive stages of religious development elementary education, secondary education, and university education. For the sake of clarity, Tamura's relational analogies between these three spheres of development may be charted as follows:

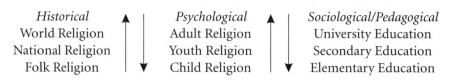

Historical		*Psychological*		*Sociological/Pedagogical*
World Religion		Adult Religion		University Education
National Religion		Youth Religion		Secondary Education
Folk Religion		Child Religion		Elementary Education

Drawing on Coe and others, Tamura takes considerable pains to describe the unique characteristics of each discrete developmental stage, but the point he wishes to drive home above all else is the importance of seeing all of these stages in invariant relation to each other.

> Just as the basis for the future perfection of language exists in the stuttering words of a child, we can see the outline of the religion of the university in the religion of the elementary child. Social consciousness and religious consciousness are in an inseparably intimate relation to each other.[27]

On the basis of this developmentalism, Tamura is building a careful rationale for a more tolerant approach to Japan's religious pluralism than that taken by the missionaries who often rejected Japanese religions out of hand.[28] He says, "Religion cannot somehow transcend or leave off the sociological and psychological situation of a certain people."[29]

In the section describing the characteristics of a child's religion, Tamura explains how Shinto and Buddhism contribute positively to the development of Japanese religious consciousness. Because a four- or five-year-old child cannot possibly grasp the concept of a formless, immaterial, spiritual God, he says it is important to utilize visible, concrete objects when teaching about God.

> Children need a religion that can be seen. The use of things such as Shinto mirrors and Buddhist idols is essential in cultivating the religion of the child. Through such things a religious spirit is nurtured.[30]

He says that only using words may have a bad effect on children since they are all "idol worshipers." Unlike most of the missionaries, Tamura acknowledges that the Japanese churches may have something to learn from Shinto and Buddhist practices of nurture.

Besides further distancing himself from the missionaries, Tamura's positive appraisal of Japanese religions also reflects his missional apologetic, even evangelistic concern. In his autobiography, he joyfully recounts his experience of being invited to a Buddhist summer institute in 1916 to speak on the principles and practices of Christian Sunday Schools.

> In spite of all of our efforts to date, I never even dreamt I would be given an opportunity to speak to such a crowd about Christianity. Not only was it the first time for most of these Buddhist priests to see a Christian pastor, it was the very first time for them to hear a long (two hour) speech by a pastor.[31]

Because of the efforts of Tamura and others, many Japanese Buddhist temples devised their own version of the Sunday School, mimicking the principles and methods of the churches. This would not have been possible if he had clung to the exclusivism of the missionaries. Again, this sensitivity toward his missional situation should not be mistaken for some facile syncretism. As we will see below, Tamura's approach to the other Japanese religions might be called a critical or positive exclusivism.

As I have already mentioned, Tamura sought to correlate the history of religions with the developmental growth from childhood to youth to adult. This correlation comes from his reading of the theory of recapitulation in Coe, Thorndike, and Davidson. Of that theory, Coe says,

> Recapitulation theory is a special and recent form of an idea, long held, that there is some sort of parallel between child life and the "childhood of the race."[32]

But rather than simply explain the Western view of recapitulation, Tamura is more interested in applying the idea to the Japanese missional situation of religious pluralism. Here his appraisal of Japan's religions takes a different form than what we have seen so far.

> Children are ruled by desire. The child is far more interested in himself than in others. The child's wants are completely selfish. . . . Early peoples were self-seeking just like children. They prayed to gods for their own needs. . . . When you visit Japanese Shinto shrines, you find the words *Taiganjoju* (attainment of one's desires) everywhere. If your desire is not attained, the gods are no longer considered to be gods. Also, the fashion of saying that the *Inari* (harvest or guardian deity) or the *Kannon* (god-

dess of mercy) of a certain Buddhist temple is currently popular is also a result of the principle of self-interest. Today in our country, the fact that we have Shinto, Buddhism, and only a minority of believers in Christianity shows that, from a religious point of view, the citizens of Japan are still kindergartners. We have not yet advanced beyond the religious elementary school.[33]

While it is easy to criticize Tamura's negative portrayal of Japanese religions here, his words need to be read as a Japanese missional *apologia* for the relative superiority of Christianity. Further, since Tamura has nothing less than the transformation of the entire nation as his goal, his critical application of developmentalist theory to Japan's religious situation also needs to be read as a positive and prophetic alternative to the government's educational program of nationalistic indoctrination.

Tamura is intuitively struggling with the difficult practical theological task of correlating theological and social science norms in order to provide a critique of an educational practice that he thought was holding the Japanese people back from making the leap into an increasingly globalized modernity.

In today's society that is becoming increasingly global, we have planes that fly in the sky and trains that run underground, making for a convenience of transportation, and we can learn what is going on throughout the entire world in a single day. Such a society cannot be satisfied with folk or nationalistic religion. Because social consciousness has progressed this far, the development of religious consciousness must keep up. We need an exceptionally noble idea of God and faith. Isn't the basic principle of Christianity that all humanity are both children of God and siblings one of another?[34]

Tamura's contemporary readers would understand this as a subtle but thoroughgoing attack on the Ministry of Education's policy of using the Imperial Rescript to systematically indoctrinate Japanese children into the invented, pseudo-religious *ethos* of Japan's "folk" or "nationalistic" ideology. On the basis of his belief in the developmentalist paradigm, Tamura argues that an increasingly interconnected world needs the universal faith of a world religion.

He goes on to argue that the world religions that preceded Christianity (i.e., Confucianism, Buddhism, Judaism, and Zoroastrianism) were all, in their own ways, preparations for Christ's coming. He then says that, since no person greater than Christ has come into the world over the past two thousand years, it is clear that Christianity is the ultimate religion. Like Coe who compares Buddhist self-denial with Christian asceticism and contrasts both to true Christian self-denial which always has a positive social aim,[35] Tamura's ultimate theological norm is the self-denying moral disposition of Jesus.

> Just as homo sapiens is the end of evolution, Christianity is the end of religions. When one arrives at Christ, one has entered the religion of the university. When a person can pray like Christ, "My Father, if it is possible, let this cup pass from me; yet not what I want but what you want," they have awakened to the real truth of world religion for the first time. If one had not received the religious education of the "university," one would not be able to pray like this.[36]

The notions of a believer "arriving at Christ," or "being able to pray like Christ," show that Tamura, again like Coe, replaces the "Christ of dogma" with the "Christ of experience."[37] In general, Tamura took his lead from Coe, who was convinced that experiential religion was much more in keeping with the rationality of modern science.[38] Tamura concludes the chapter by reiterating his view that the development of societies and persons occurs on parallel trajectories. The advance from folk to national to world religion is analogous to the advance from elementary to secondary to university education. Therefore, "religious and social consciousness must progress together hand in hand."[39]

The third chapter of *The Principles and Practice of Religious Education* is titled "The Goal of Religious Education." Here Tamura reiterates his belief that the goal of religious education is the "education of Christianized, good citizens."[40] In this chapter he addresses the imperial government's program of indoctrination even more directly. He begins by recalling an intriguing encounter he had in New York with a certain Dr. Shiraishi in his student days. Shiraishi had told Tamura about his experience of accompanying a Japanese marquis on a European tour.

> The marquis said, "I always thought that politicians used religion for the purpose of gaining the favor of religious people, but on this trip, when I met Bismarck in Germany and Gladstone in England and engaged in long, relaxing conversations with them, I was very shocked to discover that both men are true religious believers." I (Shiraishi), too, have since decided to abandon the idea of manipulating religion for political purposes.[41]

Tamura tells this story in support of the positive role that religion should play in a modern nation's sociopolitical life.

Given this basic premise, he then builds an argument for the importance of religious education in Japan's public educational policy, stating "There is nothing as important as religion in human life."[42] To counter those Japanese educators who saw no substantive or constructive role for religion in public education, he quotes Nicholas Murray Butler, then president of Columbia University.

> There are five legacies of humanity; firstly literature, secondly art, thirdly science, fourthly society, and fifthly religion. Maintaining their proper sequence, education's task is to correctly put these legacies to practical use.[43]

Building toward his critique of what he saw as the Japanese government's "religionless" education, Tamura concludes, "It is impossible to educate human beings without religion. Education that undermines the true character of humanity can not be called education."[44]

After reminding his readers that psychology provides the proper scientific basis for religion in the modern period, he launches into his carefully worded critique and proposal. On the one hand, he admits that the absence of religion in Japan's national system of education may be an unavoidable reality in the light of historical circumstances. Here he is referring to the forced opening of Japan by the countries of the West and Japan's strong sense of a need to quickly catch up. In its rush into modern industrialization, Japan had little time to attend to religious questions. On the other hand, he offers a practical example of how the Japanese government might positively approach the religious needs of its citizens, mentioning that while the U.S. and French governments do not offer any government-sponsored religious instruction in their public schools, they actively encourage the various churches to provide religious education.

He then complains that Japan has taken the "exact opposite approach" of the United States and France. Carefully choosing his words, he says,

> Just because there is no language that encourages faith in Buddha or God in the Imperial Rescript, to conclude that the spirit of the Rescript is opposed to religion is exceedingly foolish. In his book entitled *The New Education*, Mr. Tanimoto strongly criticizes the policy adopted by the Ministry of Education. While Japan boasts about being one of the five great world powers, it is an unprecedented nation from the point of view of not providing religious education for its citizens. This is a huge error on the part of the authorities at the Ministry of Education. In the schools estab-

lished by national tax revenues, if our Japanese religions which display such a mutual hostility to each other do not in their present state posses the ability to teach, then individual Shintoists, Buddhists, and Christians must certainly be called upon to provide religious education under the direction of the Ministry of Education. It is a sad fact that, as a result of having chosen this wrong path, religion has been thoroughly banished from Japan's educational world. Isn't it said that "A nation without religion will perish"? Buddhism would do. Shinto would do. Why isn't religion taught as part of the education of Japanese citizens?[45]

On the one hand, Tamura allows that Shinto or Buddhism could, hypothetically, provide the basis for a substantive religious education, but then he goes on to claim that those Japanese religions had lost their spiritual and moral power by being thoroughly conventionalized.

> In Japan, we have deeply-rooted, non-religious, conventionalized versions of Confucianism, Shinto, and Buddhism. . . . Because of the influence of common morality on Buddhism, Japanese *Bushido* has gradually lost all of its spiritual power, resulting in the heartbreaking deterioration of Japanese morality.[46]

Again, any savvy contemporary reader would have recognized the radical and subversive nature of Tamura's critical analysis. While he never comes out and states it directly, the unmistakable charge he is making is that the Japanese government's "top-down" program of indoctrination into the imperial cultus embodied a flawed conception of both religion and education.

For Tamura, the nature of religion sets the proper direction for religious education. In other words, educational methods must flow from the content of the particular religion. Further, because true religion is always rooted in personal experience, Tamura was convinced that a living faith and authentic religious disposition would never be induced by indoctrinating people into the ideology of Japan's nationalistic creed. Tamura's point that the Japanese government had taken the opposite stance from the United States and France meant that, while offering government-sponsored quasi-religious (not religious!) indoctrination (not education!) in their public schools, they actively discouraged the various religious groups from providing religious education.

Knowing full well that a frontal attack would have made him the easy target of ultranationalists, he did not openly suggest the repudiation of the Imperial Rescript. Rather, he wisely suggested that a more liberal interpretation of the Rescript would support his critical proposal. As one who deeply loved Japan, he never directly criticized the emperor, but especially in light of his placement of the Shiraishi story, he took direct aim at the bureaucrats in the government who he believed were manipulating the imperial mythology for their own political ends.

In terms of Sanneh's thesis, Tamura was striving, against overwhelming odds, to de-stigmatize Japanese sociocultural and political structures in order that they may become bearers of the truth of Christian faith. Looking back at Tamura's prescient warning and proposal through the lens of the subsequent history of the Japanese empire, we may characterize him as a prophetic and public missional-ecumenical practical theologian who clearly rejected the top-down imposition of the imperial ideology without ever rejecting his beloved emperor. As I have mentioned previously, Tamura's view should be called a qualified Christian patriotism.

After his criticism and proposal for reform, he mentions a trip he had made to the West in 1919 and reports that in every country he heard desperate cries for the reform of religious education from public educators. These postwar calls to reform all agreed on the need to "put people first." He recounted that current social problems, such as labor and human rights issues, were seen to revolve around the basic issue of the person. In light of these personalistic trends in the West, Tamura makes one of the clearest statements of how he envisioned the goal of religious education in the Japanese context.

> We will solve all of these related problems if we produce good citizens. The goal of religious education is in the building up of Christianized, good citizens. Character is not something that can be built in one night. It is completely foolish to think you can create good citizens in a day or two. Do we think that we will create "good citizens" simply by teaching history, geography and an ethics devoid of flesh and blood in our schools? Or when we look at the character of those who teach children, how is it that there are so many pitiful ones? How can we expect teachers without character to train people of character? Our Japanese educators are actually trying to do something preposterous like this.[47]

Because Tamura is convinced that the nurture of "good-citizens" is a noble goal that will require much patience, he concludes it is foolish for the government to think they can quickly produce real character through their program of indoctrination. Tamura's objection to the government's teaching of imperial doctrine also reflects the religious education movement's harsh criticism of the churches' authoritarian methods of teaching of the catechism.[48]

Clearly, Tamura was convinced that Christianity's emphasis on personal character gives it a great advantage over the other Japanese religions. Still, he is deeply critical of Christian leaders, including Sunday School leaders, who had ignored the recent advances in studies on childhood, psychology, pedagogy, and religious studies and the light these studies shed on the development of character.

> From a Christian perspective, one's sins are certainly forgiven the moment one believes in Christ. However, while the basis for character may be laid in that moment, it is not a completed character yet. Character is progressively constructed from the child to the youth to the adult.[49]

In light of this new scientific knowledge, he calls on all of Japan's religious leaders to join hands with Japan's public educators in the task of progressively nurturing the personal religious experience and character of Japan's children, youth, and adults. He concludes the third chapter by restating the goal of religious education.

> The goal of religious education . . . is making Christianized, good citizens who will take their place in society and perform one's vocation without any regret.[50]

Having presented Tamura's critical appropriation of the norms of the North American religious education movement within the volatile Japanese context, I will conclude this chapter by considering the biblical and theological norms informing his mature work.

The Child the Center of Christianity

I will focus on this small book because it presents Tamura's mature biblical and theological views and shows how he draws on these interpretive strategies and "norms of practice," as well as those drawn from the religious education literature, to support his proposal for fundamental changes in the religious educational practices of the Japanese churches and public schools.[51] While this book reflects his continuing ecumenical conversation with the "best theories and practices" suggested by scholars in the West, Tamura remains completely focused on the missional tensions of the Japanese situation. Since, as we have already seen, he was so deeply invested in such contextual missional issues as improving the conditions of women and children, Tamura locates his progressive proposals for religious education in polemical opposition to the missionaries and the Japanese pastors whom he saw as unreflectively perpetuating the imported practices of the missionaries.[52]

The basic proposal of *The Child the Center of Christianity*, a book representing the fruit of twenty-five years of missional and ecumenical practical theological engagement and reflection, may be stated as follows: *If Christianity is ever to take root in and transform Japan's non-Christian social, political, and cultural context, the Protestant churches must decisively turn from a programmatic focus on the evangelization of adults to the careful, lifelong formation of children, youth, and adults.*

Charging that the missionaries had essentially replicated American and British practices of religious education in Japan, he complains that "we have no religious service especially for children" and that "it is absurd to think that the Sunday School is sufficient for the children."[53] He says further that the missionaries and native pastors give little attention to the Sunday School themselves and instead entrust this work "to the ladies and to untrained young people. The result is a very imperfect and unsatisfactory institution."[54] This *ad hoc* approach to the Sunday School provided children little opportunity for cultivating "a spirit of reverence for God."[55] Saying that traditional Buddhist and Shinto services were more effective in nurturing a child's religious affections, Tamura says, "Our Christian leaders have no settled and deep conviction of the importance of cultivating the spiritual life of the children."[56]

He then points out that Japanese children, unlike their American or British counterparts, received no religious training at home to serve as a basis for the work of the church. Since the atmosphere of the Japanese home is "usually anti-Christian," Tamura asks, "When and where shall we give the child training in the devotional life?"[57] Because of the lack of a regular and holistic Christian nurture, Tamura laments that most Japanese Christians, unlike Japanese Buddhists, have unfortunately not developed any religious sentiment or *habitus*. He mentions Robertson Nicoll's *The Incarnate Saviour*,[58] which depicts the decisive influence of religious nurture on Jesus himself as a child. Reflecting on his own pastoral experience, he reiterates a familiar point.

> My conviction that has grown out of my fifty years of ministry is that it is too uphill work to make good Christians out of grown people. Their habits are too strong. And even when they are persuaded to embrace Christianity, and promise to follow Jesus, the habits of years make it difficult for them to stand fast and cling to the Cross. We must begin planting Christian principles in the heart in childhood if we would have them be true Christians when they are adults.[59]

Beginning in 1918, his congregation at Sukiyabashi Church had instituted two worship services, one for children and one for adults. After this initial period of trial, they then decided to expand to four services — for kindergartners, elementary schoolers, middle and high school youth, and adults. This worship-centered approach to educational ministry was a creative practical theological response to a sociocultural context in which Christianity was still a marginalized newcomer among Japan's traditional religions. Tamura thought of the educational ministry at his church as a kind of laboratory, a humble Japanese version of the Union school of religion.

> By this method we are cultivating a devotional spirit in all ages, beginning with the little children and continuing it step by step up to mature years. We have been hoping to set an example to other Christian workers, whereby they might profit by our experiment. But the results have not been what we anticipated. The missionaries and Japanese pastors persist in clinging to their old methods and ignoring the science of habit. "Train up a child in the way he should go, and when he is old he will not depart from it."[60]

I will now present the dominant biblical and theological norms and interpretive strategies supporting Tamura's proposal. On the surface, Tamura's views mirror those that accompanied the North American religious education movement.[61] However, there are subtle differences that reflect the unique tensions of the missional situation of the Japanese church that are still instructive for practical theologians in this subdiscipline today.

Revealing how completely he had accepted the then-popular view of a radical bifurcation in the New Testament between Jesus and Paul, Tamura opts for a synoptic gospel–centered hermeneutic as his critical response to Japan's evangelism or conversion-centered missionary churches. He consistently sets Jesus, the "champion of the child," in stark opposition to Paul and his "childless theology." This opposition reads like a modern version of the ancient doctrine of the "Two Ways." Paul emphasizes sin and salvation, but Jesus emphasizes "the proper valuation of the child."[62] Paul stresses evangelism or preaching, while Jesus centers on education or teaching.[63] Paul's dramatic experience of conversion leads him to stress sudden conversion, reformation, and rescue,[64] while Jesus gives much more weight to slow incremental growth, formation, and prevention.[65] Paul looked backward to the forgiveness of past sins, while Jesus looked forward to the coming of the kingdom of God. Paul is doctrinal and abstract where Jesus is narrative and concrete. Paul saw sin as a disposition while Jesus saw it mostly in terms of moral action.[66] Paul supports the negative "Don't" culture Tamura saw embodied by the puritanical missionaries, but Jesus champions the positive "Do" culture that Tamura saw reflected by the progressivist leaders of the REM. While this dramatic divorce between Paul and Jesus is problematic both exegetically and theologically, it is important to remember that Tamura, as a missional-ecumenical practical theologian, was drawing on a contemporary trend in biblical studies to critique the Japanese church's emphasis on evangelism instead of education.[67]

Because Tamura makes the arguable claim that the focus of the mission of Jesus was first and foremost on "the nurture of the child and loving appreciation of the child,"[68] his portrayal of Jesus himself varies from the deeply insightful to the highly fanciful. For example, wanting to depict Jesus as one who was positively engaged in society and not negatively withdrawn from it, he refutes Rabbi Klausner's claim that Jesus was somehow associated with the Essenes. In contrast to the austere John the Baptist, he portrays Jesus as "a great lover of home and children" who was never a stranger to celebrations and feasts.[69] Further, critical of those artists who painted "sad and meditative"[70] pictures of the face of Jesus, Tamura imagines that the fact that Jesus attracted children implies that his face must have been much more welcoming than such sour portraits suggest.[71] He depicts Jesus as the "divine Friend" of children who had a "smiling and inviting face."[72] Tamura says that this biblical truth, which had been forgotten for long centuries, was being rediscovered by contemporary psychology.[73]

Interestingly, the face of Jesus is also a dominant theme in Loder's interdisciplinary work in psychology and theology. Utilizing the post-critical epistemology of Polanyi, Loder uses the rich phrase "the self-confirming presence of a loving other" to correlate the "proximal" face of the mother or primary caregiver with the "distal" face of Jesus.[74] While Tamura lacks Loder's methodological sophistication, he shows that he also intuitively grasped this "proximal-distal" relation between human and divine caregiving by referring to Jesus' emphasis on the mother and child relation. He says, "He touched the sacred fountain of society when he exalted the mother and the child."[75]

Tamura also depicts Christ as a poet. Quoting from Georges Berguer, he says,

> a poet is a man who feels the universe taking life within himself, who sees in the spectacles of everyday existence the reflection of higher verities which the human eye hardly dares to contemplate.[76]

He lists some striking images from the gospels ("fishers of men," "city on a hill," "light of the world") to show how Jesus "himself exhibits a child spirit wherever he goes."[77] Tamura links the child's immersion in nature with the spontaneous poetic impulse evident in the metaphors Jesus used in his teaching.

> Mark the poetical sentiments He so beautifully expresses. He is walking in a world as fresh as the world of a child. Jesus is a marvelous poet who never wrote a line of verse, but His whole tone reveals the soul and sentiment of a poet. He is the first child poet in the world. His poetic genius is one of the discoveries of the Twentieth Century.[78]

While there is more than a touch of romanticism here and perhaps even a projection of his deepest personal longings for his own lost childhood, Tamura's depiction of Jesus as a "child poet" should also be understood as a missional apologetic. He creatively recasts Jesus as an itinerant poet sage, an image that would have been very familiar with his Japanese readers who were well acquainted with itinerant *haiku* poets such as Bassho and Issa.

Tamura even portrays Christ as a psychoanalyst! He refers to Freud's, Jung's, and Adler's explorations of "the deepest stratum of the unconscious mind" and calls the discovery of the "untold harm repression has wrought in human lives" a new "revelation."[79] He then describes the "dominating power" of "Don't!" in contemporary schools, homes, and churches.[80] Such "negative instruction" of children is universal, Tamura says, and it sadly continues even into young adulthood with a new list of pious moral restrictions such as "Don't smoke, Don't swear, Don't gamble, Don't misuse the Sabbath day, Don't enter the theatre or the dance hall." This is meant as a direct jab at the lifestyles of the puritanical missionaries and their Japanese disciples. Tamura says that, instead of a list of prohibitions that only tempt them, young people long for "something permissible and positive."[81]

He says that such a positive way is precisely the educational approach of Jesus and contrasts his own early childhood nurture in Confucian morality with Christ's approach.

> From a child we were trained by the negatives of Confucius. We felt a new thrill when we first read the moral code of Jesus. He fills life with affirmatives. Herein he differs from the Pharisees and Confucius. He does not dwell on what we must not do, but what we may do that will be uplifting and beneficial. He lays stress on the positive not on the negative.[82]

Jesus speaks of his own coming in the positive terms of fulfillment rather than the negative terms of destruction. Tamura creatively interprets Jesus' approach in contemporary psychoanalytic terms as a negation of repression.

He wishes to see developing in human lives not a repression but a larger fulfillment. He would take that which is the heart of man and develop it into good words, good deeds, good intentions. Christ is a practical Psycho-Analyst. About 2000 years ago, long before the present psychology had explored man's sub-conscious mind and discovered the danger from repression, Jesus had taught positive righteousness.[83]

Tamura anticipates that the anti-modernist missionaries and their Japanese followers would reject his psychological approach, just as they had rejected the concept of evolution. To these naysayers, he responds,

But as the study of evolution has done great service in disclosing scientific truth, so psychology is coming to the front with its great benefits to child education. We are not guilt of blasphemy when we speak of Jesus as a Psycho-Analyst.[84]

While it is tempting to dismiss Tamura's portrayal of Jesus as isogetical romanticism, and while he clearly lacks a nuanced methodology in making these interdisciplinary connections, he is struggling to bring some of the insights of contemporary culture into positive dialogue with the legalistic faith he observed in the missionary-founded Japanese churches. While his approach often reflects the stark either-or oppositions of the modernist epistemology, Tamura never shied away from critiquing the churches in light of his understanding of the gospel.

I will now present some examples of Tamura's contextual biblical exegesis. In chapter twenty-six, "Christ was Homesick in Gethsemane," Tamura offers a highly contextual reading of the Gethsemane narrative. He knew from personal intercultural experience as an exchange student that "homesickness is a distressing disease" and tells the story of a missionary woman who, overwhelmed by homesickness, had actually repacked her bags and returned home the very day she arrived in Japan.[85] After presenting the tragic account of the final hours of Jesus' life, he imaginatively indwells the gospel narrative, exploring what Jesus might have been feeling in Gethsemane. In contrast to the tradition that depicts the Gethsemane agony in terms of Jesus' painful consciousness of having to bear the world's sin as its Savior, Tamura suggests an alternative reading of this story.

But to my mind that (bearing the world's sin) was not his foremost thought. He realized he was the Son of God and to do the Father's will was his great privilege. Therefore he cries in the midst of his grief and pain, "Oh my Father! all things are possible unto Thee; take away this cup from me; nevertheless, not what I will but what Thou wilt." He realized that as the Son of God, this must be his duty. Benjamin Warfield says "Christ put the child in the same situation with himself." He was feeling as a child feels who is away from his human father. He was intensely homesick for his heavenly Father, just as a young child is when away from home. Certainly Jesus was human.[86]

Following the same line of argument, Tamura next launches into a discussion of the meaning of the word "heavy" that appears in Matthew: "He (Jesus) began to be sorrowful and very heavy," and Mark: "He began to be sore amazed and very heavy." Pointing out that the old lexicographers say that the Greek word for "heavy" (αδημονειν) originally meant "away from our people," Tamura interprets it to mean "homesick." "He was longing for his Father's house at this critical time. What a comforting thought that our Saviour was homesick!"[87]

At first sight, this interpretation may look like a flight of romantic fancy, but it is actually a contextual Japanese reading of the passion narrative that needs further explanation or, more appropriately, "cultural translation."[88] Clearly, Tamura's main purpose in this entire book has been to convince his readers that modern psychology demonstrates that Christianity truly is, contrary to the past and present views and practices of the churches, a child-centered faith. Because this insight carried the force of a new revelation for Tamura, in this context it is not surprising that he rereads the entire gospel narrative in its light. But, as we have seen over and over again, he is never content to simply present the theories of Western psychology in some abstract, de-contextualized form but constantly strives to press them into service to the missional situation of Japan. In this process, sometimes wittingly and sometimes unwittingly, he quite naturally and freely draws from the storehouses of his native culture and personal experience.

To return to the present case of Jesus' agony in Gethsemane, Tamura focuses not on what Jesus as Savior was feeling for wayward humanity but on the intimate familial relation between the Son and the Father. While this alternative perspective is not meant to reduce Jesus to a mere human being, Tamura knows that his depiction of this tragic longing of the Son for the household of the Father will deeply resonate in his Japanese readers' hearts and minds. Theologically, you might say that Tamura understands the sorrow of Jesus in the garden primarily on the level of intra-divine relations, arising from the Son's deep sense of filial obligation toward and love for the Father. This reading clearly reflects a Confucian *habitus* in which filial piety, or steadfast devotion to one's parents, forms the primal bedrock of identity. Beyond this more explicit cultural dimension, Tamura's painful memory of having to depart his birth home forever as an eleven-year-old boy surely contributed to his own sensitivity to the sorrowful longing that the Son felt for the fellowship of the Father's household.

Carrying forth the "child" theme, Tamura next poignantly describes an English painting of Jesus leaving the judgment hall of Pilate.

> He is met by a woman with a little child in her arms and with deep sympathy for Jesus in her face. But Jesus' eyes are upon the child rather than on the face of the mother, as if he were feeling keenly the security and confidence of this little one on its mother's bosom. He was yearning for the time when he could once more be in the bosom of the Father.[89]

Again, this view of the cross-bound Jesus longing for the "security and confidence" of the Father's care draws attention to the intra-divine *pathos* implicit in this narrative.

Finally, Tamura follows Jesus as he carries his cross along the final road to his death.

> Behind him follows a small group of pious women from Galilee, weeping bitterly for his shameful sufferings. Turning backward, Jesus looks with loving pity on these mothers and says "Weep not for me, but weep for yourselves and for your children." In Gethsemane, at Pilate's judgment bar, and even on the "Via dolorosa" facing toward Calvary, the World's Redeemer is thinking of the children. He is always solicitous for their welfare.[90]

While there is certainly room here for a more nuanced interdisciplinary methodology, Tamura's passionate reading of scripture in conversation with modern psychology and his ecclesial location engender fresh, imaginative insights into the Christ of the gospels which are still worthy of the church's consideration.[91]

Again, at the beginning of chapter twenty-seven, "Christ's Last Commands," Tamura follows Jesus to the cross, where "we cannot endure to look upon the awful agony which distorts his face."[92] Tamura continues to contemplate the psychological state of Jesus, reminding us that, as in the Garden, Jesus' first spoken word from the cross is "Father." Tortured and homesick, the crucified Jesus "appeals to his Father in heaven," but Tamura reminds us that, in this moment, "he is also mindful of his earthly mother."[93] For a contemporary analogy, he reiterates the awful story of the sinking of the *Titanic* when "even mature men in their frenzy of fear called for 'Mother'!"[94] Tamura comments on Jesus entrusting Mary to John's care:

> At that critical moment, the unconscious stratum of the mind was appealing to mother-love. We never escape from the impression made in childhood. Mother is a living reality to us long as we stay in this world. At this tragic hour, Jesus does not forget his mother. He reveals his kindness and love for her in his feeling for her lonesomeness when he has left her. Is there any privilege for children higher than repaying the tender love of a mother?[95]

Again, while it is easy to hear this as mere sentimentalism, it is another example of Tamura's biblical hermeneutic that weds the modern psychological and pedagogical "turn to the child" to Confucian familialism.

Other examples could be multiplied to show how deeply Tamura had swallowed the biblical and theological norms of the REM. However, while his theology was one-sided and his polemic sometimes harsh, his intention was always the formation of a robust missional church that would be an effective witness to the gospel in the context of modern Japan. In terms of his practical theology, it is especially significant that Tamura tried to hold on to some of the tensions between the evangelical and progressive approaches to Christian religious education when, in the North American unfolding of this story, such tensions dissolved into hardened factions that still persist today. Because of the pre-Constantinian missional situation of the Japanese church, Tamura strained to achieve some positive apologetic, albeit methodologically *ad hoc* correlation between the gospel, church, and contemporary culture.

As an example of this apologetic concern, he recounts the story of a Buddhist student from Kyoto who had come to Tokyo to examine how the new religious pedagogy was actually practiced in Tamura's congregation. In a tone that reminded Tamura of Celsus's second-century attack on Christianity,[96] the Buddhist student asserted "that if Christianity would take hold of the children in this way, there would be no future for Buddhism in Japan."[97] This shows that Tamura was conscious of the similarities between the early church's experience of sociocultural displacement and the contemporary missional situation of the tiny Japanese church.

This consciousness shows up in his acute awareness of the contextual differences between the Japanese and North American churches. For example, explaining the rationale for his radical call to the Japanese churches for a moratorium on preaching to adults in order to concentrate on the nurture of children, he begins with the premise that "there is a vast difference between children born in a Christian land and in an unchristian land."[98] Tamura says that evangelistic methods work in the United States because the whole culture was subconsciously permeated by the "sentiment" or "complex" of Christian faith. In a so-called Christian land, even adults who have been estranged from the church for many years often respond to the invitation of an evangelist because of this background. Turning to the Japanese situation, Tamura asks, "Growing up in a Buddhist environment, how can one expect a Christian complex to be developed? Most of our missionaries and native preachers seem pitifully ignorant of this psychology."[99] This reading of the missional situation in light of the norms of psychology and scripture leads him to suggest practical theological rules of art for the Japanese context.

> We are learning that it is not safe to trust strictly American methods of evangelism in such a country as Japan. . . . Most of our native Christians are abnormal in their allegiance to Jesus, and are easily tempted away from the church. I have been preaching the Gospel in Japan for fifty years. I ought to know by this time pretty well the secret of success or failure in our work. My long experience bears witness that when we begin with the child to make Christians, the greater part of them are secured permanently for the church, and when they stray away, many of them embrace the golden opportunity to come back like returning prodigals to their Father's house.[100]

In a way that partly anticipates the work of James Smart and other more churchly minded North American Christian educators, Tamura struggled, without the assistance of dialectical theology's criticism of religious education, to forge some positive synthesis between evangelical and progressivist faith and practice.[101] At one point he says, "The Kingdom of God does not come spontaneously, but with definite planning backed by prayer and energetic effort."

Tamura's views on the relation between conversion and nurture represent a creative synthesis between Bushnell and Coe. In the missional situation of nineteenth-century New England, Bushnell, unlike Coe and Tamura, did not set up a rigid opposition between the *paideia* and conversion patterns found in the New Testament, but tried to maintain a place for evangelical discontinuity (divine initiative!) in his positive view of Christian nurture within the organic matrix of the family. While Bushnell was struggling to mediate the old New England Puritanism with romantic or transcendentalist reactions to the enlightenment, Tamura tried to find a balance between his native *ethos,* the evangelicalism of the missionaries, and the pragmatic and positivist "scientific" empiricism of the religious education movement. Not surprisingly, Tamura vacillates between the positions of Bushnell and Coe. On the one hand, sounding more like Bushnell than Coe, he admits that children "also should be saved out of their sins." On the other hand, in his positive portrayal of Timothy's conversion with organic metaphors ("like the growth and ripening of fruit"[102]), he seems to side with Coe over Bushnell.[103] While the stark REM dichotomies between gradual and sudden conversion, evolution and revolution, formation and reformation are intended to score rhetorical points for Tamura's case for taking the child seriously, these oppositions also are revelatory of his personal struggle to restate the received tradition of faith in a contemporary idiom that suited the Japanese context.

A recent comment by the retired president of Tokyo Union Theological Seminary suggests that the Japanese Protestant churches ignored Tamura's practical theological proposals. Referring to the need for building stronger and more committed congregations, Matsunaga Kikuo writes,

> Our history reveals that a lot of energy and time were spent in evangelism, leading non-Christians to be baptized, but not so much emphasis was given to the true sense of "pastoral care," by which I mean, the nurturing and training of individual Christians into the Body of Christ, how to work with one another as parts, as organs of a human body, namely Jesus Christ, to become a constituent of the divine *Kahal,* or *Ecclesia.* Therefore, according to a recent statistic, the average Christian life of a Japanese Christian is only 2.8 years! This means that quite a number of the Japanese are baptized in the name of Jesus Christ but after less than three years they lose their Christian commitment and perhaps their faith in Jesus Christ.[104]

At the beginning of the next, final chapter, I will bring the case study of Tamura into critical conversation with my initial critique of North American practical theology and suggest how contemporary practical theology may be greatly enriched by deeper and broader engagement in missional and ecumenical practice and reflection. While I focus on practical theology here, I also think that such missional-ecumenical engagement and reflection would also open up exciting new research horizons for biblical, historical, and systematic scholars who are pathically committed to the church.

CHAPTER SIX

Toward a Missional-Ecumenical
Model of Practical Theology

The Contemporary Significance of Tamura's
Missional-Ecumenical Approach to Practical Theology

Having examined in considerable detail the difficult social, political, and cultural situations in which Tamura worked and his own efforts to propose practical theological "rules of art" for those situations, my task now is to positively relate this missional-ecumenical case study to the critical questions raised by my initial discussion of contemporary practical theology. For the sake of clarity, I will first offer a brief assessment of Tamura's theological, epistemological, and ecclesial views.

(1) Since Tamura's biblical and theological views increasingly followed the personalistic, moralistic, utopian, synoptic gospel–centered norms of the religious education movement,[1] I find little to commend them except in those places where the missional situation of the Japanese churches leads him to deviate from the views of his ecumenical conversation partners.

(2) With the exception of his creative indigenous attempt to overcome the modernist fragmentation between reason, emotion, and will, his epistemological views are also dominated by the norms of the North American religious education movement.

(3) I believe that the major and enduring significance of Tamura's case for practical theology is found in his reasoned, passionate, and active wrestling with the complex missional-ecumenical ecclesial questions that arose as his own congregation and other Japanese Protestant churches

sought to bear witness to the gospel within the confusing conflux of local Japanese and global Western social, political, and cultural realities.

In Chapters One and Two, I made the charge that, even in face of the de-
mise of Protestant hegemony and the dramatic shift in the center of global
Christianity from the northern to the southern hemisphere, North American
practical theologians have not paid adequate attention to either local
missional or global ecumenical questions with which the church must wrestle
if it is to resist becoming captive to some local cultural *habitus*, political ideology, or world-denying mysticism. Especially in the face of the new risks and
possibilities of accelerated globalization, local congregations that are becoming increasingly aware of the inescapable missional tensions within their own
contexts need to devise theologically appropriate means for deepening their
awareness of and conversations with churches in different spheres of the
ecumene. Tamura's lifelong engagement in both local missional and global ecumenical work has much to teach church-minded practical theologians today
who are beginning to acknowledge that the North American churches are
languishing in a hitherto unknown exile within an increasingly post-
Christian social, political, and cultural milieu.

In Chapter One, in partial agreement with Chopp, I criticized the theoretic correlationalists who tend to view the church merely as an opportunity
for empirical analysis or interpretation. I also criticized Chopp for only lifting
up certain distant Christian communities that affirmed her personal ideological convictions. Neither group of correlationalists offers a truly ecumenical
vision of the Christian church. In the first case, the church is in danger of being deflated to the level of phenomenological object useful for testing some
local academic theory. In the second case, certain churches are in danger of
being inflated to the level of idealized object useful for supporting some local
ideological agenda. Axiologically, the criterion in both cases appears to be the
pragmatic utility of the church in promoting either an individual theorist's
research program or politics. Epistemologically, both options of "empirically
tested theory" and "ideologically tested praxis" misapprehend the church by
trying to make it conform to what Torrance calls "an external or alien framework of thought."[2]

The post-critical epistemology of Polanyi and Torrance, which I examined in Chapter One, suggests that the church cannot be adequately described
and interpreted as an object of investigation without the pathically invested
personal disposition that waits patiently, in the words of Torrance, for the
"field of reality to disclose itself to us in the complex of its internal relations
or its latent structure."[3] What seems to be absent in both correlational models

is this epistemic virtue I referred to in Chapter One as the *pathic self-investment of* indwelling. While the modernist rationality claims that pathic personal involvement may lead to a menacing loss of objectivity, the post-critical rationality claims, on the contrary, that passionately indwelling a field of investigation that one really wants to know and explain will actually lead to a greater degree of "objectivity." Rather than allowing the field under investigation to disclose the most appropriate way for it to be apprehended, the correlationalists often use the church to support local research programs and politics. While I have pointed out that Loder's work overlooks the missional and ecumenical bipolarity of the church, his passionate investment in the field led him to reformulate the core problematic of practical theology within the more field-appropriate epistemic boundaries of the God who in Jesus Christ is revealed as a personal Triune community of redemptive and sanctifying love.

In light of both these shortcomings and new directions, I want to turn again to consider Tamura's case. I have emphasized over and over that, in terms of social, political, and cultural capital, the fledgling Japanese churches were a dramatic contrast to the powerful North American churches, which had both the motivation and the means to send and support missionaries to faraway places like Japan. Tamura's case reveals that the genesis and development of the minority Japanese Protestant churches reflects a complex confluence of personal, national, and international factors. Tamura himself embodied these daunting "exilic" tensions. For example, without denying the importance of the personal influence of missionaries like Miss Park or Mr. and Mrs. Carrothers, he honestly confesses that he and many other disenfranchised samurai converts had initially believed the gospel because they thought it provided the only viable means toward the end of building a strong modern Japan. In other words, he freely admits that the motives were mixed from the outset. There was severe pressure for Japan to catch up with the West — and Christianity, which held powerful ideological sway within the nations of the West, was seen quite naturally by many Japanese as an external means to an internal end.

As we have seen, however, things didn't turn out the way that the young, patriotic Tamura had envisioned. Over and over again, he found himself at odds with other Japanese Christians, with the missionaries, and with the nationalist policies of the Japanese government. What factors contributed to these painful yet creative conflicts? First of all, after being appointed at the age of twenty-two as the first Japanese pastor of the First Presbyterian Church in Tokyo (Ginza) and serving there for two years (1880-1882), Tamura went to the United States, where he studied theology at Auburn and Princeton Theological Seminaries and psychology at Princeton University (1882-1886). More than any other experience, this intercultural experience helped launch him on his career as a practical theologian.

For example, while not wishing in any way to idealize the nineteenth-century American families whom Tamura encountered as a student in the United States, the prescient tracts *The Japanese Bride* and *The Rights of Children* would never have been written without such intense personal, intercultural, ecumenical encounters. While much more might be said here, both the personal and academic engagement with the broader *ecumene* gave Tamura and certain other early Japanese converts a "glocal" sense of Christian identity that combined healthy doses of continuity and discontinuity with the North American churches and their historical traditions. This dialectic of continuity and discontinuity is most evident in Tamura's mature work, as he personally engaged the literature of the North American religious education movement for the purpose of building up his own church, society, and nation.

In addition to the analytical and disjunctive modernist modes of thinking and discourse he learned from Western theorists, we have also seen how Tamura's approach continued to reflect, albeit on a tacit level, his own cultural *habitus*, which stressed a harmonious personal integration of reason, emotion, and volition and a strong sense of public duty. This conflict between modernist and traditional epistemologies is behind the creative yet contradictory directions of his own work. For example, while intuitively reaching toward a more holistic approach to religious education, his rhetorical portrayals of the either-or distinctions between child-centered education and adult-centered evangelism, conversion and nurture, love and judgment, teaching and doctrine, Jesus and Paul, etc., all reflect the dualistic modes of thinking he picked up from the North American literature.

Though I have only made indirect reference, vis-à-vis the convoluted social, political, and cultural situation of Meiji Japan and the WSSA Conference held in Tokyo, to the overwhelming political, economic, and cultural hegemony of the Western powers during the late nineteenth and early twentieth centuries, it was precisely the global expansion of Western power that helped underwrite and transmit the project of modernity with its presumption of universality and disjunctive modes of thinking that characterize the modern critical mind. Further, while it is partly an anachronism to call the missionaries colonialists or imperialists, the modern missionary movement would have been unthinkable without the political, economic, and cultural strength of the Western powers. Needless to say, whether they were personally in favor or opposed to the emerging discoveries of modern science, the missionaries were bearers and transmitters of the distinctive traditions of their homelands as well as of their particular understanding of the gospel of Jesus Christ. I have mentioned that there was considerable diversity among the missionaries in Japan, and that they were not the only foreigners on the scene.

This meant that the highly literate and patriotic first generation of Japanese church leaders like Tamura had to struggle to sort out their own understanding of the gospel within the turbulent confluence of the following four major factors: (1) their relation to the missionaries and the Western churches who sent them; (2) their approach to contemporary intellectual developments in the West; (3) their desire to see their churches become strong and independent; and (4) their hopes for their beloved Japan to become a strong modern nation-state.

In Tamura's case, while trying to faithfully introduce the latest North American theories of religious education, his personal missional involvement in the Sukiyabashi Church and beyond made him keenly aware of the ambiguities in applying those theories to the very different and constantly shifting social, political, and cultural context in which the beleaguered Japanese churches found themselves. Because he was painfully aware of the gap between theoretical ideal and practical ecclesial reality, the form of his rhetoric more often resembles polemic than sober academic deliberation. Caught between what Sanneh calls the dynamics of relativization and de-stigmatization,[4] the early Japanese Protestant churches were in the process of moving from missionary churches to indigenous churches. In consideration of the fact that these were churches in a constant state of flux, we might forgive Tamura for often giving in to a clarion call approach to practical theology.

By contrast, the North American liberal Protestantism that gave birth to the religious education movement was in its heyday. It is helpful to think of these stark contrasts between the church-culture tensions in North America and Japan by employing an analogy from the figure-ground reversal of gestalt psychology. For "mainline" North American Protestant theorists of religious education, the church was a sociocultural "given," forming the tacit *ground*, while the challenges of modernity (evolution, social psychology, democratic educational theory, historical biblical criticism, etc.) were in the foreground of the *figure*. With the church as *ground*, the North American religious education movement came to center increasingly on academic, empirical inquiry, most notably within the Union School of Religion that had been home to such theorists as Coe, Elliot, Hartshorn, and Fahs.[5]

Clearly the figure-ground relation took a very different shape in Japan. Though he painstakingly studied and introduced the work of the North American theorists, the problem of the existence or survival of the minority

Japanese church was always in the foreground of the *figure* for Tamura. In contrast to the North American situation, the church in Japan was not and still is not, after almost 150 years, a cultural "given," in spite of its significant influence on human rights, education, medicine, and social welfare.

Thus, in place of the academy, the fledgling church where he pastored was the locus of inquiry for Tamura's distinctive missional-ecumenical approach. This simple fact, that the local congregation was the locus of Tamura's work, is exactly why his case represents a very different reading of the history of the religious education movement than the one commonly recounted by scholars in the West. Tamura was not only interested in studying his congregation, he was also desperately trying to nurture them as members of the "one body of Christ" within the shifting social, political, and cultural circumstances of Meiji, Taisho, and early Showa Japan. Whereas North American theorists like Coe theoretically repudiated the evangelical approach to Sunday School from the vantage point of the halls of academia, Tamura had to articulate and "market" the new model of religious education as a viable contextual, missional approach that would strengthen the churches and lead them to an even more robust faith than that experienced under the evangelical approach. With the very survival of the church always up for grabs in Japan, Tamura tried to link religious education more positively to the evangelistic mission of the church than did the North American theorists. As I said earlier, it is in this sense that he anticipates the work of Smart and others who had the benefit of the later dialectical critique of the religious education movement.

However, to further complicate the situation, while Japan's distinctive cultural identity should have provided a trustworthy tacit *ground* for this intercultural dialectic, the transmission of Protestant faith and the North American theories of religious education occurred precisely when Japan was struggling to clarify and even reinvent its own cultural identity while rapidly modernizing as a nation-state. The reflexive tension embodied in the policy of "Japanese Spirit-Western Learning" *(Wakon-Yosai)* meant that many leading Japanese thinkers gradually came to see modernity as a Westerncentric project embodying fundamentally alien values such as the Enlightenment myth of the autonomous individual.[6] Being on the "receiving end" of the process of Westernization, what should have been the *ground* of Japanese cultural identity was constantly drawn into a chaotic, reflexive tension with Western values and modes of thought.

Given this confusion, Tamura's theological convictions, which evolved from a more orthodox evangelicalism to a thoroughgoing liberalism, need some final comment. Reflecting the decisive influence of the theological liberalism that also inspired the North American religious education movement, I discussed in the previous chapter how Tamura strongly privileged the synoptic portrayal of the human Jesus over the Johannine divine logos or the Pauline crucified and risen Christ the Lord. Under the sway of the new historical-critical approaches to the Bible, he freely picks those parts of the canon that best suit his rhetorical and pedagogical purposes. In a word, Tamura's Jesus is the champion of the child because the Japanese churches were completely neglecting the child. In spite of the obvious problems with the Jesus-Paul bifurcation, even this shows how Tamura remains personally engaged as a missional-practical theologian who was never content merely to import the latest findings of Western biblical scholars.

As I mentioned above, his ideal portrayal of the Son-Father relationship reflects another felicitous ecumenical convergence between the North American social gospel and his Confucian *habitus*. It seems reasonable to assume that there were other tacit personal factors at work here. Wanting to avoid the kind of psychological reductionism to which Tamura himself often falls prey, my goal in the following analysis is only to suggest some of the personal impulses informing Tamura's child-centered practical theology. Firstly, we can easily imagine that his own adolescent experience of being severed from his birth parents at his adoption is a significant emotional factor that had impact upon the theological reflection behind his strong attraction to Jesus' reputed elevation of the child. His irreparable breaches with his former colleagues in the Presbyterian Church and the anti-modernist missionaries were likely influenced by this childhood trauma. By placing children — not adults! — at the very center of the Christian gospel, Tamura perhaps was unleashing some of his own anger toward those adults whom he felt had betrayed him at different stages of his life: his birth parents at adolescence, his Japanese Christian peers in young adulthood, and certain conservative missionaries in his middle years.

Secondly, there is little doubt that his anti-doctrinal, ethical reading of the Son-Father relation was also aimed indirectly at Uemura Masahisa, the former friend of Tamura's youth who had been his nemesis for more than thirty years following the *Japanese Bride* incident. From 1901 to 1902, Uemura, the leader of the Japanese Presbyterians who had revoked Tamura's ordination, had engaged in well-publicized debates with Congregational leader Ebina Danjo concerning the relation between God and Christ in the incarnation. These well-publicized debates took place just around the time of Tamura's conversion from evangelism to religious education.

While fiercely committed to the formation of a Japanese church that was independent from the foreign missions, Uemura's progressive evangelicalism *(Fukuinshugi)* also sought to maintain some positive theological continuity with the historical creeds and doctrines of Christianity.[7] On the other hand, though Ebina reportedly did not intend to deny the doctrines of the Christian church, following the liberal theological trend of the time, he believed that Japanese Christians were not beholden to doctrines that were thought to be nothing more than "explanations of the religious consciousness of Christians in the ancient world."[8] Stated positively, Ebina believed that Japanese Christians were free to find their own indigenous expressions of Christian truth. Dohi says, "Ebina understood the relationship between God and man in terms of the Confucian ethics of the relationship between father and child, which was a fundamental part of his religious understanding."[9] With the added support of modern pedagogical theory and psychology, we have seen that this was also Tamura's view. In their debates, Uemura accused Ebina of having a deficient view of Christ precisely on this point. Dohi summarizes Uemura's criticism of Ebina.

> For Ebina, Christianity was the highest form of the awareness of the father-child relationship, based upon his own experience. It follows that the relation between Christ and Ebina becomes like that between an older and younger person, and Christ is no longer a savior who redeems the sins of humanity. Ebina says that God shows his love in Christ, and man comes to know the love of God in Christ. This love is seen in the redemptive action of Christ, who offered himself as a sacrifice on the cross. This act of Jesus is God's act. Therefore, unless one recognizes Christ as God, one cannot know the love of God. However, Ebina maintains that every man has something divine within him, and so Christ shares this divinity, too. Although he says that he sees the love of God in Christ, his view of God is based on an ambiguous pantheistic argument.[10]

As a way of expressing his own bitterness toward Uemura and the church that had deposed him, it seems obvious that Tamura deliberately sided with Ebina.

Nevertheless, in spite of his anti-Uemura stance, we have also seen how he struggled to preserve some connection to the evangelical orthodoxy in which he was reared. Further, unlike Ebina who drew analogies between Shinto and Christian teachings, Tamura maintained a critical view of the way that the imperial Shinto mythology was being manipulated by bureaucrats in the Ministry of Education. While it may seem inconceivable to North American readers that Tamura could really hold a bitter grudge *(urami)* against Uemura for more than thirty years, it needs to be remembered that, in this

Confucian society, one's place of belonging (*shozoku* or *ichi*) within a particular nexus of intimate social relations forms the bedrock of one's identity. There is no greater humiliation for a Japanese than to be rejected by one's peers. In spite of this tragic personal breach with Uemura, Tamura attended Uemura's funeral and wrote his very last book about him and Uchimura Kanzo two years before his own death.[11]

In Chapter One, with the help of Fowler, Torrance, Hütter, Harvey, and others, I criticized the inordinate impact of the so-called Enlightenment rationality on contemporary North American practical theology, and I made the further claim that this intellectual tradition itself needs at last to be understood as belonging to a distinctive local, cultural *habitus*. Such an awareness was clearly lacking among the first-generation leaders of the religious education movement. From Tamura's position on the "receiving end" of modernization, the religious education movement seemed a dramatic new and objective truth with the power to change Japan. While exportation of these theories under the West's political, economic, and military hegemony was an unintended consequence of modernization, I have found nothing in the early writings of the North American religious education movement and little even in recent North American practical theology that suggests that churches and theologians in other spheres of the *ecumene* should critically and cautiously engage these theories within their own local contexts. One can only imagine how Tamura's work might have been significantly different if he had been welcomed as an equal partner into positive ecumenical dialogue with the North American theorists.

While such an ecumenical awareness would enrich the international discussion of practical theology, such an awareness is still lacking. Today, in the midst of the escalating "clash of civilizations" predicted by Samuel Huntington and others,[12] the case for increased personal, ecumenical engagements among theologians seems even more pressing. This book is a small attempt to imagine what such open-ended personal, theological dialogue, in which participants are cognizant of their missional and ecumenical riches and limitations in Christ, might look like.

What might Tamura's case signify for North American practical theologians today? I believe that the hardened theory versus praxis options of the correlationalists and the tacit individualism of Loder's transformational model might be moderated and even overcome by the kind of passionate personal participation in local missional tensions and global ecumenical conversations that we witnessed in Tamura's life and work. While his own theology and epistemology often reflected the fashionable norms of the North American religious education movement, he was never completely captive to those alien cultural norms because of his personal missional involvement at Sukiyabashi Church. In other words, this missional side of the critical tension between his local and global engagements is evident in the way he wrestled to find some continuity between the evangelical and liberal approaches to religious education. Further, while he maintained a patriotic love for Japan till his death in 1934, he was also able to criticize Japanese society, politics, and culture precisely because of his personal ecumenical involvement with Christians in the United States and elsewhere. Again, this ecumenical side of the critical tension between his local and global engagements is evident in *The Japanese Bride, The Rights of Children,* and his subtle but unmistakable critique of the government's educational manipulation of the emperor system.

At this juncture, I want to summarize how I see Tamura's work as an example of a "missional-ecumenical" approach. Tamura's work represents a creative conjunction of the following two interpenetrating spheres of action and reflection: (1) *Personal Missional Engagement at the Congregational Level;* (2) *Personal and Academic Engagement Across Cultures.* I will comment briefly on each and what it may suggest for practical theology today.

Personal Missional Engagement at the Congregational Level

It is not an insignificant fact that Tamura helped lead Japan's religious education movement while pastoring a congregation. I have observed that the critical reflection that comes from this kind of long-term, personal involvement in the life of a congregation is missing from the deliberations of many leading North American and European practical theologians today. As I pointed out in Chapter One, I think Chopp is correct to criticize the use of the congregation to confirm one's theories. Without wanting to deny a proper place for congregational studies in practical theology, such empirical research does not obviate the need for long-term, personal engagement in the life of a congregation. In the post-critical terms I addressed in Chapter One, I believe that we practical theologians must personally "indwell" specific situations of Christian practice (preaching, teaching, caring, witnessing, etc.) for a significant period of time, allowing the fields of practice under investigation to disclose the ways they are to be properly evaluated and improved. In order to grasp the complex social, cultural, and political contingencies of the missional situation within which a congregation practices its faith, one must be personally involved for a significant length of time. While empirical studies are helpful for disclosing general trends within, across, and beyond local congregations, the missional situation in its depth can only be grasped after a long period of personal involvement. If we take seriously Schleiermacher's view of the practical theologian as one "in whom an ecclesial interest and a scientific spirit are united,"[13] we sacrifice ecclesial commitment on the altar of empirical research, to our peril. While I am not suggesting a return to the so-called "clerical paradigm" of practical theology, I am claiming that serious academic reflection in this discipline will not be undermined but rather strengthened by an "ecclesial interest." For practical theologians today, Tamura is a positive exemplar of Schleiermacher's bi-focal perspective.

Personal and Academic Engagement Across Cultures

As we have already seen, Tamura was thoroughly conversant with the literature of the North American religious education movement. He also developed a special interest and considerable competency in contemporary biblical studies. On the personal level, beyond his close association with certain missionaries in Japan, Tamura sustained long-lasting, mutually edifying relationships with North American Christians he had met during his many travels abroad. In other words, Tamura worked with one eye on the missional situation of Japan and the other on the *ecumene*. As I pointed out at considerable length in Chapter Two, this commitment to mutual, intercultural enrichment across the *ecumene*, which is found in nascence in Paul's Letter to the Romans, is a serious need today. In spite of the positive direction of the international discussion among practical theologians today, it must be admitted that this discussion has not yet discovered ways to fully include our colleagues in the non-Western world. This xenophobic tendency is not limited to practical theology but extends to all of the subdisciplines of theology. Again, as I pointed out in Chapter Two, in spite of all the talk about the globalization of theological education in North America, few Western institutions and theologians have shown any serious interest in dialogue with their counterparts in the non-Western world.[14] In spite of the radical demographic shifts in the makeup of the *ecumene*, there is still a perception that those in the West determine and teach the proper modalities of rational reflection, and those in the non-West passively learn. Given this situation, it is not surprising that the so-called "international" discussion in practical theology continues to be dominated by North Americans and Europeans. If we really believe that we have gifts to share with each other, we must seek new ways to converse. If we fail to repent of such paternalism, how are we any different from those missionaries who sallied forth so long ago to enlighten the heathen? Again, Tamura is a positive exemplar of a locally grounded, ecumenically engaged practical theologian.

Tamura's lifelong appreciation for and commitment to the twin missional-ecumenical foci of the church suggests that the critical academic work of practical theologians today would be greatly enriched by (1) personal participation in, reflection on, and guidance of the core Christian practices of a local congregation, and (2) personal participation in practical theological work within churches in spheres of the *ecumene* where the views of self, other, and ultimacy are a significant contrast to those held by one's own culture.[15] These two simple proposals should not be mistaken as a call for the cessation of serious academic practical theological reflection. On the contrary, inasmuch as the "one body of Christ" is the core epistemic field of action upon which practical theology necessarily reflects, these two simple proposals are an invitation to significantly deepen and expand the work of this discipline by more active local and global engagement. Negatively, without this two-directional ecclesial involvement, I believe that the recent calls for the "globalization of theological education" will amount to little more than empty talk. Positively, such deliberate local and global involvements are likely to (1) enrich our understanding of and appreciation for the profound local social, political, and cultural contingencies embodied by the global *ecumene;* (2) bring to light some of our own tacitly held cultural assumptions that have influenced our own epistemological and theological approaches; and (3) aid us in the construction of theories and rules of art that are more biblically and theologically faithful to a wider range of local expressions of faith as well as the catholic unity of the "one body of Christ."

In the next, concluding section, I offer an example of what I have called the missional-ecumenical model. Since I examine some of the differences and similarities between the Japanese and American views of the self and briefly consider how such understandings may help to enrich the international discussion of practical theology, this discussion is also a further commentary and fitting conclusion to my initial discussion of North American practical theology and my case study of Tamura as a proto-missional-ecumenical practical theologian.

A Tale of Two Selves in Japan and the United States

> Nearly all the wisdom we possess, that is to say, true and sound wisdom, consists in two parts: the knowledge of God and of ourselves. But, while joined by many bonds, which one precedes and brings forth the other is not easy to discern.[16]

John Calvin, always the scrupulous reader of scripture, opens his *Institutes* by dramatically stating the profound mystery at the depth and center of human

145

life as a bipolar relationality between our knowledge of God and our knowledge of ourselves. For Calvin, knowledge of God and knowledge of self represent a *relationality in distinction* or a *distinction in relationality*. The Divine/human *relation* suggests a two-dimensional pattern:

(A) *Knowledge of God illuminates knowledge of self*

and/or

(B) *Knowledge of self illuminates knowledge of God.*

In modern theology, while Friedrich Schleiermacher, following the (B) pattern, tended to emphasize human intuition, feeling, and experience, Karl Barth, following the (A) pattern, insisted on the priority of the divine self-revelation of the Word of God in Jesus Christ. Actually, in the French edition of 1560, Calvin himself makes a stronger statement about the normative direction of this relationality: "In knowing God, each of us also knows himself."[17] Following Calvin and Barth, the Divine/human *distinction* suggests an essential corollary: *Christian faith rejects the conflation or confusion of knowledge of God with knowledge of self.* However, in the wake of Schleiermacher's *die Allmacht der Subjektivität* (preeminence of subjectivity), the appearance of a violation of this distinction understandably invited Feuerbach's and later Freud's reductions of religion to an illusory projection of subjective wishes or unconscious drives. In spite of the deep modernist ditch between theology and philosophy, the epistemological question of the relation between knowledge of God and self has persisted into postmodernity. It is a thorny question that practical theology cannot avoid. Clearly, the human self is a bewitching enigma that, while transcending every reified theoretical formulation, still tempts us to deeper reflection on our actual experience.

In the history of psychoanalytic theory, there is a revealing evolution from Freud's depiction of childhood self-differentiation primarily in terms of the Oedipal/Elektra conflict of ages four or five to D. W. Winnicott's theory of *transitional phenomena* and Heinz Kohut's theory of *self objects,* both of which claim that the process of self-differentiation is rooted much earlier in infancy.[18] Of course, these contrasting and sometimes conflicting theories of the self are not unrelated to the fact that Freud practiced his art with neurotic adults, while Winnicott worked with infants and young children and Kohut with narcissistic adults. As the well-worn arguments from the history and philosophy of science claim, theoretical knowledge is always, to a lesser or greater extent, conditioned by the location and personal commitments of the human observer.

Given the present context of increasing globalization, practical theological reflection on the self may be enriched by extending the discussion across cultural contexts. I will reflect on my personal experience in Japan, where I have spent twenty years teaching in church-related colleges and a seminary as a mission co-worker of the Presbyterian Church (U.S.A.). Inside and outside of classrooms, faculty meetings, and churches, I have experienced and observed profound differences in the Japanese understanding and expression of the self. I was trained in the United States to teach Christian education and studied the modern Western theories of human development that have informed and sometimes dominated this practical theological discipline since the early twentieth century. I was responsible for teaching courses that covered this material, but I observed from the outset that certain aspects of those theories simply could not adequately account for the actual Japanese experience, concept, and expression of the self.[19] *Surely I didn't have to completely reject my American education as useless, did I? Did I have anything worthwhile to contribute to the educational ministry of the struggling Japanese churches and Christian schools?* Such questions haunted me.

It occurred to me that perhaps the root of my dilemma was an unwitting theoretical "presumption of universality," even before a theory had been corroborated across cultures.[20] *Didn't such a presumption impede the process of genuine scientific inquiry? Might this "presumption of universality" be an unconscious intellectual residue of the modern era of Western colonial and imperialistic domination?* As a Christian, I could not overlook these questions without doing violence to the self-understanding and experience of my Japanese students, because I believe that the Triune God, revealed among us in Jesus Christ, embraces all humanity, in both our common and particular conditions of giftedness and fallenness, with suffering and triumphant redemptive love. Thus, in my teaching practice, I found myself constantly making intuitive, contextual theoretical "adjustments" or "corrections" in order to try to include and embrace the actual self-knowledge and experience of my students.[21]

My criticism of contemporary practical theology and the case study on Tamura suggest that, in order to better understand and more effectively nurture Christian faith within today's increasingly multicultural societies, practical theology needs a more comprehensive and flexible anthropological framework that is both biblically and theologically sound and can help to account for the actual contingencies of the human self as it is actually experienced, understood, and expressed in different cultures. This is a small attempt to suggest what such a missional-ecumenical approach might look like. In a personal dialogue with scripture, theology, psychoanalysis, sociology, and anthropology, I will examine some of the salient differences and similarities between the Japanese and American views of the self and briefly consider how such understandings may help to enrich the international discussion of practical theology.

I will begin with a brief consideration of the anthropology of Paul, the missionary apostle to the Gentiles. This discussion is intended to build on the exegesis of Romans 12 in Chapter Two.

Participation in Christ, Belonging to Others, and Realistic Self-Assessment

Through faith in Christ, or perhaps more appropriately, the faith of Christ, Christians embody and express, albeit imperfectly, a particular self-relationality that consists in three complementary modalities. The definitive modality is, of course, the baptismal relation to the Lord who "died for the ungodly" (Rom. 5:6). As I tried to show in the exegesis at the opening of Chapter Two, Paul's view is that *participation in Christ* is primarily communal and secondarily personal. "The death he died, he died to sin, once for all; but the life he lives, he lives to God. So you must consider yourselves dead to sin and alive to God in Christ Jesus" (Rom. 6:10-11). Elsewhere, referring to the completed and yet-to-be fulfilled dimensions of the new humanity *in Christ,* Paul writes to the Colossians, "You have died and your life is hidden with Christ in God" (Col. 3:3). In Galatians 2:19b-20, Paul speaks of his personal experience of the dialectical identity that grounds his self-understanding: "I have been crucified with Christ; and it is no longer I who live, but it is Christ who lives in me. And the life I now live in the flesh I live by the faith in (or 'of') the Son of God, who loved me and gave himself for me."

Again, this should not be read as supporting a privatistic, individualistic, or mystical view of faith, because the baptismal pattern of dying and rising in Christ sets the public direction for the second modality of self-relationality which is *mutual belonging with others.* The ultimate horizon of this community of Jews and Gentiles justified and reconciled in Christ is the "whole creation" (Rom. 8:22). As I tried to show in my exegesis of Romans 12 in Chapter Two, this means that Christians in any one place and time need the spiritual enrichment of *koinonia* with Christians in different places and times. Paul never envisioned an enclosed communitarianism but an open, missional-ecumenical community witnessing, by the power of the Spirit, to the God who in Christ is revealed as the redeemer of the world. The third modality of self-relationality, *realistic self-assessment,* is a mark of participation in this highly differentiated yet inextricably united eschatological community. Within this missional-ecumenical community of the Spirit, particular gifts are distributed by God to serve God's ends in and beyond the church. To repeat, Paul sees the Christian self as characterized by (1) *participation in Christ;* (2) *mutual belonging to others;* and (3) *realistic self-assessment.* Clearly, *relationality or belonging,* not self-sufficiency or autonomy, are the primary distinguishing marks of Christian self-identity for Paul.

In the following story, I narrate a personal experience of what British psychoanalyst Christopher Bollas calls the "simple experiencing self" and the "complex reflecting self" to illustrate how a Japanese Christian, with a different understanding of the self, challenged my own internalization of one of the more loaded symbols of our shared Christian faith. In *Being a Character: Psychoanalysis and Self Experience,* Bollas describes the distinction between the "simple experiencing self" and the "complex reflecting self" as follows:

> The simple experiencing self and the complex reflecting self enable the person to process life according to different yet interdependent modes of engagement: one immersive, the other reflective. When I am "in" the dream, although as a simple self I perceive dream objects, even more importantly I endure deep experiences there. Recollection and interpretation of the dream's meaning do not necessarily address the essence of self-experience gained by the simple self's movement through the events of the dream, but the complex self possesses a different psychic agenda: the aim of this position is to objectify as best as possible where one has been or what is meant by one's actions.[22]

"Was Judas Saved?"

I'll never forget the day a colleague at Tokyo Union Theological Seminary, whom I'll refer to as Dr. K, presented me with a signed book of his sermons that had just been published upon his retirement from the church he had been pastoring for some years. After bowing deeply with deferential gratitude to my senior colleague for his gift, I returned to my office and, having some time before my next class, opened the book of sermons to peruse the table of contents. One title immediately leapt off the page: "Was Judas Saved?" I quickly found and started reading the sermon which was based on Matthew 27:3-5.

> When Judas, his betrayer, saw that Jesus was condemned, he repented and brought back the thirty pieces of silver to the chief priests and elders. He said, "I have betrayed innocent blood." But they said, "What is that to us?

See to it yourself." Throwing down the pieces of silver in the temple, he departed; and he went and hanged himself.

The title was tantalizing and threatening at the same time: *Was Judas saved? Of course Judas was not saved! Was he?* I responded in my mind with a mixture of confident indignation, an almost insatiable curiosity, and more than a hint of self-doubt. Personally, I had unconsciously internalized the popular American characterizations of Judas, the paradigmatic "bad guy who gets his just deserts," the lone "assassin," who not unlike Lee Harvey Oswald in our own time, fully deserves to be loathed for his despicable crime. *"Was Judas saved?"* The very question, it seemed to me at the time, bordered on irreverence or even blasphemy. Perhaps it was the forbidden nature of the question itself that lured me on. I had never heard a sermon that seriously addressed this question in an American church. The *Harper's Bible Dictionary* starkly expresses the familiar solution to this question. "Upon reflecting over what he had done, Judas experienced remorse and sought to undo his evil deed (Matt. 27:3-4), but it was not possible."[23] Judas is without hope!

As I read through the sermon, I found myself fidgeting in my chair and growing increasingly edgy. I felt torn, for on the one hand, I deeply respected Dr. K as a humble brother in Christ and a competent exegete of scripture — *after all, he had a Ph.D. in New Testament from Heidelberg* — while on the other hand, I was sure that I had properly settled the fate of Judas long ago in keeping with sound theological tradition. Strangely, Dr. K's challenge to my introjection of the Judas symbol brought something hidden deep within my self into consciousness, and the elicitation was simultaneously cognitive and emotional. Perhaps because of my trusting, personal relationship with the sermon writer, I felt free to explore this unconscious mental and emotional terrain.

This type of emotional identification with a co-worker is a daily experience in Japan where, perhaps as a kind of "psychic pressure release valve" to the strict formality of social relations, a certain freedom or playfulness is allowed for the mutual indulgence of narcissistic dependency *(amae)* even within the context of well-defined hierarchical relationships. In classical psychoanalytic terms, the *amae* relation is analogous to the *transference* that takes place between a therapist and client or, in terms of Winnicott's theory, the safe *holding environment* provided for the child by the omnipresent, but non-intrusive mother. At the time I discovered the sermon, I had already lived and worked in Japan for more than ten years and had naturally internalized some aspects of Japanese psychology and behavior. Still, while feeling safe enough to explore Dr. K's curious sermon, something inside of me was simultaneously struggling to fortify some inner wall, to objectify and thereby transcend this Japanese rereading of this infamous tale of betrayal.

My heart and mind were racing to get to the end of the sermon to determine whether or not my colleague's answer to the haunting enigma of Judas was intellectually convincing. I scanned my gray matter, trying to predict some of the ways he might try to resolve the issue. *Isn't there a sense in which Judas is enlisted to fulfill salvation history? Isn't God's mercy in Jesus Christ big enough to include Judas Iscariot?* Upon reflection, I realized that my attempt to adjudicate the situation of conflict raised by the sermon was a repressive psychic move. In terms of James E. Loder's theory of transformational logic, the downward psychic drive toward adaptation during the painful *interlude for scanning* is often overpowering.[24] Undoubtedly, the conjectures that appeared on the screen of my consciousness were a defense mechanism thrown into the service of keeping my unconscious, internalized Judas symbol safely under psychic lock and key. In psychoanalytic terms, my ego was employing its habit of using deductive reasoning to try to protect my "self" from the threat of a radical reinterpretation of a cherished unconscious symbol.[25]

Nevertheless, the "*amae* transference" had occurred, and I couldn't easily dismiss my trusted colleague's faithful exegesis of the plain sense of this biblical text. Dr. K points out that Matthew is the only gospel that reports the tortuous story of Judas's repentance, confession of faith, and suicide, and tellingly, Matthew's simple account is patently free of all the anathemas the biblical and post-biblical tradition has heaped upon the betrayer of the Lord. The text portrays an utterly crushed man teeter-tottering on a narrow psychic precipice between life and death. Judas is a self painfully severed from himself or, theologically, a broken sinner who, in the way of all broken sinners, acknowledges his sin by repentance ("he repented") and indirect confession of faith in Jesus ("I have betrayed innocent blood"). Dr. K points out that Matthew's placement of this text is theologically suggestive because the betrayal of Peter (Matt. 26:69-75) and the suicide of Judas (Matt. 27:3-5) are poignantly punctuated by the report of Matthew 27:1-2.

> When morning came, all the chief priests and the elders of the people conferred together against Jesus in order to bring about his death. They bound him, led him away, and handed him over to Pilate the governor.

The context suggests that, in relation to the One who is about to be executed, the denial of Peter and the betrayal of Judas may not be as dissimilar from each other as Western church tradition has assumed. Though this reading was very convincing, I found myself throwing up one final resistance to thinking of Peter, the great apostle who admittedly denied the Lord three times, and Judas, the betrayer of the Lord who is called "the son of destruction" in John 17:12, as standing in exactly the same relation to the execution of Jesus. *But isn't the suicide itself sufficient proof of damnation?*

Suddenly, in a rare moment of intercultural enlightenment, it occurred to me that while I, as an American, always viewed suicide as a negative, selfish, or unredeemable act worthy only of shame and even contempt, Dr. K could be more sympathetic since the Japanese have reserved an honorable place for suicide for those who have lost all hope of reconciling with themselves, their community of belonging, or the deity. This doesn't mean that suicide is ever viewed as a happy event in Japan, but Japanese are able to express a deep sense of compassion in the midst of the tragic loss of those who choose to exchange their present life in the desperate hope of a better future one. While we Americans glory in "happy endings" and "success stories," Japanese tradition is replete with the noble failures of courageous "losers."[26] Also, while our American aesthetic sensibility generally tends toward a flashy, colorful permanence and certainty, the Japanese aesthetic expresses a muted, pale ephemerality and uncertainty. I thought again. *Maybe there really is another way to read this story.*

Some of the questions appearing in my consciousness revealed that Dr. K's words had moved me beyond the level of defense mechanism. I thought of the striking parallel to the legend of Jonah, who had also betrayed God's call. The repentant prophet had offered himself to be thrown into the sea in order to still the storm that had overtaken their ship bound for Tarshish.

> He (Jonah) said to them, "Pick me up and throw me into the sea; then the sea will quiet down for you; for I know it is because of me that this great storm has come upon you." (Jon. 1:12)

I was launched into a playful, imaginative and emotional digression that bordered on free association. *Hadn't God saved Jonah when he cried "out of the belly of Sheol"* (Jon. 2:2)? *Do I really see my self or other selves as recipients of God's unconditional love and forgiveness? Might our Western reading of the Judas symbol be fundamentally flawed? Could it be that my vilification of Judas (Judah in Hebrew) as a damnable scapegoat veils the unconscious yet pervasive anti-Semitism that has characterized much of the history of Western Christianity? Is it possible that our collective internalization of the Judas symbol (Judah = Israel) is an archetype of the church's hatred of the Jews for allegedly handing Jesus over to be executed?*

While Dr. K is careful not to elevate Judas to heroic status or to see his death as redemptive in any way, he is profoundly empathic, even sympathetic, with this member of the twelve who, in Matthew's portrayal, could no longer bear to face the Lord, his community of belonging, or himself. As an "I" bereft of every relationality, with no place to stand in relation to God, other, or self, Matthew's Judas is *no self*, a liminal spiritual condition that serves as the ground for his final act. Accordingly, Judas fatefully carries out the burlesque command of the religious leaders ("See to it yourself") and, from a Japanese perspective, does the only honorable thing remaining by hanging himself.

My mind continued to reel at some of the implications of Dr. K's sermon. *Hadn't the crucified Jesus, at the moment of his death, welcomed into Paradise a similarly repentant sinner who confessed, like Judas, "This man has done nothing wrong"* (Luke 23:41)? *As repentant sinners who confess Jesus Christ with the faith and hope that forgiveness and salvation have a much surer ground beyond the self in the God who, according to our common creed, "descended into hell," aren't we all essentially in the same groundless, "no-self" predicament as Judas? If there is evidence of repentance and confession of faith, however tortured and flawed, doesn't the gospel proclaim that damnation is not remotely within the realm of possibility for the God who is revealed in the face of the crucified and risen Lord who "saw to it" on our behalf?*

Finally, I could look into the face of Judas and recognize — not some damned stranger — but an aspect of my self, in the actuality of my own frequent conscious and unconscious betrayals of my Lord, those with whom I am in intimate relation, and myself. Dr. K had helped me to confess my own Judas heart and to sense anew the depth of God's saving love. I felt as if the liberating gospel Word had been transposed into a new, richer, and more wondrous key. With repentance and gratitude for the Word of forgiveness, I quietly responded, *Amen.*

Is it accidental that the writer of this sermon was a non-Western Christian who felt free to probe playfully the meaning of Judas's suicide within both the context of his own cultural location and the sheltering matrix of the gospel Word? Might the faith of the Western churches that originally planted the seeds of the gospel in places like Japan be enriched today by hearing the gospel afresh, sometimes as if for the first time, from sisters and brother in Christ with sufficient cultural distance from Christendom? These are questions that cannot be ignored by the global church if we will dare to continue to believe, with the apostle Paul, that we are truly "one body in Christ, and individually members one of another" (Rom. 12:5).

Whether one agrees or not with Dr. K's rereading of the Judas symbol is not the real issue here. The deeper question is how and why, in the terms suggested by Bollas, the same religious object (the Judas symbol) can elicit such radically different self-experiences.

I will now turn to a brief consideration of some of the thorny epistemological questions that must be faced in order to discern real similarities among the differing cultural conceptions of the self while embracing those differences.

Humility in the Face of the Unity and Variety in the Order of Creation

Our age of globalization is witnessing technological improvements in the speed of communication and transportation that have vastly extended our consciousness of and contact with the extraordinary varieties of cultures in the world. While globalization is a parallel development to the modernization that began in the sixteenth century, "the process has accelerated through time and is currently in the most rapid phase of its development."[27] From our cultural location in the West, our growing knowledge of non-Western cultures has sabotaged some of the universal claims of the venerated grand narratives of modernity, and for this we can be thankful. Some philosophers claim that the resultant loss of certainty has left us with no forms of human knowing beyond local forms.

On the one hand, in thinking about the self I want to resist the radical estimation of our time as a kind of confused, *all-knowledge-is-local-knowledge* Babel world in which we may never really talk *with* but only *past* each other. While the difficulties of communicating across cultural barriers should never be underestimated, the conclusions of the postmodernists ultimately lead to a theologically and morally unacceptable nihilism. At the same time, to speak authentically of the human self in terms that would be recognizable to different peoples, we need to take cultural differences much more seriously than has often been the case during the era of Western theoretical hegemony. Shouldn't we pay close attention when confronted with expressions of the self that resist reduction to the categories of Western theories and, in some cases, call some of the core assumptions of those theories into question? Thus, rejecting both the epistemological extremes of an unrelenting modern positivism and a radical postmodern relativism, I will seek a moderating framework comprehensive enough to embrace the breadth of actual expressions of the human self in Japan and the United States.

Though Japan is a thoroughly "modernized" nation in terms of technology and science, it has still not experienced the Enlightenment "turn to the self" taken for granted, as we saw in Chapter One, by North American practical theologians. In his now-classic study titled *The Thought of Japan*, Japanese sociologist Maruyama Masao writes,

To state it point blank really opens up a whole can of worms, because our country has not experienced any philosophical tradition — even in terms of a negation — in which the self has been advocated historically or nurtured as a core concept or as an axis of coordination and, whether one likes it or not, this lack of emphasis on the self has bequeathed a character of mutual interdependency to the ideals and philosophies of every historical era.[28]

In sharp contrast to the intellectual traditions of the modern West, in which the freedom, rights, autonomous moral agency, and critical distantiation of the individual have dominated political, scientific, philosophical, and theological discourse, Japanese academic thought occurs within what Fortmann calls a "maternal womb of collectivity"[29] that values, above all else, intense loyalty toward the particular school of thought *(gakuha)* in which one was nurtured and to which one owes one's existence. A disciple *(deshi)* is expected to faithfully imitate his or her mentor *(sensei)* over a long period of apprenticeship before daring to make any personal, creative contribution. From the Western view of the self, this looks like slavish conformity, but the Japanese see this deep respect for the matrix of tradition as a sign of maturity and wisdom. Although the situation is changing today, relationality and belonging, not individuality and autonomy, are the core values of the Japanese self, and as hard as it is for North Americans to imagine, *we-consciousness,* not *I-consciousness,* characterizes mature relationality.

These presuppositions about the self are evident in Dr. K's conclusions about Judas. Rather than seeing the betrayer of the Lord as an autonomous moral individual who must be held accountable for his actions, Dr. K sees Judas firstly as a brother in Christ, a chosen, though failed member among the community of Jesus' disciples. Judas is caught within an entangled web of tragic circumstances from which he has absolutely no power to extricate himself. Knowing well the common betrayals that characterize even the closest human relationships, Dr. K sees Judas as a fallen brother and his predicament as one with which he could easily identify. I, on the other hand, had seen Judas as a traitor, someone so radically separate from me as to eliminate the possibility of any empathy or identification. To me, the fact that Judas was chosen by Jesus to be a member of the twelve seemed irrelevant in light of his villainous betrayal. While Dr. K was able to confess an affinity, empathy, or identity with Judas the betrayer, I had effectively banished him to hell in keeping with the scapegoating tradition of the West. Dr. K deeply identifies with Judas in his liminality as "no-self," a man with no "standing place" *(tachiba)* because, theologically, he knows that the *extra nos* character of

God's grace in the cross of Jesus Christ is the only sure ground of Christian faith.

To help us understand this identification, Nakamura Hajime describes the blurring of subject and object that is reflected in the structure of the Japanese language in *Ways of Thinking of Eastern Peoples*:

> In the original language, there is no word that expresses the object as opposed to the subject. The word *mono* may mean a person as subject as well as a thing as object. In such a situation, it cannot be expected that the word *shiru* (to know) will be employed to denote the cognition of objects existing apart from knowing subjects. In other words, the emphasis is put on the understanding of the inner experiences and on the feelings or mutual understanding among men, as shown by the usage of *Nasake o shiru* (to understand the feeling) and of *Hito to shiri au* (to understand each other). Chiefly directed toward the expression of human relations, the pure Japanese language has no word corresponding to impersonal or purely objective "knowledge" or "cognition." Largely as a result of Western influence have the Japanese people attained any degree of scientific self-consciousness and objective perception — that is, the perception of things as distinguished from perceiving subjects. . . . Japanese people for the most part tend to make little of objects unless they are related to familiar human relations.[30]

Dr. K's response to Judas points to the *participatory character* of the Japanese self-other relationality which has been characterized by Japanese theologian Yagi Seichi as a "mutual interpenetration of subject and object, I and Thou, Self (Christ living in me) and ego."[31] Bollas elegantly captures the empathic exchange I experienced with Dr. K as a conjuring of spirits that transcends rigid self-other distinction. His language points to the need for a more open way of thinking about the self than what the modern West has proposed:

> As we move through the object world, breathing our life into the impersonal, we gather and organize our personal effects. As we collide with other subjectivities, we exchange differing syntheses, and leave the other with his or her inner sense of our self, just as we carry the spirit of the other's idiom within our unconscious. We can conjure these spirits within us as we evoke the name of the other, although what we deeply know is only ever partly thought, and strangely defies the codes of thought we have valued so highly in Western culture. And of ourselves, I

think it can be said that we are spirits, that we shall scatter our being throughout the object world, and through the winds of interforming human mutualities. A dream that defies its content, it enjoins the world through the dream work. We will have had, then, a spiritual sense, a notional grasp of the force to be what we have been, and this presence, valued yet ungraspable, is consolation amidst the human march to wisdom's end, punctuated, as always, by the question mark.[32]

Where might we find an epistemological framework comprehensive enough to embrace these different cultural experiences of the self? While I will not repeat what I said in Chapter One, it is my conviction that the epistemological and theological work of Torrance, Polanyi, Loder, points in the right direction. It may be helpful for readers to review that material in Chapter One before moving on in the present discussion.

At Play in the Matrix Uniting Subject and Object

The idea that the symbols (scripture, creeds, liturgies, theology, devotional literature, art, etc.), or in psychoanalytic terms, the *objects* of Christian faith are sufficiently multivalent to be capable of evoking a wide range of responses in Christians from differing cultural locations is not so astounding. But what happens when we move beyond simple acknowledgment of this fact to serious reflection on some of its underlying reasons? I have tried to describe how, in Bollas's terms, there are distinct forms of self-experiencing because of the very different ways the self is respectively normed within the social holding environments of Japan and America. In describing some of these differences, Joseph Tobin makes a helpful distinction between psychology and ethnopsychology in his insightful essay on "Japanese Preschools and the Pedagogy of Selfhood."

> The difference (between Japanese and American selves) may be less one of psychology than of ethnopsychology, less a difference between Japanese and Western psyches than in the way the dimensions of the self are portrayed and evaluated in Japan and the West. In Japan, unlike in America, circumspection, circumlocution, formality, ceremony, ritual, and manners are viewed as vehicles for expressing as well as masking pleasure and for realizing rather than for binding the self. Less likely than Americans to view social conformity as a sign of weakness of character, joining the group as a betrayal of individuality, or ritualized public discourse as

hypocrisy, Japanese value the *omote,* formal dimension of the self, as well as the *ura,* more spontaneous dimension.[33]

To illustrate how the two-tiered public/*omote* and private/*ura* self is normed in Japan, I will briefly introduce the Asian concept of energy *(Ki),* which refers to the basic, dynamic life force that fills heaven and earth and structures the universe. *Ki* is also thought to flow through each individual's body, feelings, or spirit. Acupuncture or *shiatsu* massage, Asian medical practices that are also popular in the West, attempt to regulate the flow of this cosmic energy which is believed to flow along meridians in the body. In the public/*omote* sphere, to "withhold *Ki*" *(Ki wo haru),* or resist displaying more feeling than is considered appropriate, is a sign of maturity. In the private/*ura* sphere, there is no need to "withhold *Ki.*" Further, to discern what the other is thinking or feeling, one "withdraws one's *Ki*" *(Ki wo hiku),* or calmly distances oneself from one's inner emotional state. This tactic is used, for example, in business negotiations to silently persuade the other to take your side. Again, in the private/*ura* sphere, there is no such need to "withdraw *Ki.*" In Japan, a mature and successful adult is one who has mastered the art of discerning how to draw a sharp line between one's public and private lives *(koshi no kejime wo tsukeru).* Of course, this line between private and public exists in the United States also, but the actions of the Japanese public-self are ritually circumscribed to a far greater extent.

Bollas speaks of the infinite varieties of ways we think, feel, or dream our selves through the contingent, daily encounters with the objects of our world.

> We all walk about in a metaphysical concrescence of our private idioms, our culture, society, and language and our era in history. Moving through our object world, whether by choice, obligation, or invitational surprise, evokes self states sponsored by specific objects we encounter. In a very particular sense, we live our lives in our own private dreaming.[34]

Reflecting the cultural norms of the West, Bollas accents the private modality of self-experience, but I wish to expand his insight by suggesting that, in addition to the self's "private idiom" and "private dreaming," there is also a normative "public idiom" and "public dreaming" of the self that contribute greatly to the overall consciousness and identity of the self. This public idiom, which is grounded in the mythical norms that are more or less tacitly shared by the participants in a particular culture, is just as powerful in the *I-oriented West* as in *We-oriented Japan.* In spite of the modern separation between the self and the collectivity, culture is not just a field that is external to or separate from me through which I, as an individual, experience my self, but a field in which others and I actively and playfully participate and through which we, as a particular community to which we both belong, nurture our distinctive collective self-consciousness. Whether we are Japanese or American, our selves are such a complex amalgam of private and public idioms and dreamings.

The metaphor of play seems the best way of describing how we gradually internalize the cultural norms that form such a huge part of our self-identity and experience. Referring to the work of Johan Huizinga, Wolfhart Pannenberg describes how we "play" our selves into identity.

> Playing together, in its various forms, is to be seen in all modes of communal life, including even cult. On the other hand, playing also forms the biological basis of all free and creative activity of individuals. Thus the theme of play links together the question of the identity of the individual, with the further question arising out of the previous one, regarding the shared world in which individuals are given the opportunity for achieving their personal identity.[35]

Based on his clinical work with young children, British psychoanalyst D. W. Winnicott postulates an intermediate area of experiencing between the infant and the mother, which "throughout life is retained in the intense experiencing that belongs to the arts and to religion and to imaginative living, and to creative scientific work."[36] While inner reality and external life both contribute to this intermediate sphere, it is neither completely subjective nor completely objective but a paradoxical interplay between inner and outer spheres of consciousness.

As Christians, whether Japanese or American, our understanding of the self is also mediated by the scriptures of the Old and New Testament, which make normative claims about actualities that are not always borne out in our daily experience. You might say that scripture is the matrix of our "shared dream," our "sphere of illusion," which we believe is actually truer or more real than any or all of the counterclaims of our particular cultures. Take, for example, Paul's view of the Christian self as one who, through participation in Christ and belonging to others, begins to soberly assess his or her gifts. Where and how is this counterintuitive, counter-cultural scriptural view of the self communicated? I want to suggest that the worship of the church, where, by the power of the Holy Spirit, Jesus Christ is really present to do what we cannot do, is the primary Christian holding environment in which we are granted freedom, over and over again across a lifetime, to playfully test out the "reality" of the gospel. Theologian Geoffrey Wainwright speaks of worship as "the explicitly religious form of play."[37] Bollas talks about the risk of play in terms of the possibility of being "born again."

> In play the subject releases the idiom of himself into the field of objects, where he is then transformed by the structure of that experience, and will bear the history of the encounter in the unconscious. To be a character is to enjoy the risk of being processed by the object — indeed, to seek objects, in part, in order to be metamorphosed, as one "goes through" change by going through the processional moment provided by any object's integrity. Each entry into an experience of an object is rather like being born again, as subjectivity is newly informed by the encounter, its history altered by a radically effective present that will change its structure.[38]

Based on the discussion up to this point, I will now attempt a description of a theoretical framework for thinking about the self.

A Tripartite, Contingent Relationality

The human self is a tripartite, contingent relationality formed and transformed over a lifetime by a complex range of determinate and indeterminate genetic, environmental, and religio-cultural factors.

The *tripartite levels of relationality* in which the self is formed and transformed are:

(1) *The other(s)-I relation, or the interpsychic or psychosocial modality;*
(2) *The I-self(ves) relation, or the intrapsychic modality;* and
(3) *The relation to a context of ultimacy, or the mythico-religious modality.*

This relationality may be pictured as three mutually interpenetrating modalities of one self, as follows:[39]

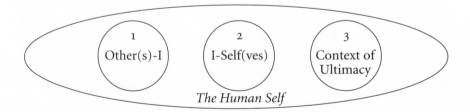

The Other(s)-I Relation

While the intellectual traditions of the modern West have tended to emphasize the differentiation or freedom of the self from the other, post-Freudian object-relations theory claims that the quality of the earliest relation of primary caregivers to the infant exercises a profound, lifelong influence on the way a person relates to others and himself or herself. For example, in describing how the infant moves "from a state of being merged with the mother to a state of being in relation to the mother as something outside and separate,"[40] Winnicott speaks of "transitional phenomena" that take place in an "intermediate area of experiencing" between subject and object "to which inner reality and external life both contribute."[41] Thus, the self is both a gift waiting to be received and a creation to be established in freedom. While it may seem too obvious to even mention, Winnicott's theory claims that the emergence of human self-consciousness is predicated on the presence of well-intentioned others, or a "good enough" holding environment. In terms of the theological anthropology I have been suggesting, (1) *always precedes* (2) or, in other words, *relationality predicates distinction*. This ordering principle suggests that a holding community of care is indispensable for the birthing, nurturing, transforming, and healing of the human person.

The I-Self(ves) Relation

In spite of appearances, even the I-self relation, or in Erik Erikson's terms, the I's reflection upon "the various selves which make up our composite Self,"[42] is not an entirely subjective process since the conscious, preconscious, and unconscious influences of others are never completely absent even in the purest self-reflection. While Descartes sought to demonstrate that the self's irreducible ground for certainty was the *cogito,* even the rationalist's "I" is not an isolated island of pure subjectivity since thinking always requires some object to think about, even if that object is thinking itself. This is a further demonstration of how *relationality predicates distinction.*

The Relation to a Context of Ultimacy

While psychoanalytic theory focuses mostly on the first two modalities of the self, I have tried to suggest a more adequate epistemological ground to help overcome the Freudian reduction of the third modality to a narcissistic illusion. Contrary to the early predictions of secularization theorists like Peter Berger, myth and religion have, for better or for worse, outlived the assault of modernity. The dialogue of theology with natural and human sciences has yielded some fruitful insights on the question of theological anthropology. The concepts of *contingency* developed by Scottish theologian T. F. Torrance and *the religious thematic* developed by German theologian Wolfhart Pannenberg provide two ways to positively account for the enduring power of myth and religion.

Torrance's argument for contingency suggests that, while the created order is in itself intelligible to human understanding, this intelligibility "cannot explain itself."[43] That is, it always points beyond itself to "the ultimate intelligibility toward which all lesser intelligibilities point." From the point of view of the Christian narrative, the argument for contingency says that the universe is ultimately conditioned by and dependent upon a personal Author. On the other hand, Pannenberg's religious thematic refers to the universal human longing for an all-encompassing, unified vision of the world beyond the individual in which individuals may participate vis-à-vis "jointly affirmed meanings."[44] The religious thematic is the web or universe of meaning that underlies the shared lives of individuals in a given cultural situation — "a life springing from a shared center that transcends the limitations of individuals."[45]

While I am asserting that psychoanalytic theory does not provide an adequate picture of the self, it does not, except perhaps in its extreme Freudian form, obviate a more serious consideration of this third modality of the human self. Isn't it possible, for example, for Winnicott's description of infant-mother relationality to be interpreted in light of the arguments for contingency and the religious thematic? Winnicott describes the development of the self as a three-step movement from (1) the illusion of omnipotence and total fusion with the mother, to (2) the shared illusion of the "transitional sphere" where reality is tested by playful engagement, to (3) the stage of disillusionment in which a gradual diffusion of transitional phenomena across a wider range of experience (emotion, dream, art, religion, etc.) takes place. The self's journey between "me" and "not-me" parallels what Pannenberg calls the "exocentric centeredness" of the human spirit. The self's movement beyond itself without losing one's self hints at a movement toward a relation to a context of ultimacy. Theologically, the self appears to be contingently directed beyond itself toward an ultimate horizon of relationality and meaning which, in Christian terms, is the Creator God who is revealed in the divine person Jesus Christ.[46]

While the three modalities of the self are universal across cultures, the relative weight a culture ascribes to each self-modality will result in radically differing expressions of the self, or *public self-idiom*. In cultures where the public self-idiom is governed by a *we-orientation*, there is a pronounced accent on the other-I relation. *Loyalty* to one's group of belonging is considered the most highly valued public virtue. In cultures where the public self-idiom is governed by an *I-orientation,* there is a pronounced accent on the I-self relation. *Freedom* of individual decision is considered the most highly valued public virtue. Cultures whose public self-idiom is governed by a *religious-orientation* accent the relation to a context of ultimacy. *Faithful observance* of religious practice is considered the most highly valued public virtue. In spite of the relative cultural accents on one of the three self-modalities, the other two will always find some expression, albeit in less direct, private, and even subversive ways.

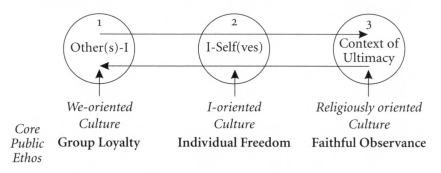

Since I have focused only on the *we-orientation* of the Japanese self and the *I-orientation* of the American self, I will not comment on *religiously oriented* cultures here, though it is not difficult to imagine how India or certain Islamic cultures might be understood in those terms. In the *we-oriented* public culture of Japan, expressions of the I-self modality are relegated to more private, subversive, aesthetic, and religious contexts. The mythico-religious modality that tacitly undergirds Japanese identity continues to exert a profound influence.[47] By contrast, in the *I-oriented* public culture of the United States, the other-I modality is often experienced and expressed as a source of "superego" pangs of conscience, a threat to self-actualization and the ironic American obsession with conformity. Its "mainline" mythico-religious orientation is characterized, on the conservative side, by a moralistic emphasis on individual salvation from personal sins and, on the liberal side, by an ideological concern for issues of social and ecological justice and human rights. Conservatives tend to downplay the social witness of the church while liberals tend to downplay the call to personal conversion and discipleship. In terms of their cultural self-identity, it is not difficult to discern their deep *I-oriented* affinity to each other.

As I have already mentioned, French sociologist Pierre Bourdieu's theory of practice is helpful in trying to understand the cultural variations in self-praxes. Bourdieu uses the term *habitus* to describe the pre-reflective informal dispositions that order a particular social or cultural world. *Habitus* discloses what a given people consider to be reasonable and unreasonable, possible or impossible.

> The conditionings associated with a particular class of conditions produce *habitus,* systems of durable, transposable dispositions, structured structures predisposed to function as structuring structures, that is, as principles which generate and organize practices and representations that can be objectively adapted to their outcomes without presupposing a conscious aiming at ends or an express mastery of the operations necessary in order to attain them.[48]

Habitus is always interest-oriented and its influence is especially strong where normative rules of action are not made explicit — a point of particular interest for practical theology.[49] In a global age that is, for better and for worse, witnessing the reemergence and assertion of ethnic self-identity, the recognition, respect, and celebration of difference and otherness is perhaps the most urgent task facing the Christian, and indeed, the world community today.

In the concluding section, I will offer some brief personal observations of how the private and public idioms are expressed in distinctive ways in the religious lives of Japanese and American Christians and how I think the educational ministry of the churches today may be greatly enriched by exploring and reflecting on such distinctions across the *ecumene.*

Conclusion: A Missionary Confession

In a nearly complete reversal of my earlier presuppositions about what a "good missionary" should be, I have realized that we do not lose our cultural particularity and become cosmopolitan citizens of a kind of Christian United Nations the moment we confess Christ as Lord. Even though our Japanese sisters and brothers in Christ draw spiritual water from the same religious objects (scripture, ecumenical creeds, theology, etc.), the way Christian faith is expressed in the worship, preaching, teaching, and organizational styles of the Japanese church is strikingly different from that of the North American churches whose missionaries, by and large, originally planted the Japanese churches in the nineteenth century. For example, most Japanese Protestant churches founded before World War II carefully preserve the non-formal patterns of worship introduced by the North American missionaries in the nineteenth century. The undisputed place of prominence is still given to the sermon, which averages between thirty and forty minutes, and there is often little trace of the influence of the liturgical renewal that followed in the wake of Vatican II. The value of keeping faith with one's received tradition clearly triumphs over pragmatic, contemporary innovation.

Through baptism and profession of faith, we have been brought into a new relationship with God in Christ and joined to the human community of the church, which Ephesians describes as "God's household, built on the foundation of the prophets and apostles, with Christ Jesus himself as the chief cornerstone" (Eph. 2:19b-20). Our unity in Christ is a divine gift we should not take lightly. At the same time, as members of this worldwide community in Christ, we continue to embody and express our particular cultural self-identities. Over long centuries, the staggering diversity of the church has been the source of much bitter misunderstanding, tension, and division. Our spiritual unity in Christ has often been pitted against our actual cultural diversity.

As a North American Protestant engaged in intercultural mission for fifteen years in Japan, I must honestly confess that it has been much easier to believe that our unity in Christ, more than our cultural diversity, is a good gift of God. Even after one has more or less mastered the language, there is a constant level of frustration in having to do little daily things in a very different way. Without denying this personal frustration, I do not conclude that my American self-idiom is better, just that it's different. And the opposite is surely true for my Japanese students and colleagues. Still, looking at this intercultural phenomenon in a theological perspective, I've tried to suggest in this book that it's possible, and perhaps even imperative in these increasingly perilous times, to conceive of our cultural diversity, like our unity in Christ, also as a good gift of God.

What might happen if practical theologians really began to take the rich diversity of the *ecumene* more seriously today? Clearly, a longing for this kind of engagement is one factor behind the trend to include the issue of globalization, for example, in virtually every recent discussion of North American theological education. In spite of such discussions, it is still far from clear that theologians and institutions have really grasped the import of this issue for the nurture of church leaders and lay people.[50] While I am under no illusion that educational programs alone will lead the people of God to *metanoia*, I wonder if more intentional personal engagement with and reflection on other ways of being Christian might not help broaden our view of the working of divine grace in our earthen vessels.

As an example of the direction that such intercultural practical theological engagement may take, I will briefly characterize how the play of Christian worship is differently expressed in American and Japanese societies today and how this knowledge may, at the very least, enlarge our appreciation for the working of divine agency across very different cultural fields and may even enrich our understanding of the gospel. It is often commented that contemporary American social life creates in many people a feeling of being cut off from any sense of a community that provides nurture over a lifetime. This seems to be especially true of the middle-class suburban lifestyle, which moves across a multitude of unrelated locations such as workplace, school, shopping mall, vacation spot, and church. In this harried and fragmented lifestyle, American Christians seem to long in the church's worship, or in small groups, for an experience of communal (horizontal) relationality. In *Sharing the Journey: Support Groups and America's New Quest for Community,* Robert Wuthnow critically describes the spirituality associated with this longing.[51]

By contrast, the structures of contemporary Japanese society seem to create a feeling for many people of being too connected and even smothered by one's main community of belonging (i.e., workplace, school, family, neighborhood, etc.). For example, Japanese businesspeople are virtually required to eat lunch and supper together with their work peers every day. Women who send their children to kindergarten or elementary school are expected to participate in PTA groups. Junior and senior high school and college students who join extracurricular clubs incur specific duties, and the "proper" performance of those duties is often strictly enforced by the senior members of the club. In short, in sharp contrast with the fragmented disconnect that characterizes contemporary American culture, Japanese society is a collection of different spheres of belonging that operate with clearly defined roles and obligations. It is therefore not surprising that Japanese Christians appear to seek an experience of individual (vertical) relationality in the church's worship. The church is a place where one can be alone with God, free from the ceaseless demands of one's sphere of belonging. Some Japanese thinkers have criticized the extremely individualistic orientation of Japanese Christians.[52]

To reiterate, American Christians seek communal healing while Japanese Christians seek individual healing. Put another way, the expressive worship styles of many American Protestant churches seem too noisy from the Japanese point of view, while the solemn non-liturgical styles of many Japanese Protestant churches seem too quiet from the American point of view. Further, Japanese pastors are taught to expunge personal stories or jokes from sermons, because they are thought to only draw attention to oneself and away from God. By contrast, American pastors are taught to make the text relevant or risk losing the attention of the congregation and maybe even one's job! Such stark contrasts in the understanding and expression of "proper" Christian worship in Japan and North America could be multiplied, but these few should suffice. In conclusion, while Japanese and American Christians are nurtured by the same "objective" texts of Christian faith, we respond to those texts through the particularities of our sociocultural experience. This naturally gives birth to huge differences in our expressions of faith.

In some of the darker moments of my missionary sojourn, I have been tempted to wonder whether we are finally understanding and expressing the same Reality. Even allowing for significant differences in English and Japanese scriptural and creedal translations, I have wondered how the same texts can give birth to such different religious views and expressions. Of course I believe that we are worshiping the same God! But where do I learn that? What is the basis for that conviction?

Like other Christians, I bring the doubts that haunt my soul with me to worship, and place them freely and playfully before God. In the presence of Christ and his people, I confess again the very familiar words of the creed as if for the first time, "I believe in the holy, catholic and apostolic church, the communion of saints," and I am brought into the light of God's Truth which helps expose my untruth.[53] In this light, I repent over and over from my cultural prejudices and expectations about what the Japanese church should or should not be. Only then can I begin to imagine that the very cultural differences that puzzle me are surely a great delight to the Lord who made heaven and earth.

When we consider this dilemma in light of Christian faith, it may seem reasonable at first glance to hypothesize that a Japanese Christian and an American Christian are at a distinct advantage in understanding each other because they share a common "language" that transcends both English and Japanese. With hopeful enthusiasm, we sing "In Christ there is no East or West," but once the worship service ends, we awaken to the reality that we do not suddenly lose our cultural particularity and become cosmopolitan citizens of a kind of "Christian United Nations" when we confess Christ as Lord. When one looks at the 150 years of Protestant mission in Japan, which included a bitter and brutal war between Japan and the countries that sent the missionaries, we are forced to conclude that, in spite of all wistfully pious and romantic voices to the contrary, there is nothing magical about this "shared" Christian language that automatically ushers believers from two very different cultures into genuine dialogue and understanding.

While it is tempting to retreat back into the safety of our own institutional enclaves where we often do not have to seriously address the reality of profound cultural difference, the current world situation suggests that the Lord of the church is calling us to a whole new level of positive ecumenical engagement. We know from personal experience that the most educative experiences of Christ are often found in the hard facticity of his being not yet fully known, for it is there that a gracious God calls forth and sustains our human responses of faith, hope, and love. Since the only true and sure basis of ecclesial unity is, as the hymn subtly proclaims, "In Christ," to confess Christ means also that we have despaired of the possibility of finding any other basis for Christian unity, in either culture or ideology. In the face of much evidence to the contrary, the church believes that our unity in Christ will be realized in God's hopeful future. Playfully and joyfully opening our hearts and minds to the genuinely different faith perspectives and experiences of culturally different selves who have also been called to participate in the life of Christ and his church will surely enrich our understanding of the One who delighted enough in our common humanity to journey into this far country for our salvation. The Christian confession of the Triune, relational God provides an enduring, comprehensive, and creative mode of rationality for encountering and rejoicing in the polymorphic understanding of the human self as it is actually embodied in the wonderfully diverse cultures of the earth.

Imperial Rescript on Education

Know Ye, Our Subjects:

Our Imperial Ancestors have founded Our Empire on a basis broad and everlasting and have deeply and firmly implanted virtue; Our subjects ever united in loyalty and filial piety have from generation to generation illustrated the beauty thereof. This is the glory of the fundamental character of Our Empire, and herein also lies the source of Our education. Ye, Our subject, be filial to your parents, affectionate to your brothers and sisters; as husbands and wives be harmonious, as friends true; bear yourselves in modesty and moderation; extend your benevolence to all; pursue learning and cultivate arts, and thereby develop intellectual faculties and perfect moral powers; furthermore, advance public good and promote common interests; always respect the Constitution and observe the laws; should emergency arise, offer yourselves courageously to the State; and thus guard and maintain the prosperity of Our Imperial Throne coeval with heaven and earth. So shall ye not only be Our good and faithful subjects, but render illustrious the best traditions of your forefathers.

The Way here set forth is indeed the teaching bequeathed by Our Imperial Ancestors, to be observed alike by their descendants and the subjects, infallible for all ages and true in all places. It is Our wish to lay it to heart in all reverence, in common with you, Our subjects, that We may all attain to the same virtue.

Official English translation from Robert Hall, *Education for a New Japan* (New Haven: Yale University Press, 1963), pp. 162-63.

APPENDIX B   *Twentieth-Century Sunday School* (1907)

Book One: General Principles

1. *The Mission of the Sunday School:* What Is Education?; The Significance of Education; The Religious Factor; Where Religious Education Should Be Practiced; Two Methods of Evangelism: Conquest and Education; The Necessity of Education; Education over "Revival"; A Great Misunderstanding; The Means of Saving the World; Conclusion; Questions and Suggestions

2. *The History of the Sunday School:* Rooted in Ancient Past; The Jewish System; The Birth of the Sunday School; Gloucester's Robert Raikes; The First Sunday School; The Progress of the Sunday School; The Greatness of Wesley; The Methodist Church's Sunday School; Conclusion; Questions and Suggestions

3. *The European and American Background of Religious Education and a Warning to Our Country's Childhood Educators:* Religion Is a Nation's Life; Germany; The Great Ends of Education; France; England; The United States; The Religious Education Association; Conclusion; The Necessity of Religious Education in Japan; Japan's Molding of a Deformed Citizenry; Questions and Suggestions

4. *The Teaching of Christ Concerning Children:* Christ Is the Champion of Children; Christianity Is the Religion of Children; Children as the Pattern of Those Who Will Enter Heaven; Children as the Ambassadors of Christ's Perfect Joy; The Value of Children; The Sin of Those Who Neglect the Education of Children; Christ Receives Children; Christ's Command to Educate Children; Children as the Model of Those in Heaven; The Mother as the Child's Guardian Angel; Conclusion; Questions and Suggestions

5. *The Connection of the Family and Sunday School:* The Necessity of Family Education; The Divine Administration of the Family; The Greatest End of the Family; The Error of Parents and Its Reasons; Practices of the Family; The Connection of the Sunday School and Family; Questions and Suggestions

6. *The Pastor's Duty Concerning the Sunday School:* The Reason Pastors Are Not Passionate About the Sunday School; The Function of the Pastor; The Position of the Pastor; A Valuable Pastor; Nineteen Rules for the Pastor Concerning Sunday School; Conclusions; Questions and Suggestions

7. *The Relationship Between the Sunday School and the Community Based on Childhood Educational Principles:* The Organization of a Community; The Two Great Institutions for Religious Education; Instruction and Training; Trumbull's Wisdom; The Great Principles of Progress; Theory and Practice; The Child Is Active; The Great Mission of the Community; The Order of the Child's Psychology; System of Yearly Apprenticeship; The Sunday School and the Community; The Fate of the Church; The Words of Aristotle; The Words of William James; The Error of Today's Churches; The Role of the Sunday School and the Community; Conclusions; Questions and Suggestions

Book Two: Administrative Methods

1. *Principles of Administration:* Based on New Educational Theory

2. *Rules:* The Necessity of Rules; The Rules of Sukiyabashi Church's Sunday School; Questions and Suggestions

3. *Classrooms:* The Necessity of Classrooms; Using Curtains for Dividers; Opening on Different Days; What Is the Sunday School?; Conclusions; Questions and Suggestions

4. *Materials:* Necessary Materials; Chairs for Children; Musical Instruments; Blackboards; Maps; Hymnals and Music; Bells; Combs and Metal Washtubs; Divisional Banners; Offering Box; Attendance Book; Questions and Suggestions

5. *Expenses:* Contributions; The Example of Toyohashi Church; Questions and Suggestions

6. *Pupils:* Problems of Gathering Pupils; Qualifications of Pupils; Sunday School Is Not a Playground; The Strength of a Good School; Inexcusable Methods; Problematic Errors; Individual Work; Teacher's Work; Church Member's Work; Publicity; Finding a Place in Each Town; Competition; Giving Awards, Conclusions; Questions and Suggestions

7. *Age Divisions:* The Necessity of Divisions; Norms for Age Divisions;

Age; Ability; How to Make Age Divisions; Pre-School; Elementary; Youth; Young Adults; Research Lessons; Teachers of Divisions; Promotion to the Next Division; Graduation Diploma; The Responsibility of Placing Pupils in Divisions; The Introduction to the New Life; The Names of Divisions; Problems in Organizing Divisions; Conclusions; Questions and Suggestions

8. *Lessons:* Bible; Uniform Lessons; The Benefits and Problems of Fixed Lessons; New Lessons; Conclusions; Questions and Suggestions

9. *Executing Order in the Sunday School:* The Time of Sunday School; The Approach of Sunday School; The Execution of Order in Sukiyabashi Church's Sunday School; Questions and Suggestions

10. *Offerings:* The Necessity of Offerings; The Experience of Sukiyabashi Church's Sunday School; Things to Consider Concerning Offerings; The Use of Offerings; Offering Time; Speaking of the Purpose of Offerings; How to Collect Offerings; Determining the Purpose of Offerings; Questions and Suggestions

11. *Rewards and Punishments:* Dealing with Withdrawals from Sundays School; Giving Rewards; Medals and Banners; Cards; Things to Consider Concerning Rewards; Questions and Suggestions

12. *Songs:* Music and Singing Is the Heart of Children's Education; Songs Used in the Sunday School Should Be Rich in Variations; Various Ways of Singing; Questions and Suggestions

13. *Head of the Sunday School:* Head Is Like the Coxswain of a Boat; Election of the Head; Qualifications of the Head; A Strong Will; A Warm-hearted Piety; Business Ability; Sixteen Rules Concerning the Head's Work; Questions and Suggestions

14. *Officers of the Sunday School:* The Necessity of Officers; Greeter; Musical Director; Treasurer; Secretary and Vice-Secretary; Librarian; Questions and Suggestions

15. *Teachers:* Teacher Is Like a Butterfly; The Best Way to Attract Teachers; Five Qualifications of a Teacher; Five Rules for Preparing to Teach; Forty Rules for Teachers; Questions and Suggestions

16. *Executive Committee:* The Place Where Sunday School's Coal Is Supplied; The Place of the Executive Committee; The Period of the Executive Committee; The Business of the Executive Committee; The Chair of the Executive Committee; A Unified Executive Committee; Occasions for Delivering Lectures and Promoting Fellowship; Questions and Suggestions

17. *Books:* Books Teachers can Use; Books Pupils can Use; The Habit of Reading; Rules for Contributing Books and Reasons for Problems in Contributing Books; Questions and Suggestions

18. *Miscellaneous Meetings:* The Sociable Nature of Children; Musical

Gatherings; Outdoor Activities; Christmas Celebrations; Flower Day; Easter; Pupils' Birthdays; Questions and Suggestions

19. *Conclusion:* Japanizing our Administrative Methods; Executing Administrative Methods; Questions and Suggestions

Book Three: Teaching Methods

1. *General Principles:* Instructional Principles; Socrates' Question; Educating the Human Child; God's Clever Judgments; The Ordering of Education; The Great Principle of Modern Psychology; The Pupils of the Sunday School and Their Five Divisions; Questions and Suggestions

2. *Infancy:* God's Most Wonderful Creation; A Mysterious Reality; The Common View Is Mistaken; The Situation of the Infant; The Brain's Center ("The Animal Stage"); A Baby's One Voice and One Smile, Religious Animal; The Misunderstanding of Teachers; (1) The Achievement Stage; (2) Learning with Objects; (3) The Stage of Imitation; Education of Love; Froebel's Words; (4) Activity Is the Infant's Life; The Greatest Sinner in an Infant's Life; (5) Music and Singing; The Pupils' Enemies; (6) The Religious Truths That Should Be Taught in This Stage; There Are No Atheists Among Infants; (7) The Classroom for This Age Group; The Infant's Heaven and Earth; The Infant's View of God; (8) The Language of the Infant; (9) One Truth at a Time; (10) Long Stories Are Prohibited; Questions and Suggestions

3. *Pre-School:* Development in the Pre-School Stage; (1) The Age of Imagination; The Confusion of Object and Imagination; (2) The Religious Truths That Should Be Taught in This Stage; The Pre-Schooler's View of God; (3) The Pre-Schooler's Curiosity; Ways to Get Their Attention; Actual Examples; (4) Understanding Through Imitation; Teacher as a Living Lesson; (5) Learning Through Encouraging Activity; Speaking with One's Hands; The Motto of This Stage; (6) The Age of Eager Listening; (7) The Age of Strong Superstition; The Only Way to Leave Superstition Behind; (8) The Age of Wanting to Fight; The Reasons for This; (9) The Pre-Schooler's Feelings Are Deep; (10) The Qualifications for Teachers; Questions and Suggestions

4. *Childhood:* The Pattern of Development; The Transitional Stage; (1) The Age of Memorization; (2) The Era for Developing Good Habits; Carpenter's Words; The Motto of This Stage; (3) The Desire to Read; (4) The Age of Relative Obedience; (5) Imitating; (6) The Leak Period; The Qualifications for Teachers; (7) The Age of Inclination Toward Social Relationships; (8) The Religious Truths That Should Be Taught in This Stage; (9) The Age of Vitality; Actual Examples; (10) Things for Teacher to Consider; Questions and Suggestions

173

5. *Youth:* Stanley Hall's Words; The Age of Revolution; Differences in Male and Female Growth; (1) The Age for Appealing to Reason; The Center of Instruction; (2) Teaching Boys and Girls Separately; (3) The Age of the Appearance of Inherited Characteristics; (4) Two Extremes into Which Youth Easily Fall; The Age When It Is Easy for the Teacher to Give Up; (5) The Interest in Reading; Daughter's Test; (6) The Era for Developing Independence; The Error of Crushing the Will; (7) The Intelligence of Youth; The Era for Testing the Teacher's Patience; (8) The Age of Misunderstanding Others; Spencer's Words; (9) The Age of Daily Dreams; (10) The Age of Being Conscious of One's Relationship to God; The Best Age for Becoming a Christian; Leading the Pupil's Future; Questions and Suggestions

6. *Young Adults:* Life's Turning Point; (1) Era of Interest in Philosophical Thinking; (2) Period of Greatest Activity; Active Children vs. Active Young Adults; (3) Age of Suspicions; (4) Respecting Individuality; The Case of Freud; (5) The Age of Practice; One Great Psychological Principle; (6) Individual Instruction; (7) No Shortcuts to Education; (8) The Goal of the Sunday School; The Place of Religious Education; Questions and Suggestions

7. *Conclusions:* The Effect of Child Psychology on Education; The Child Is a Species of Human Being; Our Church's Need for Resolve; The Writer's Hopes; Questions and Suggestions

There are two appendixes, the first providing a brief synopsis of some of the one hundred English books Tamura deemed most relevant to this subject and which, he says, contributed greatly to his own work. The second appendix contains actual samples of useful documents and advice. He divides the first appendix into twenty-one books on the Sunday School (including Burton and Matthews's *Principles and Ideals for the Sunday School*), six on Children's Rights (including Harrison's *A Study of Child Nature*), four on Childhood (including McKinney's *After the Primary, What?*), two on Adolescence (including G. Stanley Hall's *Adolescence*), ten on the Study of Children (including Dewey's *The School and Society*), five on Child Psychology (including King's *The Psychology of Child Development*), twelve on Children's Religion (including Bushnell's *Christian Nurture*, Coe's *The Spiritual Life* and *The Religion of a Mature Mind*), three on Heredity (including Bradford's *Heredity and the Christian Problem*), nineteen on Teachers (including Brumbough's *The Making of a Teacher* and James's *Talks to Teachers on Psychology*), thirteen on Pedagogy (including Butler's *The Meaning of Education* and Davidson's *A History of Education*), and four on the Use of the Blackboard.

APPENDIX C *The Rights of Children* (1907)

Table of Contents

"Barthian Theology and
Religious Education,"
Sunday School, April 1933

Editors' Introduction

While there are various opinions about Barth's theology, it is without question a hot topic these days, and from the perspective of religious education, it is a theology that should not be overlooked. Rev. Tamura has a great interest on this point and has expressed it here. Of course, his article does not claim to treat either the whole of the so-called "crisis theology" or religious education. It is better to be able to speak of the problems of both in more detail at a later time. The editors are also very concerned about this issue, and we expect Rev. Tamura's essay, like a fuse, to ignite a thorough discussion. We hope that those who stand in both camps of religious education and crisis theology will add their words to the controversy.

1.

Last year, Barth's voice came within earshot for the first time in our country like the high-pitched barking of a wild dog. There have already been six or seven Barthian theological books published in our country that are receiving the attention of readers. Though it hardly needs to be mentioned, Barth's theology is not the latest theology, but it is the most elaborate version of old Calvinism. There is not a huge difference between Barth and the theology I learned in the United States at Auburn and Princeton Theological Seminaries. Thus the seeming amazement and wonder of our Japanese translators and readers of Barth has had little effect on me. In the present twentieth-century stabilized situation of Japanese theology, it has surely created wind and waves, and I am a little wary that it may stir up animosity between Presbyterians and Methodists. I think that rather than spending all of our energy on theological arguments, we should not get sidetracked from the task of zealously and faithfully seeking the salvation of our country. Already, those who are infatuated with Barth are taking an aggressive posture, and are employing abusive slogans like "impoverished theology," "drunken theology," "spineless theology," and "demonic theology" to characterize the claims of other theologies. This 76-year-old man feels the need to warn them to moderate their attacks.

Because Barthian theology has spread its wings in so many directions at once, it is of course not going to be possible to criticize it adequately in one day or night. It is so new that it has not only not yet taken shape as a systematic theology, but Barth himself, it seems, does not even want to construct a systematic theology. Since he uses the ingenuous motto of "a bird in flight" to characterize his approach, he is freed of any need to become fixed. There is little room for doubt that his opinions ten years ago and his opinions today are different. His main strategy in the Romans Commentary was to lay down the gauntlet at the feet of his enemies. That book has already gone through five editions in fifteen years, and with each new edition, the form of the "bird in flight" appears to be higher and higher up in the blue sky. Because his writing makes even native German readers suffer, Japanese are even all the more likely to find it tough going. Unfortunately, the Romans Commentary, the pride of Barth, has still not been translated into any other languages. In this paper, I want to set a narrow focus and limit myself to the main points regarding the Barthian view of religious education.

2.

Before entering into my critique, however, even though my theological position is different than his, I want to say that I wholeheartedly respect Professor Barth. As far as I know, even though there are Japanese who have introduced Barth's ideas here, no one has commented on the value of the Japanese Barthians yet. One of the biggest reasons behind the tremors Barth's theology has created in the German religious world is surely Barth's personality. Unfortunately, through these Japanese introductions, our readers are put in contact only with a man with a chilling theology, and I feel they are unable to touch the real man who, in his own context, is aflame with a sacred fire. Rather than choose the life of a preacher, Barth settled into writing theology.

He is a prophet of the miserable dark world brought forth by the first world war. He is a lone preacher and patriot who proclaims there are no gods to depend on outside of God. Further, he is a faithful explicator of the doctrine of the reformed church. To those within the threatened Germanic civilization, he is proclaimed a saviour, and to the reformed church, he is called a defender of doctrine. His voice is volcanic, impassioned, and revolutionary. He calls all of the work of the present civilization the devil's doing, addresses everyone in every direction — liberal theologians, mystics, fundamentalists, scientists, psychologists, educators, scholars of religion — and he criticizes them one at a time and denounces them all. He essentially and thoroughly demolishes emerging contemporary science and society, and wants to establish a new world based on God. Personally, I think he truly is a great, outstanding man, and to class him with the likes of Japan's Nichiren[1] would be no exaggeration. Before his learning, energy, zeal, and patriotism, I feel compelled to bow my head low. If someone like Barth were to rise up within our Christian circles in Japan, surely they could move our citizens who are bearing the weight of the present national crisis. I am praying for someone like Barth to arise among those who are engaged in religious education, someone who burns with a similar patriotic love, who could face death and burn with a holy fire for the salvation of our nation, who would give complete heart and strength for the children of our nation!

3.

If we characterized Barth's theology in a word, it could be expressed by the single phrase, "God is God, humans are human." God and human beings have absolutely no relation. God is in heaven, is eternal, and without limit. God is the creator, the absolute other. Humans are limited as created beings, restricted by time. Between God and humanity there is an absolute restriction of traffic. Between humanity and God, there are no roads or bridges. Human beings are innately depraved. The baby, child, youth, and adult must bear the consequences of being thrown into the fire of hell. To know God, approach God, or have fellowship with God in the power of wisdom is an absolute impossibility. It is useless to look for the glory of God in the cosmos, to try to understand God's revelation in history, and absolutely impossible to hear God's voice in our conscience. Even if we read or teach the Bible, this provides no path to know God. Even if we pray, God has no ears. It is like speaking on the telephone without a line; there is no voice. Thus, teaching and prayer are useless. The sole way of knowing or drawing near to God is through the saving logos, the divine Christ, that is, we are saved through the word of God and for the first time may enter the presence of God; then we pray and are heard by God and our new life as Christians opens up. Thus, Barth's theology is a theology of one golden phrase and a theology of salvation. He has no interest in the historical Jesus, his character, his teaching; there is absolutely no weight given to his embodied humanity. In Barth's theology, only salvation and resurrection in Christ are indispensable. As a result, teaching and praying in the Sunday School are of no avail. The matter that must be settled first is the salvation of children. There is no other theology that gives as much weight to the doctrine of atonement as Barth's. The love of enemies, good works, the entire life is, by faith, a continuous conversion through the word of God, that is Jesus Christ, as we become children of God for the first time. Anyone who takes a quick glance at these words will realize at once that religious education and Barth's theology are like the south and north poles which can never approach each other. To put it bluntly, they are as different as white and black.

4.

The Barthians' theology is a great enemy of religious education and essentially a destroyer of our work. There is not a single reference to children in their work, and of course, they take no notice of something like religious education. Religious psychologists like Coe, Platt, or James are despised and called names like the devil. In a high voice, they shout, "Return to Calvin!" "Return to the Reformers!" "Return to Paul!" However, not one says a word such as "Return to the Jesus of the Synoptic Gospels!" On the question of children, Paul and Jesus are absolutely opposed to each other. We religious educators need not lend an ear to anyone but Jesus! When we read the Gospel of Mark, Jesus clearly and confidently, without so much as a single doubt, taught that God is our father and human beings are his children. Taking a child in his arms, he grasped the key of the kingdom of heaven, saying the greatest thing in the kingdom of heaven is a child. He said that those who receive the child receive him, while he compared those who neglect the education of a child to those who cast themselves into the sea and perish. Jesus was the great discoverer of the value of children and their champion. On this point, Confucius and Buddha pale in comparison to Jesus. There is one certainty under heaven, which is that our religious education is built on the foundation of the word of Jesus! Our mission of religious education is to see to it that not even one of these children of God who comes into this world is left to wander alone. We may say that evangelism is a negative task that guides a wrongdoer into a good direction, but religious education is a positive task that prevents the development of the wrongdoer. This is the only way to make our nation a nation for God. The building up of God's kingdom on earth as it is in heaven is our great mission. Who dare say this is the task of the impoverished? Who dare say this is the task of the drunkard? Who dare say this is the task of the spineless? Who dare say this is the task of the devil? We will think, speak, and act like Jesus and promote the great gospel to the world. Both in name and reality, we want the spirit of the Yamato nation (Japan) to be in accord with the divine kingdom. This is the precious task of religious education.

Endnotes

Notes to Chapter One

1. Edward Farley, *Theologia: The Fragmentation and Unity of Theological Education* (Philadelphia: Fortress, 1983).

2. In an article titled "Culture and Coherence in Christian History," the historian of missions Andrew Walls poignantly asks, "How does the expression of the faith compare among Temple-worshipping Jew, Greek Council Father, Celtic monk, German Reformer, English Puritan, Victorian Churchman? How defective would each other think the other on matters vital to religion? . . . And yet I believe we can discern a firm coherence underlying all of these, and indeed, the whole of Christianity. It is not easy to state this coherence in propositional, still less in creedal form — for extended creedal formulation is itself a necessary product of a particular Christian culture. But there is a small body of convictions and responses which express themselves when Christians of any culture express their faith. These may perhaps be stated thus: 1) The worship of the God of Israel . . . ; 2) The ultimate significance of Jesus of Nazareth; 3) That God is active where believers are; 4) That believers constitute a people of God transcending time and space." Andrew Walls, *The Missionary Movement in Christian History: Studies in the Transmission of Faith* (New York: Orbis, 1996), pp. 23-24.

3. See Reinhard Hütter's brief synopsis of the legacies of Kant and Schleiermacher in "The Knowledge of the Triune God: Practices, Doctrine, Theology," in Buckley and Yeago, *Knowing the Triune God: The Work of the Spirit in the Practices of the Church* (Grand Rapids: Eerdmans, 2001), pp. 24-25.

4. See Stephen A. Schmidt, *A History of the Religious Education Association* (Birmingham, AL: Religious Education Press, 1983); and Mary C. Boys, *Educating in Faith: Maps and Visions* (Kansas City: Sheed & Ward, 1989).

5. In the introduction to *Developing a Public Faith*, Osmer says that the *descriptive-empirical* task asks, "*What* is going on in a specific domain of practice?; the *interpretive* task asks *Why* is this going on in this domain of practice?; a practical theologian's *norms of practice* influence the question of 'What *ought* to be going on in this domain of practice?'; and the

rules of art (Schleiermacher's *Kunstregeln*) are open-ended, 'how to' suggestions for guiding future practice. In any given model of practical theology, these four tasks are not necessarily engaged in a neat order, but they can be teased out by careful reading." Richard Robert Osmer, ed., *Developing a Public Faith: New Directions in Practical Theology — Essays in Honor of James Fowler* (St. Louis: Chalice Press, 2003).

6. James W. Fowler, "Practical Theology and Theological Education: Some Models and Questions," *Theology Today* 42, no. 1 (April 1985): 54-55.

7. Mathew L. Lamb, *Solidarity with the Victims* (New York: Crossroad, 1982).

8. Rebecca S. Chopp, "Practical Theology and Liberation," in *Formation and Reflection: The Promise of Practical Theology,* ed. Lewis S. Mudge and James N. Poling (Philadelphia: Fortress, 1987), pp. 120-38.

9. Lamb, *Solidarity with the Victims.*

10. Osmer, *Developing a Public Faith.*

11. James E. Loder, "Normativity and Context in Practical Theology: The Interdisciplinary Issue," in *Practical Theology: International Perspectives,* ed. Friedrich Schweitzer and J. A. Van der Ven (Frankfurt am Main and New York: Peter Lang, 1999), pp. 359-81.

12. James W. Fowler, Sam Keen, and Jerome Berryman, *Life Maps: Conversations on the Journey of Faith* (Waco: Word Books, 1978); and James W. Fowler, *Stages of Faith: The Psychology of Human Development and the Quest for Meaning* (San Francisco: Harper & Row, 1981).

13. For example, arguably the most notable theoretical construction in this field during the post-1960s period, Thomas Groome's *Christian Religious Education,* draws on both the theories of Fowler and Jean Piaget, one of the *ur* sources for Fowler's own stage theory of faith development. Thomas Groome, *Christian Religious Education: Sharing Our Story and Vision* (San Francisco: Harper & Row, 1980).

14. Groome, a Roman Catholic, and Robert Pazmino, a self-identified evangelical, are representative of the broad-ranged acceptance of Fowler's work. It is interesting to note, however, that Pazmino's most recent work, *God Our Teacher: Theological Basics in Christian Education* (2001), draws more on Loder than Fowler. Cf. James E. Loder and James W. Fowler, "Conversations on *Stages of Faith* and *The Transforming Moment,*" *Religious Education* 77, no. 2 (1982): 133-48; and Craig R. Dykstra and Sharon Parks, eds., *Faith Development and Fowler* (Birmingham, AL: Religious Education Press, 1986).

15. Fowler, "Practical Theology and Theological Education," pp. 54-55.

16. Lamb, *Solidarity with the Victims.*

17. Fowler, "Practical Theology and Theological Education," p. 56.

18. Fowler, "Practical Theology and Theological Education," p. 55. Perhaps one of the reasons that Fowler himself strives to describe the interaction of divine and human initiative is his proximity to the actual concerns of the churches. While I will not comment here on what I see as some of the problems with Fowler's own integration of theology and the human sciences, his work shows that a correlational approach does not, by definition, have to ignore the relation between divine and human praxis. Beyond Loder's critique (via Ebeling) of Fowler's use of the word "faith," my own research with Japanese junior college women also raises unresolved questions about faith development's handling of non-theological and theological resources. Thomas J. Hastings, "Parameters of Faith Among Japanese Junior College Women: An Initial Inquiry Based on Fowler's Theory of Faith Development," *Japanese Reli-*

gions 16, no. 4 (July 1991): 49-81; and "Beyond Autonomy and Belonging: Toward a Global Vision for Christian Nurture," *Japan Christian Review* 60 (1994): 79-95.

19. I use the word *habitus* in Bourdieu's technical sense. *Habitus* discloses the normative boundary conditions of what a given collectivity considers to be reasonable and unreasonable, possible or impossible. "The conditionings associated with a particular class of conditions produce *habitus*, systems of durable, transposable dispositions, structured structures predisposed to function as structuring structures, that is, as principles which generate and organize practices and representations that can be objectively adapted to their outcomes without presupposing a conscious aiming at ends or an express mastery of the operations necessary in order to attain them." Pierre Bourdieu, *The Logic of Practice* (Stanford, CA: Stanford University Press, 1990), p. 53.

20. One recent example of this growing sensitivity to the cultural location of the theologian is the biblical studies approach called "cultural exegesis." See Fernando F. Segovia and Mary Ann Tolbert, eds., *Reading from This Place: Social Location and Biblical Interpretation in the United States* (Minneapolis: Fortress Press, 1995); and *Reading from This Place: Social Location and Biblical Interpretation in Global Perspective* (Minneapolis: Fortress Press, 1995).

21. Fowler, "Practical Theology and Theological Education," pp. 56-57.

22. Fowler, "Practical Theology and Theological Education," pp. 56-57.

23. Thomas F. Torrance, "The Making of the 'Modern' Mind from Descartes and Newton to Kant," in *Transformation and Convergence in the Frame of Knowledge: Explorations in the Interrelations of Scientific and Theological Enterprise* (Eugene, OR: Wipf & Stock, 1980), pp. 38, 40.

24. Hütter, "The Knowledge of the Triune God," in *Knowing the Triune God*, p. 27.

25. Hütter, "The Knowledge of the Triune God," in *Knowing the Triune God*, pp. 27-28.

26. Robert Jenson, "How the World Lost Its Story," *First Things* 36 (October 1993): 20; and Barry Harvey, *Another City: An Ecclesiological Primer for a Post-Christian World* (Harrisburg, PA: Trinity Press International, 1999), p. 103.

27. Jenson, "How the World Lost Its Story," p. 103.

28. Thomas F. Torrance, *Space, Time and Resurrection* (Grand Rapids: Eerdmans, 1976), p. 2. Commenting on Torrance's linkage of epistemological and cosmological dualism, Elmer Colyer says, "Those who operate with an epistemological dualism of the human knower over against the world out there, rather than with an interactive and personal human epistemic agency, will be predisposed to cosmological dualism (with its radical separation or yawning chasm between the universe and God) which is inhospitable to an interactive God-world relation, and therefore to the active agency of God as the sufficient reason for the astonishing and subtle intelligibility of the universe and its openness to active human agency at the center of Torrance's reformulation of the main point of the cosmological 'argument.'" Elmer M. Colyer, *How to Read T. F. Torrance: Understanding His Trinitarian and Scientific Theology* (Downers Grove, IL: InterVarsity, 2001), p. 203.

29. George Lindbeck says this approach "interprets doctrines as noninformative and nondiscursive symbols of inner feelings, attitudes, or existential orientations." *The Nature of Doctrine: Religion and Theology in a Postliberal Age* (Philadelphia: Westminster Press, 1984), p. 16.

30. Lamb, *Solidarity with the Victims*, pp. 76ff.

31. Chopp, "Practical Theology and Liberation," p. 123.

32. David Tracy, *Blessed Rage for Order: The New Pluralism in Theology* (New York: Seabury Press, 1975); and *The Analogical Imagination: Christian Theology and the Culture of Pluralism* (New York: Crossroad, 1981).

33. Carl S. Dudley and James D. Anderson, *Building Effective Ministry: Theory and Practice in the Local Church* (San Francisco: Harper & Row, 1983).

34. Chopp, "Practical Theology and Liberation," p. 124.

35. Chopp, "Practical Theology and Liberation," p. 125.

36. Chopp, "Practical Theology and Liberation," p. 133.

37. Fowler, "Practical Theology and Theological Education," p. 55.

38. Loder, "Normativity and Context in Practical Theology," p. 359.

39. James E. Loder, *The Logic of the Spirit: Human Development in Theological Perspective* (San Francisco: Jossey-Bass, 1998), p. 37. In the article I will examine in more detail below, Loder says that this *tertium quid* situation is "the key problem common to interdisciplinary methodology in practical theology. It is problematic because, under the surface of the interdisciplinary discussion, it introduces an alternative reality that is not explicitly accountable to the terms of the theology-human science dialogue itself. By so doing, these approaches subvert the central problematic of practical theology as a discipline. The tacit dimension not only controls, in an unexamined way, the outcome of the dialogue but connotes an ethos within which it is assumed that the results of the dialogue must take place." Loder, "Normativity and Context in Practical Theology," p. 362.

40. See also Loder's creative analogy between Hiltner, Farley, Pannenberg, and liberationist approaches to interdisciplinarity in practical theology and the *ethoi* of Manchester, Athens, Berlin, and Delphi. Tongue in cheek, Loder asserts that the alternative *ethos* of Jerusalem seems to be conspicuously absent in these approaches. Loder, "Normativity and Context in Practical Theology," pp. 364-65.

41. Loder, "Normativity and Context in Practical Theology," p. 359.

42. The doctrine of the coherence of two natures, divine and human, in the one person of Jesus Christ was clarified in the Chalcedonian formulation of 451 CE.

43. Loder, "Normativity and Context in Practical Theology," p. 359.

44. If we take Loder's theological approach beyond Chalcedon back to the Trinitarian ground that Chalcedon presupposes, we can positively state that, since the Triune mission of the God/man Jesus Christ to the glory of the Father, in the power of the Holy Spirit, through the witness of the church, on behalf of all creation, inseparably joins the being and act of God and humanity, the dualistic practical theological arguments in favor of either theory or praxis become inconsequential. Such a Trinitarian development also brings the decisive issue of the grounds for the church's participation in the mission of God into clearer relief than Loder's Christocentric formulation.

45. As I will show in my case study of the ways that the North American theories of religious education were introduced into Japan by Tamura Naomi, the modern development of practical theology is replete with examples of theorists and practitioners who gave in to the temptation to take theology hostage to the human sciences or, as a reaction, the human sciences to theology.

46. Osmer, *Developing a Public Faith.*

47. Loder, "Normativity and Context in Practical Theology," p. 359.

48. See David H. Kelsey, *Proving Doctrine: The Uses of Scripture in Modern Theology* (Harrisburg, PA: Trinity Press International, 1999), pp. 185-92.

49. Loder, who in *The Transforming Moment* expressed a deeper affinity with the Lutheran theological tradition mediated mainly by Kierkegaard, rediscovered the Reformed tradition through his reading of Torrance. Specifically, it was in Torrance's work on the dialogue between science and theology that Loder found a comprehensive and convincing theological and scientific examination and critique of the hopelessly dualistic *habitus* of the contemporary Western mind which I described above in conversation with Fowler's own critique. Seeing most contemporary practical theology as hopelessly devoted to non-theological, dualistic, and therefore non-scientific modes of rationality, Loder turned more and more to Torrance's "theological science" for insights in *The Knight's Move* and *The Logic of the Spirit.* James E. Loder, *The Transforming Moment* (Colorado Springs: Helmers & Howard, 1989); James E. Loder and Jim W. Neidhardt, *The Knight's Move: The Relational Logic of the Spirit in Theology and Science* (Colorado Springs: Helmers & Howard, 1992); and James E. Loder, *The Logic of the Spirit.*

50. Thomas F. Torrance, *The Ground and Grammar of Theology* (Charlottesville: University of Virginia Press, 1980), p. 93.

51. See n. 28 above.

52. Torrance, *The Ground and Grammar of Theology*, p. 94.

53. Torrance, *Space, Time and Resurrection*, pp. 1-2.

54. Torrance, *Space, Time and Resurrection*, pp. 1-2.

55. Torrance, *Space, Time and Resurrection*, p. 7.

56. He claims that a "revelation-independent" natural theology thrived during those times when the church lapsed into dualistic modes of thought wherein "knowledge was allegedly derived by way of abstraction from sense experience or deductions from observations." Torrance, *The Ground and Grammar of Theology*, p. 76.

57. By means of an analogy to the reconstrual of geometry as four-dimensional within the unitary view of the universe in Einsteinian physics, Torrance seeks to reclaim a proper place for natural theology *within* the unified field of revelation opened up under the incarnation of the eternal Son of God. "If natural theology is to have a viable reconstruction, it can only be on the basis of a restored ontology in which our thought operates with a fundamental unity of concept and experience, or of form and being, within a contingent but inherently intelligible and open-structured universe." Within this unified field of inquiry, natural theology finds "its proper place and status within the area of overlap between natural science and theological science, that is, within the overlapping of created and uncreated intelligibility where natural science presses its inquiries in one direction and theological science presses its inquiries in another direction." Torrance, *The Ground and Grammar of Theology*, pp. 77, 86-87.

58. Torrance, *The Ground and Grammar of Theology*, p. 46.

59. In this reading of history, the ancient church's struggle with regnant Greco-Roman cultural conceptions becomes much more than a political move to enforce doctrinal conformity as a means of consolidating ecclesial power. (Torrance, *Ground and Grammar*, p. 47.) Actually, the history between Nicea and Constantinople shows that Arianism was not so easily defeated. Given the large number of Arian-tending bishops, if the church had only been interested in institutional benefits, the compromise of the *homoiousious* ("similar sub-

stance") over the *homoousios* ("same substance") would have easily carried the day. See Frances Young, *From Nicaea to Chalcedon* (Philadelphia: Fortress Press, 1983) and Donald McKim, *Theological Turning Points: Major Issues in Christian Thought* (Atlanta: John Knox Press, 1988).

60. Torrance, *The Ground and Grammar of Theology*, p. 47.

61. Torrance, *The Ground and Grammar of Theology*, pp. 46-47.

62. See Loder and Neidhardt, *The Knight's Move*.

63. These terms are borrowed from George Hunsinger's description of the Chalcedonian Christology in "Karl Barth's Christology," *Disruptive Grace: Studies in the Theology of Karl Barth* (Grand Rapids: Eerdmans, 2000), pp. 131-33.

64. Torrance, *The Ground and Grammar of Theology*, p. 30.

65. Thomas F. Torrance, *The Mediation of Christ* (Colorado Springs: Helmers & Howard, 1992), pp. 3-4.

66. Again, the conviction here is that any field under investigation will only disclose its inner intelligibility when it is apprehended in ways appropriate to its actual nature. In other words, the "object" exercises a definitive marginal control in the knowing event. Put another way, the inquirer's questions must first be rigorously *directed by* an object under investigation before they may properly be *directed to* that object. By acknowledging the epistemological priority of the object over the investigator, Torrance is seeking to get below the surface to what he calls a field's "being-constituting relations or 'onto-relations.'" Torrance, *The Mediation of Christ*, p. 47.

67. Polanyi says, "It is not by looking at things, but by dwelling in them, that we understand their joint meaning." Michael Polanyi, *The Tacit Dimension* (Gloucester, MA: Peter Smith, 1983), p. 18.

68. In speaking of the passions of the scientist, Polanyi says, "I want to show that scientific passions are no mere psychological by-product, but have a logical function which contributes an indispensable element to science." Michael Polanyi, *Personal Knowing* (Chicago: University of Chicago Press, 1958), p. 134.

69. My description of *pathos* is informed by Walter Brueggemann's description of the prophetic literature of the Hebrew scriptures: "the sense of fracture and abrasion between what is at hand and what is promised." Walter Brueggemann, *The Creative Word: Canon as a Model for Biblical Education* (Philadelphia: Fortress Press, 1982), p. 12. See also Reinhard Hütter's definition of *pathos* in *Suffering Divine Things: Theology as Church Practice* (Grand Rapids: Eerdmans, 2000), pp. 29-32.

70. Loder, "Normativity and Context in Practical Theology," p. 359. In terms of Loder's transformational logic, *the pathic self-investment of indwelling* is potentially brought to a new depth and intensity in the second movement, the *interlude for scanning*, where new insight or discovery is waiting to break in upon the knower, but also where the downward psychic drive toward adaptation is often overpowering. In many educational contexts, this is where an *ethos* that values quick, easy and painless "answers" subverts the kind of cruciform investigation that is "unto transformation." See Loder, *The Transforming Moment*.

71. Loder, "Normativity and Context in Practical Theology," p. 361.

72. Loder, "Normativity and Context in Practical Theology," p. 360.

73. Loder, "Normativity and Context in Practical Theology," p. 370.

74. Loder, "Normativity and Context in Practical Theology," p. 370.

75. The New Testament's emphasis on the eschatological community as the locus of divine transformation is obscured by the English translation of the word "you" to indicate both the singular and plural usages that are, of course, clearly distinguished in Greek. In Paul's letters, which were mostly addressed to one or more churches, the plural usages of "you" naturally dominate. Beyond this obvious linguistic evidence, however, is the far more important conviction that the *ecclesia*, and not the discrete individual, is portrayed by Paul as the primary sphere of God's transforming work in Christ.

76. Torrance, *The Mediation of Christ*, p. 67.

77. Loder, *The Transforming Moment*.

78. Loder, *The Logic of the Spirit*, pp. 46-55.

79. Karl Barth, "The Sanctification of Man," in *Church Dogmatics* IV/2, ed. Geoffrey W. Bromiley and Thomas F. Torrance (Edinburgh: T. & T. Clark, 1956), pp. 491-613.

80. I owe this insight to my conversations with Professor George Hunsinger.

81. Richard B. Hays, *The Moral Vision of the New Testament: Community, Cross, New Creation: A Contemporary Introduction to New Testament Ethics* (San Francisco: Harper, 1996), p. 204, n. 11.

82. Roland says, "It dawned on me that it is not simply that we view things differently, coming from varied cultures (Hall 1959: 128-164), but that our very inner emotional-cognitive makeup is of another order. . . . I realized that the whole elaboration of the psycho-analytic theory of personality in its many variations is Western-centric. . . . Much of it is clearly related to the clinical data of Western personality in societies emphasizing individual-ism. Although psychoanalysis repeatedly claims to deal with universals of psychological makeup and ideal norms of mature human functioning, yet these universals, ideals, and norms were frequently contradicted in Japan and India. And when these norms of develop-ment and functioning have been applied by psychoanalysts to Asians, Africans, and others, the inevitable results are that they are seen as inferior or psychopathological — *a theoretical position that is tenable only if one assumes the inherent superiority of Western civilization and psyche*. When not used normatively, the central developmental constructs are simply not very relevant to persons from these other cultures" (italics mine). Alan Roland, *In Search of Self in India and Japan: Toward a Cross-Cultural Psychology* (Princeton: Princeton University Press, 1988), pp. xv, xvi. I will return to this issue in more detail in Chapter Five.

83. Gerben Heitink, *Practical Theology: History, Theory, Action Domains* (Grand Rapids: Eerdmans, 1999), pp. 29-30.

84. Hays, *The Moral Vision of the New Testament*, p. 24.

85. Hays, *The Moral Vision of the New Testament*, p. 24.

86. See James E. Loder, "The Dominance of Socialization," in unpublished manuscript titled *Educational Ministry in the Logic of the Spirit* (computer printout, Princeton Theologi-cal Seminary, 2001), pp. 1-66.

87. Loder, "Normativity and Context in Practical Theology," p. 370.

88. For example, teach/διδάσκω, encourage/παρακαλέω, form/μορφή, and nurture/ἐκτρέφετε.

89. Søren Kierkegaard, *Attack upon Christendom* (Princeton: Princeton University Press, 1944).

90. Loder, *Educational Ministry in the Logic of the Spirit*, p. 28.

91. See "The Field of Human Action: A Neo-Parsonian Model," Appendix 1 in Loder, "Normativity and Context in Practical Theology," p. 379.

92. Loder describes these counterdynamics as follows: "The counterforce to this so-cialization model is transformation. Transformation takes place in all basic spheres of action, and it exposes the evidence that a deeper intelligibility underlies the system, but it is not usu-ally released except through a transformational process. Transformation occurs whenever, within a given frame of reference or experience, hidden orders of coherence and meaning emerge to replace or alter the axioms of the given frame and reorder its elements accord-ingly." Loder, "Normativity and Context in Practical Theology," p. 380.

93. Loder, "Normativity and Context in Practical Theology," p. 381.

94. Even if one does not go as far as an Augustinian argument for the *vestigia*, isn't there a possible analogy to *perichoresis*, a mutual interpenetration between these spheres of action that is supported by theology, common experience, and a post-critical methodology?

95. Rodney Stark, *The Rise of Christianity* (Princeton: Princeton University Press, 1996), p. 213.

96. See Roland Robertson, *Globalization: Social Theory and Global Culture* (London: Sage Publications, 1992), p. 27.

97. For his wonderful discussion of the four dimensions of knowing, see chapter 3, "The Fourfold Knowing Event," in *The Transforming Moment*, pp. 67-91.

98. Loder, "Normativity and Context in Practical Theology," p. 359.

99. See Catherine Mowry LaCugna, *God for Us: The Trinity and Christian Life* (San Francisco: HarperCollins, 1991).

100. See Hütter's development of Luther's view of ecclesial practices in a pneumatological framework in *Suffering Divine Things*.

101. See George R. Hunsberger and Craig Van Gelder, eds., *The Church Between Gospel and Culture: The Emerging Mission in North America* (Grand Rapids: Eerdmans, 1996), pp. 64-65.

102. While I think that the recent interest in catechesis reflects a positive acknowledg-ment of how the lines between the gospel, church, and culture have become so blurry, this in-terest is not an unambiguous development. This ambivalence is expressed beautifully by George Lindbeck in the final chapter of *The Nature of Doctrine*. On the one hand, Lindbeck says that "This method [his "cultural-linguistic" view of doctrine] resembles ancient cat022he-sis more than modern translation. Instead of redescribing the faith in new concepts, it seeks to teach the language and practices of the religion to potential adherents." At the same time, Lindbeck is gravely pessimistic about any practical application of his proposal in the current sociocultural situation of North America. "Western culture is now at an intermediate stage, however, where socialization is ineffective, catechesis impossible, and translation a tempting alternative. . . . The intertextual intelligibility that postliberalism emphasizes may not fit the needs of religions such as Christianity when they are in the awkward intermediate stage of having once been culturally established but are not yet clearly disestablished." Lindbeck leaves the reader with the paradoxical (Lutheran?) conclusion that, while postliberalism has a family resemblance to the catechesis of the early church, a renewal of catechesis today is ruled out because the churches today are so completely enculturated. "In the present situation, un-like periods of missionary expansion, the churches primarily accommodate to the prevailing culture rather than shape it." Lindbeck, *The Nature of Doctrine*, pp. 132-33.

103. While I am also opposed to the pre-1960 patterns of "one-way" missionary engagement, it has been all but forgotten that, in spite of their many sins, the missionaries also regularly reminded their "home" churches of the world's profound cultural diversity. In an age when increasing globalization has clearly not increased the level of understanding and tolerance among the peoples of the world, I do think that the North American churches and their theological institutions have much to gain from a serious reexamination of their own missionary past and a careful consideration of how they might be positively engaged in the *ecumene* today in ways more consonant with the gospel.

Notes to Chapter Two

1. George R. Hunsberger, "The Newbigin Gauntlet: Developing a Domestic Missiology for North America," in Hunsberger and Van Gelder, *The Church Between Gospel and Culture* (Grand Rapids: Eerdmans, 1996), p. 9.

2. See H. I. Marrou, "The Old Roman Education," in *A History of Education in Antiquity* (Madison: University of Wisconsin Press, 1956), pp. 229-41; and William Barclay, "Education Among the Romans," in *Educational Ideals in the Ancient World* (Grand Rapids: Baker Book House, 1974), pp. 143-91.

3. Andrew Walls, *The Missionary Movement in Christian History: Studies in the Transmission of Faith* (New York: Orbis, 1996), p. 54.

4. Barry Harvey, *Another City: An Ecclesiological Primer for a Post-Christian World* (Harrisburg, PA: Trinity Press International, 1999).

5. Of course, faith "in the church" falls under the third pneumatological article in the classical ecumenical expressions of the faith "of the church," i.e., in *The Nicene Creed* ("We believe one holy catholic and apostolic church") and *The Apostles' Creed* ("I believe in the Holy Ghost; the holy catholic Church, the communion of saints"). *The Constitution of the Presbyterian Church (U.S.A.): Part One, Book of Confessions* (Louisville: Office of the General Assembly, 1996), pp. 3, 7.

6. In Ephesians, the writer speaks of the peace between Jews and Gentiles as the unilateral gift of the crucified Christ. In Christ's body, God creates "one new humanity in place of the two" (Eph. 2:15).

7. For an excellent discussion of the *charismata* in the more problematic Corinthians context, see Richard B. Hays, *First Corinthians* (Louisville: John Knox Press, 1997), pp. 206-52.

8. See also Schleiermacher's strong emphasis on historical theology in understanding how Christians in previous ages have interpreted the "essence of Christianity." Friedrich Schleiermacher, *Brief Outline of Theology as a Field of Study*, trans. Terrence N. Tice (Lewiston, NY: Edwin Mellen Press, 1988).

9. Loder rightly places a strong emphasis on worship for practical theology. However, as I pointed out in Chapter One, he overlooks the importance of worship as a transformational communal (more than individual!) practice of discernment, which is uppermost in Paul's mind.

10. While this kind of implicit reference to later ecclesial formulations such as Nicea and Chalcedon may seem like an anachronistic kind of New Testament interpretation, clearly Paul in Romans and elsewhere expresses a highly exalted view of the Lord Jesus Christ who is

"descended from David according to the flesh and was declared to be Son of God with power according to the spirit of holiness by resurrection from the dead" (Rom. 1:3-4). The hermeneutical point I wish to make here is that, while Paul of course did not work out the doctrine of the dual nature in one person, the doctrine is not only not inconsistent with Paul, it may even be said to be implicit, only awaiting the rational reflection and expression of later church councils. For a more nuanced example of this kind of approach, see David S. Yeago, "The New Testament and the Nicene Dogma: A Contribution to the Recovery of Theological Exegesis," in *The Theological Interpretation of Scripture: Classic and Contemporary Readings,* ed. Stephen E. Fowl (Malden, MA: Blackwell, 1997); and Stephen E. Fowl, *Engaging Scripture: A Model for Theological Interpretation* (Malden, MA: Blackwell, 1998).

11. As I said in Chapter One, Loder's reconception of practical theology as a theological discipline is a vast improvement over the *tertium quid* methodologies of the correlationalists because, in the words of Torrance, he seeks to know the divine-human Subject of investigation "in the light of its own intrinsic intelligibility or *logos*." Thomas F. Torrance, *The Mediation of Christ* (Colorado Springs: Helmers & Howard, 1992), pp. 3-4.

12. Romans 6:14.

13. See Karl Barth, *Der Römerbrief,* 4. Abdruck der neuen Bearb (Munich: Kaiser, 1926, English version), pp. 441-44. In *Church Dogmatics,* Barth makes an even stronger case for the apprehension of the gift of unity and diversity in Jesus Christ, the divine-human agent of reconciliation. "Christian faith can and should be varied. . . . Although its object, the Jesus Christ attested in Scripture and proclaimed by the community, is single, consistent and free from contradiction, yet for all His singularity and unity His form is inexhaustibly rich, so that it is not merely legitimate but obligatory that believers should continually see and understand it in new lights and aspects. For He Himself does not present Himself to them in one form but in many — indeed, He is not in Himself uniform but multiform. How can it be otherwise when He is the true Son of God who is eternally rich?" Barth, "The Doctrine of Reconciliation," in *Church Dogmatics* IV/I, p. 763.

14. In other places (i.e., Romans 7 and 8), the apostle is brutally honest in confessing the common Christian experience of a raging battle, on personal and communal levels, between present experience and eschatological hope.

15. Speaking of the intimate relation between Christ and the church, Torrance says, "If atoning reconciliation between man and God is not externally but internally related to Jesus Christ, fulfilled and grounded in his incarnate constitution as Mediator, God and man indivisibly united in his one Person, then the Church of Jesus Christ cannot be thought of as only externally related to him. In the Church of Christ all who are redeemed through the atoning union embodied in him are made to share in his incarnational union with them through his birth, death, and resurrection and are incorporated into Christ by the power of his Holy Spirit as living members of his Body, the 'earthly-historical form of his existence' (as Karl Barth has called it) among us. Thus it may be said that the 'objective' union which we have with Christ through his incarnational assumption of our humanity into himself is 'subjectively' actualized in us through his indwelling Spirit, 'we in Christ' and 'Christ in us,' thus complementing and interpenetrating each other. In other words, there takes place a relation of mutual indwelling of the Father, the Son, and the Holy Spirit in the Holy Trinity." Torrance, *The Mediation of Christ,* pp. 66-67.

16. This kind of caution is behind Paul's admonition about the abuse of such gifts in the Corinthian community; see 1 Corinthians 14.

17. Jürgen Moltmann, *Theology of Hope* (London: SCM Press, 1967), p. 21. It is worth noting that Moltmann's theology of the cross was, by his own admission, partly indebted to the theological insights of the Japanese Lutheran theologian Kitamori Kazoh, author of *The Theology of the Pain of God* and former professor of systematic theology at Tokyo Union Theological Seminary. See Jürgen Moltmann, *The Crucified God: The Cross of Christ as the Foundation and Criticism of Christian Theology* (London: SCM Press, 1974), pp. 47, 153.

18. Newbigin insightfully comments on the tacit Westerncentrism of this heritage. "With hindsight, it is now easy to see how many of the self-evident truths of the Enlightenment were self-evident only to those who were the heirs of a thousand years of Christian teaching. They were not self-evident to the peoples of India or Africa." In spite of its continuing fascination with modern Western intellectual trends, I would also add Japan. Lesslie Newbigin, *Proper Confidence: Faith, Doubt, and Certainty in Christian Discipleship* (Grand Rapids: Eerdmans, 1995), p. 48.

19. In the stark words of Wilbert Shenk, "Missions within Christendom were unthinkable." Wilbert R. Shenk, "The Culture of Modernity as a Missionary Challenge," in *The Church Between Gospel and Culture,* p. 71.

20. Thomas John Hastings, "Theologie, Praxis und kultureller Habitus, Fragen zur japanischen Situation," in *Christentum und Spätmoderne, Ein internationaler Diskurs über Praktische Theologie und Ethik,* ed. Gräb et al. (Berlin: Kohlhammer, 2000).

21. Largely as a result of the work of Newbigin and his disciples, this situation is gradually changing in some North American seminaries.

22. The work of Dr. Andrew Walls and his colleagues at the University of Edinburgh's Center for the Study of Non-Western Christianity is especially exemplary in this connection.

23. See Philip Jenkins, *The Next Christendom: The Coming of Global Christianity* (Oxford: Oxford University Press, 2002).

24. See George Gallup, Jr. and Sarah Jones, *100 Questions and Answers: Religion in America* (Princeton: Princeton Religion Research Center, 1989); and Dean R. Hoge, Benton Johnson, and Donald A. Luidens, *Vanishing Boundaries: The Religion of Mainline Protestant Baby Boomers* (Louisville: Westminster/John Knox Press, 1994).

25. See Lesslie Newbigin, *The Other Side of 1984: Questions for the Churches* (Geneva: World Council of Churches, 1983); *Foolishness to the Greeks: The Gospel and Western Culture* (Grand Rapids: Eerdmans, 1986); and *The Gospel in a Pluralist Society* (Grand Rapids: Eerdmans, 1989).

26. Robert Neelly Bellah, *Habits of the Heart: Individualism and Commitment in American Life* (Berkeley: University of California Press, 1996); and Robert Wuthnow, *Sharing the Journey: Support Groups and America's New Quest for Community* (New York: Free Press, 1996); and *The Restructuring of American Religion: Society and Faith Since World War II* (Princeton: Princeton University Press, 1988).

27. John Taylor, "The Future of Christianity," in *The Oxford Illustrated History of Christianity,* ed. John McManners (Oxford: Oxford University Press, 1990), pp. 628-65.

28. Walbert Bühlmann, *The Coming of the Third Church: An Analysis of the Present and Future of the Church* (Slough, UK: St. Paul, 1974), quoted in Taylor, "The Future of Christianity," p. 637.

29. See Judith A. Berling, ed., "Incarnating Globalization in ATS Schools: Issues, Experiences, Understandings, Challenges," *Theological Education* 35 (Spring 1999): i-vii, 1-189.

30. One positive example of a move in the right direction is the recent book by Richard R. Osmer and Friedrich L. Schweitzer, *Religious Education between Modernization and Globalization: New Perspectives on the United States and Germany* (Grand Rapids: Eerdmans, 2003). In my case study of Tamura, I want to acknowledge my debt to the work of Osmer and Schweitzer and hope that my contribution will enlarge the ecumenical framework for grasping the historical and practical theological significance of the religious education movement.

31. "The Expansion of Christianity: An Interview with Andrew Walls," *Christian Century* 117, no. 22 (August 2-9, 2000): 795. The biblical reference is to Ephesians 4:1-16.

32. Walls, *The Missionary Movement in Christian History,* p. xix.

33. Walls, *The Missionary Movement in Christian History,* p. 260.

34. Walter Brueggemann has suggested the biblical metaphor of exile as an appropriate way to characterize this situation.

35. This is Stanley Hauerwas's word for the perduring temptation "to make Christianity at home in the world." Stanley Hauerwas, *With the Grain of the Universe: The Church's Witness and Natural Theology* (Grand Rapids: Brazos, 2001), p. 36.

36. A phrase I borrowed from Wuthnow, *Sharing the Journey,* pp. 18-19.

37. Barth, *Church Dogmatics,* IV/I, p. 481.

38. Rodney Stark, *The Rise of Christianity* (Princeton: Princeton University Press, 1996).

39. After I was officially appointed as a PC (USA) mission co-worker to Japan in 1988, a wise Japanese pastor told me, "Welcome to Rome in A.D. 150." Though I never forgot his words, it took many years to really grasp the depth of his meaning.

40. Craig Van Gelder, "A Great New Fact of Our Day: America as Mission Field," in Hunsberger and Van Gelder, *The Church Between Gospel and Culture,* pp. 64-65. While I generally agree with Van Gelder's analysis, his claim that the social movements of the 1960s and 1970s "collapsed the Christian culture that had been built up over a 150 year period" reads like an idealization of some former American Christian cultural consensus whose existence is historically and theologically contestable.

41. Hunsberger, "The Newbigin Gauntlet," pp. 7-10.

42. Hunsberger, "The Newbigin Gauntlet," p. 8.

43. Hunsberger, "The Newbigin Gauntlet," p. 9; Hunsberger refers to Lesslie Newbigin's "Christ and the Cultures," *Scottish Journal of Theology* 31 (1978): 11-12.

44. Walls, *The Missionary Movement in Christian History,* p. 54. Since Walls is reflecting on actual histories of gospel transmission in an *a posteriori* way, the point he is making here is, in terms of Osmer's "consensus model," "descriptive and interpretive." That is, practical theologians and missiologists should be wary of trying to extract some general "rules of art" from the pilgrim-indigenization tension for guiding future ecclesial practice.

45. Lesslie Newbigin, *Foolishness to the Greeks: The Gospel and Western Culture* (Grand Rapids: Eerdmans, 1986), p. 62, quoted in Hunsberger and Van Gelder, *The Church Between Gospel and Culture,* p. 10.

46. Hunsberger, *The Church Between Gospel and Culture,* p. 10.

47. T. F. Torrance, *The School of Faith* (New York: Harper & Brothers, 1959), p. xxxv.

48. David Yeago, "The Spirit, the Church, and the Scriptures: Biblical Inspiration and

Interpretation Revisited," in Buckley and Yeago, *Knowing the Triune God* (Grand Rapids: Eerdmans, 2001), pp. 49, 51.

49. Yeago, *Knowing the Triune God*, p. 92.

50. Yeago, *Knowing the Triune God*, p. 92.

51. Hunsberger, "The Newbigin Gauntlet," p. 10.

52. Hunsberger, "The Newbigin Gauntlet," p. 10.

53. Hunsberger, "The Newbigin Gauntlet," p. 10.

54. Walls, *The Missionary Movement in Christian History*, p. 9.

55. Walls, *The Missionary Movement in Christian History*, p. 9.

56. Harvey, *Another City*, p. 25.

57. In keeping with Japanese practice, Tamura is his family name and Naomi is his first name. I will follow this practice throughout this book when using Japanese names.

Notes to Chapter Three

1. In 1919, the Sukiyabashi congregation actually moved to Sugamo and changed names to the Sugamo Church, but I will use the earlier name to avoid confusion.

2. Tamura Naomi, *The Guide of Religious Education* [in Japanese] (Tokyo: Taisho Kindergarten Publishing, 1928). Unless otherwise noted, all translations from Japanese are my own. Readers of Japanese will note that we have not added diacritical marks to distinguish between the short "o" and the long "ou" or "oo" sounds.

3. Schmidt divides the U.S. history of the REM into four periods of twenty years each (1903-1923, 1923-1935, 1935-1952, and 1952-1970). Schmidt, *A History of the Religious Education Association*. Osmer and Schweitzer divide their recent comparative history of the U.S. REM and the German *Religionspädagogik* into three thirty-year periods (1900-1930, 1930-1960, and 1960-1990). Osmer and Schweitzer, *Religious Education Between Modernization and Globalization*.

4. Tamura, *The Guide of Religious Education*, p. 2. This book was written to commemorate the 150th anniversary of the founding of the Sunday School by Robert Raikes.

5. Tamura, *The Guide of Religious Education*, p. 2.

6. Tamura was born as Asaba Fujisaburo in Osaka to a samurai family on September 15, 1858, and was later adopted by another, wealthier Kyoto samurai family named Tamura when he was eleven.

7. Kobayashi Koichi, *The Background of Christian Education* [in Japanese] (Tokyo: Yorudansha, 1979), p. 246.

8. Hane Mikiso, *Modern Japan: A Historical Survey* (Boulder and London: Westview, 1986), p. 68.

9. Hane, *Modern Japan*, p. 68.

10. Matsumoto Sannosuke, "The Significance of Nationalism in Modern Japanese Thought: Some Theoretical Problems," *Journal of Asian Studies* 31, no. 1 (November 1971): 51.

11. Kobayashi Koichi, "Japanese Education and Christian Education," in *Dictionary of Christian Education* [in Japanese] (Tokyo: Kyodan,), pp. 395-99.

12. Matsumoto, "The Significance of Nationalism in Modern Japanese Thought," p. 49.

13. Furuya Yasuo and Ohki Hideo, *A Theology of Japan* [in Japanese] (Tokyo: Yorudansha, 1989), pp. 137-38.

14. Hane points out that Hirata, who died before Perry's arrival, had come into contact with Christian ideas through some Chinese writings. Interestingly, he shows that he "sought to provide Shinto with a clearly defined theology by presenting a monotheistic interpretation of the religion, and by emphasizing life after death." Hane, *Modern Japan*, p. 63.

15. Helen Hardacre, *Shinto and the State, 1868-1988* (Princeton: Princeton University Press, 1989).

16. Only after intense foreign pressure did the Japanese government lift the ban against Christianity in 1873.

17. The Evangelical Alliance was a union of individuals, not churches, who originally met in London in 1846 to "enable Christians to realize in themselves and to exhibit to others that a living and everlasting union binds all true believers in the fellowship of the church." They drafted a nine-point doctrinal consensus called the "Basis" that was comprehensive enough to embrace the majority of Protestant confessions. Edwin Burton, "Evangelical Alliance," in *Catholic Encyclopedia,* http://www.newadvent.org/cathen/05641a.html (accessed September 30, 2003). While its drafters did not want this consensus to be seen as a confession or creed, it significantly departs from the reformation faith on two major points. (1) While it is strong on Christ's incarnation and atoning sacrifice, it makes no mention of Christ's resurrection. It does refer to the eschatological "resurrection of the body." (2) Its second point, which affirms "the right and duty of private judgment in the interpretation of Holy Scriptures," is a radical departure from the understanding of the reformers who, while encouraging private reading of scripture in the home, gave clear priority to the public reading and interpretation of scripture in public church gatherings. See "The Second Helvetic Confession," in *The Constitution of the Presbyterian Church (U.S.A.): Part One, Book of Confessions* (Louisville: Office of the General Assembly, 1996), article 5.211, 108.

18. Robert S. Schwantes, "Christianity Versus Science: A Conflict of Ideas in Meiji Japan," *The Far Eastern Quarterly* 12, no. 2 (February 1953): 125.

19. Schwantes, "Christianity Versus Science," p. 124.

20. Hane, *Modern Japan*, p. 103.

21. See Klaus Luhmer, "Moral Education in Japan," *Journal of Moral Education*, 19, no. 3 (October 1990).

22. *Proceedings of the General Conference of the Protestant Missionaries in Japan held at Osaka, April, 1883* (Yokohama: R. Meiklejohn, 1883) and *Proceedings of the General Conference of Protestant Missionaries in Japan held in Tokyo, October, 1900* (Tokyo: Methodist Publishing House, 1901).

23. See Karen Seat, "Mission Schools and Education for Women," in *Handbook of Christianity in Japan*, ed. Mark R. Mullins (Leiden: Brill, 2003), pp. 321-42; and Thomas John Hastings, "Japan's Protestant Schools and Churches in Light of Early Mission Theory and History," in Mullins, *Handbook of Christianity in Japan*, pp. 101-23.

24. Tamura Naomi, *Fifty Years of Faith* [in Japanese] (Tokyo: Keiseisha, 1924), pp. 24-25. See also Akiyama Shigeo, *Stories of Meiji-era Personalities: A Genealogy of Christianity* [in Japanese] (Tokyo: Shinkyo, 1982), p. 193.

25. Robert Enns, "'Slander Against Our People': Tamura Naomi and the Japanese Bride Incident," *Japanese Religions* 18 (January 1993): 19.

26. Hane, *Modern Japan,* p. 104.

27. Mori had committed an act of disrespect at Ise Shrine, the main shrine of the imperial household, by allegedly poking his cane around in an inner shrine that housed some of the most sacred artifacts of the ancient imperial cult. Yamaji Aizan, *Essays on the Modern Japanese Church,* English translation of 1906 Japanese version (Ann Arbor: Center for Japanese Studies, University of Michigan, 1999), p. 160.

28. Luhmer, "Moral Education in Japan," p. 3.

29. Mark Mullins calls Uchimura's Non-Church Movement the "earliest expression of Japanese Christianity." Mark R. Mullins, *Christianity Made in Japan: A Study of Indigenous Movements* (Honolulu: University of Hawaii Press, 1998), p. 54.

30. Schwantes, "Christianity Versus Science," p. 127.

31. Schwantes, "Christianity Versus Science," p. 127.

32. Koizumi Takashi documents how, in Fukuzawa's own writings on religion, he actually embodied that instability he saw as an unavoidable aspect of Japan's coming of age as a modern nation-state. From his initial vehement opposition to Christianity as a threat to the Japanese soul and patriotism, Fukuzawa went through a number of phases in which he (1) gradually warmed up to Unitarianism; (2) asserted the superiority of Buddhism over Christianity for its softer approach to proselytism and its greater utility in the program of nation building; and (3) eventually developed his own independent and creative interpretation of Buddhist ideas in conversation with a variety of Buddhist priests and scholars. Koizumi Takashi, "Fukuzawa Yukichi and Religion," *Asian Philosophy* 4, no. 2 (1994): 109-19.

33. Schwantes, "Christianity Versus Science," p. 127. Schwantes concludes, "Knapp's tolerant attitude toward Buddhism and Shintoism and his willingness to accept the current scientific theories made his message extremely attractive to Japanese intellectuals" (p. 129).

34. Dohi Akio claims that the impact of the Unitarians was significant. "These groups denied the traditional doctrine of the Trinity and Christology. Though the churches developed by these missions in Japan remained small, their theological impact upon Japan's Christian leaders was great." Dohi Akio, "The First Generation: Christian Leaders in the First Period," in *A History of Japanese Theology,* ed. Furuya Yasuo (Grand Rapids: Eerdmans, 1997), p. 22.

35. See Appendix A.

36. Luhmer, "Moral Education in Japan," p. 4.

37. Luhmer, "Moral Education in Japan," p. 4.

38. Kobayashi, "Japanese Education and Christian Education," pp. 395-99.

39. Matsumoto, "The Significance of Nationalism in Modern Japanese Thought," p. 52.

40. Richard Drummond, *A History of Christianity in Japan* (Grand Rapids: Eerdmans, 1971), pp. 199-200.

41. Uchimura later became the founder of the indigenous "Non-Church Movement" *(Mukyokai)* and a prolific author of religious works. Like Tamura, he had also studied in the United States from 1884 to 1888 where he was influenced by evangelical Puritans and Quakers.

42. Katoh Masao, *The Spirit of the Meiji Christians and Modernity: The Christian Schools Are Founded* [in Japanese] (Tokyo: Kindai Bungeisha, 1996), pp. 68-69.

43. Yamaji, *Essays on the Modern Japanese Church,* p. 150.

44. See the careful analysis of the ambiguity of Uchimura's "two-J" (Jesus and Japan) "Christian nationalism" in Furuya and Ohki, *A Theology of Japan*, pp. 131-50.

45. Yamaji, *Essays on the Modern Japanese Church*, p. 160.

46. Yamaji, *Essays on the Modern Japanese Church*, pp. 160-61.

47. Yamaji, *Essays on the Modern Japanese Church*, p. 163. Elsewhere, Inoue wrote that the Rescript's purpose was "to govern oneself for the state. Filial piety to one's parents, friendship for brothers and sisters, this is all for the state. We must offer ourselves to the service of the state and we must die for our emperor" (p. 168).

48. Robert E. Lewis, *The Educational Conquest of the Far East* (New York: Revell, 1903), p. 59. In spite of some courageous attempts at resistance, the government's shift from an emphasis on Westernization to nationalism had a profound and lasting effect on the schools and the churches. As a way of dodging the criticism that Christianity was at odds with national identity, both the mission schools and Sunday Schools gradually began to shift their focus from evangelism and conversion to moral education and character building.

49. The reference to the "old charge," of course, is to the common feeling of antipathy toward Christianity that arose in the wake of the Tokugawa government's "sakkoku policy," which effectively abolished Roman Catholic Christianity in Japan after its initial success in the late sixteenth and early seventeenth centuries. August Karl Reischauer, *The Task in Japan* (New York: Revell, 1926), p. 80.

50. Tamura, *Fifty Years of Faith*, p. 208.

51. For example, the above-mentioned Fukuzawa Yukichi had written a similar critique of the situation of Japanese women in *Japanese Women* (*Nihon no Fujinron*, 1885) and *New Women's Education* (*Shin Joshi Daigaku*, 1889). While he said that the "family was hell" for Japanese women and called for their liberation, Takeda Kiyoko points out Fukuzawa wrote those books for the male students at his college. Takeda Kiyoko, *The Yokohama Band's View of Women: Reflections on the Japanese Bride Incident* [in Japanese] (Tokyo: Meiji Gakuin University Institute for Christian Studies, 1997), p. 9.

52. Enns, "'Slander Against Our People,'" p. 21.

53. In 1894, Tamura opened the *Jieikan* as a self-supporting boarding house for impoverished students. Changing the name to the Tamura Juku in 1904, it remained in operation until 1919. One list of forty-one former *Jieikan* boarders includes six teachers, two painters, a philosophy professor, a veterinarian, two bankers, a physics professor, a history professor, a composer, a lawyer, a pastor and professor of theology, an employee of the Japan Steamship Company, and a member of the government's communications bureau. *Research on the Tsukiji Band*, ed. Miura Tadashi [in Japanese] (Tokyo: Sugamo Church, 1986), pp. 134-39.

54. Tamura Naomi, *The Japanese Bride* (New York: Harper & Brothers, 1893).

55. Thompson was a missionary of the Presbyterian Church in the U.S.A. and husband of Mary Park, Tamura's former English teacher.

56. Tamura, *Fifty Years of Faith*, pp. 211-12.

57. Tamura, *Fifty Years of Faith*, pp. 211-12.

58. Takeda, *The Yokohama Band's View of Women*, p. 9.

59. Takeda, *The Yokohama Band's View of Women*, p. 10.

60. Tamura, *The Japanese Bride*, pp. iii-v.

61. Furuya and Ohki, *A Theology of Japan*, p. 122.

62. Nishikawa Yuko, "The Changing Form of Dwellings and the Establishment of the Katei (Home) in Modern Japan," *U.S.-Japan Women's Journal* 3 (1995): 20.

63. Takeda, *The Yokohama Band's View of Women*, p. 10.

64. Enns, "'Slander Against Our People,'" pp. 31-32.

65. Enns, "'Slander Against Our People,'" p. 33.

66. Enns, "'Slander Against Our People,'" p. 32.

67. Enns, "'Slander Against Our People,'" p. 33.

68. Enns, "'Slander Against Our People,'" p. 35.

69. The Yokohama Band is a reference to the faction to which Uemura and Tamura's other accusers belonged. Tamura was from the Tsukiji Band, a competing Tokyo faction. Tamura, *Fifty Years of Faith*, p. 231.

70. From an unreferenced newspaper article in Tamura's file in the archives of Princeton Theological Seminary.

71. See Takeda, *The Yokohama Band's View of Women*, pp. 20-24, for her analysis of the views of Uemura and Ibuka.

72. Enns, "'Slander Against Our People,'" pp. 29-30.

73. Furuya and Ohki, *A Theology of Japan*, p. 126.

74. Takeda, *The Yokohama Band's View of Women*, p. 24.

75. Takeda, *The Yokohama Band's View of Women*, p. 11.

76. Furuya and Ohki, *A Theology of Japan*, p. 134.

77. Furuya and Ohki, *A Theology of Japan*, p. 120. This serious oversight by Ohki and Furuya is probably due to the fact that they are both systematic theologians. By contrast, in his 1935 *History of Modern Japanese Christians*, published one year after Tamura's death, Hiyane Antei not only includes Tamura in his list of the forty-one major leaders of the first generation of Japanese Protestants, he makes more reference to Tamura than other such noteworthies as Oshikawa, Nijima, and Yamamuro. The only nine leaders with more references than Tamura are Uemura, Uchimura, Ibuka, Ebina, Kanamori, Kozaki, Honda, Miyakawa, and Yokoi. This suggests that Tamura continued to be a dominant figure in the Japanese church long after *The Japanese Bride*. Hiyane Antei, *History of Modern Japanese Christians* [in Japanese] (Tokyo: Kirisutokyo Shisogyosho, 1935).

78. Akiyama, *Stories of Meiji-era Personalities*, p. 21.

79. See Hastings, "Japan's Protestant Schools and Churches," in Mullins, *Handbook of Christianity in Japan*, pp. 101-23.

80. For an insightful discussion of Uchimura's dual loyalties to Japan and Jesus, see Furuya and Ohki, *A Theology of Japan*, pp. 131-50.

81. Takeda, *The Yokohama Band's View of Women*, p. 13.

82. See Furuya Yasuo, "Bushido and Christianity," in *Japanese Christianity* [in Japanese] (Tokyo: Kyobunkan, 2003).

83. George Hunsberger, "The Newbigin Gauntlet: Developing a Domestic Missiology for North America," in Hunsberger and Van Gelder, *The Church Between Gospel and Culture* (Grand Rapids: Eerdmans, 1996), p. 9.

84. Dohi, "The First Generation," p. 14.

85. Schwantes, "Christianity Versus Science," pp. 130-31.

86. Furuya, *Japanese Christianity*, p. 70.

87. *Collected Works of Uemura Masahisa*, ed. Kumano Yoshitaka, Ishihara Ken, Saito

Isamu, Ouchi, Sabura [in Japanese] (Tokyo: Shinkyo Shuppansha, 1932), 1:391. Translation from Addison Soltau, "Uemura Masahisa (1857-1925): First Generation Pastor, Christian Leader and Instinctive Proponent of Indigenized Christianity in Japan" (Th.D. diss., Concordia Seminary, St. Louis, 1982), p. 124.

88. Takeda, *The Yokohama Band's View of Women*, pp. 16-17. *Kokorozashi* is a rich Confucian term that encompasses such volitional English words as self-cultivation, ambition, will, aspiration, progress, and determination. This view of self-development is not to be confused with the modern Western idea of self-realization. Rather, it emphasizes a self-denying kind of self-development for the betterment of the entire community. Uemura remained dedicated to Christian public service throughout his long career. There were times, however, when his own theology tended more toward the pattern of nationalist syncretism, i.e., when he interpreted Japan's subjugation of Korea using the categories of the biblical conquest narrative. In December 1909, after Japan "annexed" Korea, he wrote, "And Moses called unto Joshua and said unto him in the sight of all Israel, 'Be strong, and of good courage; for thou must go with this people unto a land which the Lord has sworn unto their fathers to give them; and thou shall cause them to inherit it . . .' Japan has been related to Korea intimately and long. We feel truly that God has sworn to give it to our fathers. This conviction in the Japanese mind has been so deep-rooted that nothing should subdue it. . . . In genius, ability, and responsibility Japan is endowed with a paternal privilege over her junior neighbor. As Korea has always been a hotbed of disturbances Japan should make Korea her territory in order to lead her into civilization, and as a contribution to the advancement of mankind. It seems a most proper and reasonable thing to happen, and nobody can gainsay it." Aoyoshi Katsuhisa, *Dr. Uemura Masahisa: A Christian Leader* (Tokyo: Kyobunkan, 1941), pp. 242, 232. This quote is also from Soltau, *Uemura Masahisa*, p. 122.

89. Hunsberger, "The Newbigin Gauntlet," p. 10.

90. See Enns, "'Slander Against Our People,'" pp. 31-32.

91. In place of the Westminster, Heidelberg, and Dort standards originally introduced by the Presbyterian and Reformed missionaries and adopted in 1877, Uemura led his church toward what he perceived as a healthy theological independence that sought to preserve the continuity with the church catholic by adopting the Apostles' Creed along with their own minimalist confession. Given the numerous confessions represented by the missionaries, Uemura and other Japanese leaders naturally associated the elaborate Western creeds with schism and denominationalism. He said, "The thing I fear the most is that the church in Japan will inherit the schisms and divisions of the denominations abroad." Concerning the minimalist confession of his church, he boasts, "The Confession of Faith includes all the essentials of evangelical Christianity and excludes all the points of schism and division. It also preserves the orthodoxy of Christianity and leaves plenty of room for the future development of theology. I do not know yet whether this kind of thing has happened in the nineteenth century in any other country. Is the church with no creed free? I fear it goes to oppression. The church with too minute a creed, on the other hand, dwarfs the growth of thought and makes the church too conservative. The Confession of Faith which the Church of Christ in Japan has adopted recently is brief and simple, and comprehensive. Preserving soundness of doctrine, allowing broad freedom for strengthening the fellowship of Christians, it will give remarkable impetus to the theological development of the future. Its influence will not be limited to this country, but will go abroad far and wide." Soltau, *Uemura Masahisa*, pp. 159, 161. Like the

United Church of Christ in Japan's present confession of faith that was drafted in 1951, this earlier Japanese Protestant creed is also centered on the salvific work of Christ's cross and contains no mention of Christ's resurrection, except, of course, in the amended Apostles' Creed. When I pointed out this omission to a prominent Japanese theologian, he did not believe me and was dumbfounded after checking the language of both creeds for himself. This lack of reference to the resurrection is likely a fruit of the complex encounter between the tradition of the Evangelical Alliance, the strong naturalistic tendency in the moral tradition of Japan, and the generally positive appraisal of modern scientific positivism in Japan. See Harada Tasuku, "Japanese Character and Christianity: A Study of Japanese Ethical Ideals as Compared with Teaching of Christianity," *Pacific Affairs* 2, no. 11 (November 1929): 697.

92. Dohi, "The First Generation," p. 37.

93. Mullins describes the motives behind Uchimura's creative amalgam of continuity and discontinuity with Western Christianity as follows: "While Uchimura was clearly indebted to certain aspects of Western Christianity, he rejected the denominationalism and displacement theology of the mission churches, arguing that native traditions provided a positive foundation for Christianity in Japan. In order to create an authentic faith in Japan, Uchimura reasoned, Japanese Christians must build on this foundation independent of Western church control and finances." Mullins, *Christianity Made in Japan*, p. 60.

94. *Proceedings of the General Conference of the Protestant Missionaries in Japan held at Osaka, April 1883*, 204.

95. Reischauer, *The Task in Japan*, pp. 204-5.

96. Soltau, *Uemura Masahisa*, p. 98.

97. This dualistic inner/outer dialectic that was deeply ingrained in the structure of the modern Japanese consciousness had an important historical precedent. From the sixth century, China was the core external cultural source for Japan's internal renewal. This renewal included the introduction of Chinese Buddhism, Confucianism, and *kanji*, the ideographic writing system still in use in Japan today along with two phonetic alphabets which are also derived from *kanji*. Japan's dependent relation to China had given birth to the reflexive slogan, *Wakon, Kansai* ("Japanese Spirit, Chinese Learning"). In the nineteenth century, when the external cultural source for Japan's national renewal was Western technology and science, the ancient slogan was revised to *Wakon, Yosai* ("Japanese Spirit, Western Learning"). In regards to this "deceptively simple" slogan, Buell says, "What really happened was the invention of an 'ancient Japanese spirit,' not the persistence of a mythically preexisting cultural identity that was reinforced by the adoption of foreign techniques. . . . Absorption of external influences meant the construction, reification, and reinforcement of an idea of national identity; success in this venture meant styling this identity as essentially more 'real' than others." Frederick Buell, *National Culture and the New Global System* (Baltimore: Johns Hopkins University Press, 1994), p. 47.

98. Uchimura Kanzo, "Can Americans Teach Us Religion?" *Japan Christian Intelligencer* 1 (1926): 352-62.

99. Torrance, *The School of Faith*, pp. xxxiii-xxxiv.

100. After more than 140 years of huge foreign and native efforts, only 0.48 percent of Japanese claim to be Protestant today. *Christian Yearbook* [in Japanese] (Tokyo: Kirisuto Shinbunsha, 2003), pp. 90-91. See Hastings, "Protestantism's Perduring Preoccupation with Western Theological Texts," *Theology Today* 62, no. 1 (April 2005).

101. Karl Löwith, *Samtliche Schriften*, vol. 2, pp. 536f., quoted in *A History of Japanese Theology*, pp. 4-5. While Löwith's critique is accurate, it shows no awareness that the same fact-value dualism was increasingly present within modern Western intellectual developments.

102. For example, contextual Christian approaches to the veneration of the ancestors, marriage, family, religious education, sexuality, the rights of minorities, women, children, foreign residents, etc.

Notes to Chapter Four

1. Philip E. Howard, ed., *Sunday Schools the World Around: The Official Report of the World's Fifth Sunday-School Convention, in Rome, May 18-23, 1907* (Philadelphia: The World's Sunday-School Executive Committee), p. 276. Even before going to the United States to study at Auburn Theological Seminary, Princeton Theological Seminary, and Princeton University, Tamura had started reading the psychological literature. While he received advanced degrees both from Princeton Theological Seminary and Princeton University, he reports that he concentrated more on his psychology studies with McCosh at Princeton University than on his theological studies with orthodox Calvinists Paton and Hodge at the seminary. Tamura, *Fifty Years of Faith*, pp. 126-33, 292-93.

2. See Katakozawa et al., eds., *The Journey of the Church School in Japan* [in Japanese] (Tokyo: The Educational Division of the National Christian Council), p. 42.

3. *World-Wide Sunday School Work: The Official Report of the World's Sixth Sunday-School Convention, Held in the City of Washington, U.S.A. May 19-24, 1910* (Chicago: The Executive Committee of the World's Sunday-School Association), pp. 345-47.

4. *World-Wide Sunday School Work*, p. 346.

5. Tamura Naomi, *The Child the Center of Christianity* (Tokyo: Taisho Kindergarten Publishing, 1926), p. 1.

6. Tamura, *The Child the Center of Christianity*, pp. 1-2.

7. Miura Tadashi, "'The Children of Jesus': Tamura Naomi, the Father of Japanese Modern Religious Education," in *Research on the Tsukiji Band* [in Japanese] (Tokyo: UCCJ Sugamo Church, 1986), pp. 6-17.

8. He recalls, for example, that his first U.S. alma mater, Auburn Theological Seminary, had been founded during one of Charles Finney's revivals and also mentions the huge influence of Moody and Sankey during the 1880s while he was a student in the United States.

9. Tamura, *The Child the Center of Christianity*, p. 72.

10. Given the need for an ethical, non-supernatural, non-authoritarian, and social (non-individualistic) Christian response to the scientific paradigm of modernity, Coe had also concluded that the "contracted" methods of revivalism were passé. In *The Religion of a Mature Mind*, he says, "The chief trouble with the traditional revival is that it is not big enough to solve our problems." George A. Coe, *The Religion of a Mature Mind* (Chicago: Revell, 1902), p. 285. Later, in *A Social Theory of Religious Education*, Coe reports a similar cooling among American evangelicals. "The impossibility of continuously maintaining the emotional exaltation of the revival, and the limited response to the revival appeal, have necessitated much softening down of these contrast-effects in the every-day life of the

churches." George A. Coe, *A Social Theory of Religious Education* (New York: Charles Scribner's Sons, 1917), pp. 324-25.

11. Tamura, *The Child the Center of Christianity*, pp. 72-73.

12. Richard R. Osmer, *Developing a Public Faith: New Directions in Practical Theology — Essays in Honor of James Fowler* (St. Louis: Chalice Press, 2003).

13. Tamura, *The Child the Center of Christianity*, p. 73.

14. Drawing on the post-critical critique of the disinterested rationality of the Enlightenment, Osmer says that the *What* and *Why* tasks "stand in a mutually influential relationship." Osmer, *Developing a Public Faith*.

15. Tamura, *Fifty Years of Faith* [in Japanese] (Tokyo: Keiseisha, 1924), p. 280.

16. Tamura, *The Child the Center of Christianity*, p. 73.

17. See 1 Corinthians 5:1-8; 11:17-34; and 14:1-40.

18. In the course of my research, I discovered Tamura's personal copy of Coe's *The Spiritual Life* with what I assume, because the book had never been borrowed, are his own markings in red pencil in the library of Tokyo Union Theological Seminary. Based on my reading of Tamura's post-conversion writings, it is likely that this book was the intellectual *ur source* behind his conversion.

19. While utilizing empirical methods, in this early work Coe is careful to point out that he does not wish to deny or discount the workings of divine agency. "Empirical methods do not, then, reduce the facts of religious life to the plane of the natural as contrasted with the supernatural." Rather, he seeks to use scientific methods to understand the working of divine agency. "Every question arising in the psychology of religious experience may be understood in this way: Under what circumstances does the Divine Spirit work such a change in the minds of men?" George A. Coe, *The Spiritual Life* (New York: Eaton & Mains, 1900), p. 17.

20. Coe, *The Spiritual Life*, pp. 146-47.

21. Tamura, *The Child the Center of Christianity*, pp. 73-74. On suggestibility, see Coe, *The Spiritual Life*, pp. 128-37, 144-50.

22. Tamura Naomi, *Miscellaneous Thoughts on Pastoral Ministry* [in Japanese] (Tokyo: Taisho Kindergarten Publishing, 1928), p. 90.

23. Tamura, *Miscellaneous Thoughts on Pastoral Ministry*, pp. 91-92.

24. Tamura, *The Child the Center of Christianity*, p. 74. The association between sexual instinct and religious experience and the distinction between the religious experience of groups and individuals reflect Tamura's reading of Hall, James, Starbuck, Coe, and others.

25. Coe, *The Spiritual Life*, p. 215. In *A Social Theory of Religious Education*, Coe further refines what he means by a symmetry between all the faculties of the mind. He calls for a "socialized evangelicalism that *will not separate emotion from study or from action.* And because *it will maintain these three in vital unity,* it will obliterate the gulf that has existed between child and man, between religious education and religious experience" (italics mine). Coe, *A Social Theory of Religious Education*, p. 328.

26. While Coe later vehemently denied the rubric "practical theology" to describe what he was doing in religious education, in *The Spiritual Life*, he uses the classical practical theological terms "cure of souls" or "care of souls" to make explicit his reasons for correlating the findings of empirical science (developmental psychology) with religious experience. "Why should not the care of souls become an art — a system of organized and proportioned methods based upon definite knowledge of the material to be wrought upon, the ends to be

attained, and the means and instruments for attaining them? Such an art would require scientific insight into the general organization of the mind, and especially into the particular characteristics of the child mind, the youth mind, and the adult mind." Coe, *The Spiritual Life,* p. 21.

27. One reason that Sunday Schools so greatly outnumbered churches was that, as part of their evangelistic strategy, the mission schools and missionaries often founded Sunday Schools independently of churches. *Proceedings of the General Conference of Protestant Missionaries in Japan held in Tokyo, October 1900.*

28. Even as late as 1938, for example, only one-half (950 out of 1874) of all Protestant churches were listed as "self-supporting." Charles Igleheart, ed., *The Japan Christian Yearbook 1938* (Tokyo: Kyobunkan, 1938), pp. 376-77.

29. In 1883, the missions reported 109 Sunday Schools with 4,132 pupils as compared with 93 churches with 4,987 members. *Proceedings of the General Conference of the Protestant Missionaries in Japan held at Osaka, April 1883.*

30. August Karl Reischauer, *The Task in Japan* (New York: Revell, 1926), p. 177.

31. This Confucian term means selfless devotion for the public good.

32. While I could have chosen the term "pre-establishment," I chose "pre-Constantinian" to indicate the analogy between the minority status of the Japanese churches and the Gentile churches of the Greco-Roman empire prior to the legitimation of Christianity in the fourth century. The tension in the New Testament and pre-Constantinian churches between loyalty to Christ and loyalty to the Emperor is analogous to the experience of the Japanese converts in the Meiji period. Given the especially volatile relations of the new nation-state and the tiny church, Japanese Christians were hard-pressed to demonstrate that their love for God did not in any way undermine their love for their country.

33. In 1891, the population was around 40 million and in 1912, around 50 million.

34. *World-Wide Sunday School Work,* p. 347.

35. The "First Sabbath School" was established in 1864 for the earliest missionary children. *The Journey of the Church School in Japan,* p. 26.

36. See Coe's trenchant analysis of evangelicalism in *A Social Theory of Religious Education,* pp. 324-34, and Mary C. Boys, *Educating in Faith: Maps and Visions* (Kansas City: Sheed & Ward, 1989), pp. 13-38.

37. Friedrich Schleiermacher, *Brief Outline of Theology as a Field of Study,* trans. Terrence N. Tice (Lewiston, NY: Edward Mellen Press, 1988), p. 133.

38. See Chan Wing-Tsit, trans., *A Sourcebook in Chinese Philosophy* (Princeton: Princeton University Press, 1963).

39. Lamin Sanneh, *Translating the Message: The Missionary Impact on Culture* (New York: Orbis, 1989), p. 1.

40. The Constantinian shift may be characterized as the church's loss of its identity as an alternative polis or its tendency to identify itself with the world "as its spiritual form." Harvey says that the Cartesian shift "jettisoned the eschatological framework of early Christianity altogether, along with the ecclesial practices and relationships that sought (albeit imperfectly) to bind life in the saeculum to its beginning and end in the mystery of God's providential design." Barry Harvey, *Another City: An Ecclesiological Primer for a Post-Christian World* (Harrisburg, PA: Trinity Press International, 1999), p. 104.

41. Tamura Naomi, *Twentieth-Century Sunday School* [in Japanese] (Tokyo: Keiseisha,

1907), pp. 1-2. Because the *Twentieth-Century Sunday School* is so thorough in its programmatic scope and is so clear a demonstration of Tamura's creative practical theological use of both the theoretical and practical resources that the North American religious education movement had deemed best, I have provided a detailed synopsis of the book in Appendix B.

42. Tamura Naomi, *The Rights of Children* [in Japanese] (Tokyo: Keiseisha, 1907), pp. 6-8. I have provided a translation of the table of contents in Appendix C.

43. As the first Japanese graduate, Tamura (class of 1886) was Kagawa's (class of 1916) *senpai* (senior) at Princeton Theological Seminary. Also, in addition to his many social and church activities, Kagawa was a leader in the religious education movement in which Tamura was highly respected as a charismatic founder.

44. Tamura, *The Rights of Children*, pp. 6-8.

45. Tamura, *The Rights of Children*, preface. In the preface, he goes on to state his purpose for writing this book. "I will have no greater joy than if this book is lovingly read in Japanese families, and parents are enabled to fulfill their duty as parents by recognizing the rights of their children, loving, respecting, and educating them well."

46. Tamura, *The Child the Center of Christianity*, p. 53.

47. For a contemporary *apologia* for the Meiji family structure, see Takakusa Junjiro, "The Social and Ethical Value of the Family System in Japan," *International Journal of Ethics* 17, no. 1 (October 1906): 100-106.

48. As evidence that he was, in part, wishing to avoid a recurrence of *The Japanese Bride* incident, Tamura published *The Rights of Children* only in Japanese. Presumably to avoid every hint of any accusation of seeking to defame Japan's honor in the eyes of the West, Tamura even left off his characteristic English title on the cover. As we have already mentioned, Tamura reports that this book was strongly criticized in spite of these precautions.

49. Tamura, *Twentieth-Century Sunday School*, pp. 1-2. He goes on to touch on the recent, momentous developments in religious education in the United States. "In the United States, at the famous Union Theological Seminary, a professor of child studies and education (Coe) has become the principal in their so-called school of religion, which meets every Sunday in the chapel and classrooms of the seminary. This clearly indicates that the importance of the religious education of children is beginning to be recognized in the United States. As Dr. Bushnell said fifty years ago, 'Instead of prophetically producing believers, we should nurture them.' Children are born with the innate capacity for religious faith, and it is upon the basis of this psychological instinct that we should engage in the great responsibility of religious education" (pp. 2-3). See Harris H. Parker, "The Union School of Religion, 1910-1929: Embers from the Fires of Progressivism," *Religious Education* 86, no. 4 (Fall 1991): 597-607.

50. Coe, *A Social Theory of Religious Education*, p. 6.

51. Coe, *A Social Theory of Religious Education*, p. 55.

52. "The religious education movement . . . has been working all along upon the central issue of the present moment, the issue of democracy." George A. Coe, "The Religious Education Movement in Retrospect," *Religious Education* 39 (July-August 1944): 223, quoted in Stephen A. Schmidt, *A History of the Religious Education Association* (Birmingham, AL: Religious Education Press, 1983), p. 37.

53. If Tamura's conviction of the superiority of Christianity over the other religions of Japan sounds strange to some contemporary Western readers, perhaps Furuya's recent article

titled "The American Church and the Japanese Church: Who Is First and Who Is Last?" will help shed some light on the perspective of Japanese Christians like Tamura. In this article, Furuya reflects on his long-term experience of teaching his "Theology of Religion" course at Princeton Theological Seminary. While acknowledging that Christians surely have some important things to learn from the study of other religions, he is highly critical of the facile religious pluralism that he sees behind the "mainline" U.S. Protestant churches' loss of evangelical ecumenical nerve. "I do not think that it is a good thing that the U.S. churches have lost interest in world evangelism. The Japanese church, which is largely made up of converts from other religions or no religion, resolutely reject the religious pluralists who say that all religions are the same. As there is a continuum from the superb to the appalling within Christianity itself, so it is with all religions. The problem with religious pluralism is that it offers no way to distinguish the good from the bad in religions. What about Aum Shinrikyo or Japanese state Shinto, which forced Koreans to participate in shrine worship during World War II? The evangelistic mission of the Japanese church is focused not on Christianity as one religion among others, and certainly not on American Christianity, but on the gospel of Jesus Christ." Furuya Yasuo, *Japanese Christianity* [in Japanese] (Tokyo: Kyobunkan, 2003), pp. 44-45.

54. Tamura Naomi, *The Principles and Practice of Religious Education* [in Japanese] (Tokyo: Keiseisha, 1920), p. 136.

55. Coe, *A Social Theory of Religious Education*, p. 18.

56. This is the Latin form of Luther's much-used word *Anfechtung*, a key term in his *theologia cruxis*. This rich word refers to the testing, persecution, or suffering of the Christian for the cause of the cross of Christ. As Robert Kelly points out, Luther saw *tentatio* as a necessary experience in the training of a theologian. "The necessity of *tentatio* also means that the theologian in formation must learn to center all her/his theology on the crucified Jesus as God most visible. Any other center for theology will only result in a speculative theology of glory." Robert A. Kelly, "Oratio, Meditatio, Tentatio Faciunt Theologum: Luther's Piety and the Formation of Theologians," *Consensus* 19, no. 1 (1993): 18. See also *Luther's Works: The American Edition* (Philadelphia and St. Louis: Fortress and Concordia, 1955), 34:286-87.

57. "The people to whom a human nexus is important place great moral emphasis upon complete and willing dedication of the self to others in a specific human collective. . . . Self-dedication to a specific human nexus has been one of the most powerful factors in Japanese history." Nakamura Hajime, *Ways of Thinking of Eastern Peoples: India, China, Tibet, Japan* (Honolulu: University of Hawaii Press, 1964), p. 415.

58. Nakamura, *Ways of Thinking of Eastern Peoples*, p. 415.

59. See my discussion of Judas and the differing views of self in Japan and the United States in Chapter Six.

60. Tamura, *Fifty Years of Faith*, p. 2.

61. Tamura, *Fifty Years of Faith*, pp. 239-40.

62. Tamura, *Fifty Years of Faith*, p. 11.

63. See James E. Loder, *The Transforming Moment* (Colorado Springs: Helmers & Howard, 1989), p. 41.

64. "Religious education is not a temporary thing. It is a huge project that needs to be undertaken with a one-hundred-year plan in mind." Tamura, *The Principles and Practice of Religious Education*, pp. 100-101.

65. Stanley Hauerwas, *With the Grain of the Universe: The Church's Witness and Natural Theology* (Grand Rapids: Brazos, 2001).

66. He goes on to conclude, "the Protestant culture that made Niebuhr intelligible no longer exists, which is not to say, exactly, that it has been defeated, but that we are no longer surrounded by the spoils of its victory." Hauerwas, *With the Grain of the Universe,* p. 139.

67. See George A. Coe, *The Psychology of Religion* (Chicago: University of Chicago Press, 1916).

68. See Coe's references to missions in *A Social Theory of Religious Education* and Andrew Walls, "The Nineteenth-Century Missionary as Scholar" and "Humane Learning and the Missionary Movement," in *The Missionary Movement in Christian History: Studies in the Transmission of Faith* (Maryknoll, NY: Orbis, 1996).

69. Coe, *A Social Theory of Religious Education,* pp. 54ff.

70. Coe, *A Social Theory of Religious Education,* p. 54.

71. While a public intellectual humiliation of sorts came later to the North American religious education movement at the hands of the followers of Barth and Brunner, for example, when H. Shelton Smith abandoned the REM, it is not at all clear that this academic assault led to a transformational experience of *tentatio* for the discipline of religious education. But that is getting beyond our story.

72. For example, *The Mother and Child* (1904) and *Early Childhood Education* (1904).

73. The graded lessons were a child-friendly, developmentally graded answer to the more commonly used Uniform Lessons.

74. Tamura, *Fifty Years of Faith,* p. 295.

75. Tamura Naomi, *Sunday School Lessons Graded Series: Outline of Bible Stories, Primary Course First Year* [in Japanese] (Tokyo: Kyobunkan, 1912), fourth edition.

76. Tamura, *Fifty Years of Faith,* pp. 292-93.

77. Since the work of the NSSA was to be underwritten by a substantial unrestricted annual gift of $1,000 from American businessman Henry Heinz, money undoubtedly was a significant factor in the political struggles recounted here.

78. Tamura, *Fifty Years of Faith,* pp. 293, 337. While a fiercely independent and sometimes anti-missionary spirit was not uncommon among contemporary Japanese Christian leaders like Uemura and Uchimura, Tamura seems to have adopted the "Japanese principle" for pragmatic rather than emotional reasons. Throughout his life, he maintained positive relations with many missionaries and American friends he had made while a student in the 1880s. He called the United States his "second home" and says he could never forget the many benefits he had received from America and his American friends, perhaps most especially the moral support he received from the missionaries during *The Japanese Bride* debacle.

79. Tamura, *Fifty Years of Faith,* pp. 294-95.

80. Tamura, *Fifty Years of Faith,* p. 307.

81. Tamura, *Fifty Years of Faith,* p. 308.

82. Tamura, *Fifty Years of Faith,* p. 309.

83. Tamura, *Fifty Years of Faith,* pp. 310-11.

84. Tamura, *Fifty Years of Faith,* p. 307.

85. The report says that, at the 1893 meeting, "Mr. Thomas J. Belcher threw down a silver dollar and said it was for Japan. The secretary took up the dollar and said: 'Are there any others? This looks very practical.' A plate was passed, and three hundred and twenty-three

dollars were placed on it. That was the beginning of the interest in the World's Sunday School Association in Japan." *The Sunday School and World Progress: The Official Book of the Eighth World's Sunday School Convention, Held in Tokyo, Japan, October 5-14, 1920,* ed. John T. Faris (New York: World's Sunday School Association, 1921), p. 11.

86. Kobayashi Koichi, *The Background of Christian Education* [in Japanese] (Tokyo: Yorudansha, 1979), p. 247.

87. Andrew F. Walls, "From Christendom to World Christianity," in *The Cross-Cultural Process in Christian History* (New York: Orbis, 2002), p. 51. The original lectures may be found in James Dennis, *Foreign Missions After a Century,* Students' Lectures on Missions, Princeton Theological Seminary, 1893 (New York: Revell, 1893).

88. *The Sunday School and World Progress,* p. 2.

89. *The Sunday School and World Progress,* p. 12.

90. *The Sunday School and World Progress,* p. 16.

91. *The Sunday School and World Progress,* p. 17.

92. Hane Mikiso, *Modern Japan: A Historical Survey* (Boulder and London: Westview, 1986), pp. 157-62. Hane reports that Uchimura Kanzo, the Christian leader who was the target of extreme criticism for the *Lese Majesty Incident,* supported the Sino-Japanese War "as a just war that was being fought to assist Korea against Chinese oppression" (p. 160).

93. Gerald E. Knoff, *The World Sunday School Movement: The Story of a Broadening Mission* (New York: Seabury, 1979), pp. 83-84.

94. *The Sunday School and World Progress,* p. 21.

95. Beginning with the so-called Manchurian or Mukden Incident of 1931, which gave Japan a rationale for annexing Manchuria.

96. *The Sunday School and World Progress,* pp. 339, 342-43.

97. Tamura, *Fifty Years of Faith,* p. 314.

98. Tamura, *Fifty Years of Faith,* pp. 314-15.

99. Then Prime Minister, Mr. Hara, had even offered the National Diet (Parliament) building. *The Sunday School and World Progress,* p. 41.

100. Tamura, *Fifty Years of Faith,* p. 315.

101. *The Sunday School and World Progress,* pp. 243-44.

102. *The Sunday School and World Progress,* pp. 246-48.

Notes to Chapter Five

1. The last words of the preface read, "I want to make this book public this year since the World Sunday School Convention will be held in our beloved Tokyo." Tamura Naomi, *The Principles and Practice of Religious Education* [in Japanese] (Tokyo: Keiseisha, 1920), p. 2.

2. Tamura, *The Principles and Practice of Religious Education,* p. 2.

3. While Kitoku Kazuo's 1932 *The Principles of Religious Education* is the most thorough academic treatment of religious education theory in Japanese, it is wooden and mimetic compared to Tamura's creative practical theological approach. Though Kitoku had actually studied with Coe at Union and Columbia University in the 1920s, he clearly lacked the great passion and creative practical theological vision of Tamura.

4. At the end of the book, he mentions three Japanese books that had already appeared

on the subject of religious education: Tanimoto's *The Principles of Religious Education,* Itoh's *The Foundations of Religious Education of Children,* and Kan's *Religious Education and Sunday School Based on Child Studies.* Since all three of these books exceed five hundred pages and cover the topic of religious education with a thoroughness not seen in the Western literature, Tamura says, "From this point of view, we might conclude that Japanese are ahead of Westerners in research in this field." This claim certainly warrants further investigation. Tamura, *The Principles and Practice of Religious Education,* p. 147.

5. Tamura, *The Principles and Practice of Religious Education,* p. 1.

6. Mullins calls the missionary approach a "displacement theology." Mullins, *Christianity Made in Japan,* p. 36.

7. Stuart D. Hoffman, "School Texts, the Written Word, and Political Indoctrination: A Review of Moral Education Curricula in Modern Japan (1886-1997)," *History of Education* 28, no. 1 (March 1999): 89.

8. Tamura Naomi, "Christianity and Politics," in *Research on the Tsukiji Band,* Miura Tadashi [in Japanese] (Tokyo: Sugamo Church, 1986), p. 79.

9. Tamura, "Christianity and Politics," pp. 104-5.

10. Steven, *The Psychology of a Christian Soul,* quoted without reference in Tamura, *The Principles and Practice of Religious Education,* p. 2.

11. See George A. Coe, *The Religion of a Mature Mind* (Chicago: Revell, 1902).

12. George A. Coe, *The Psychology of Religion,* quoted without full reference in Tamura, *The Principles and Practice of Religious Education,* p. 7.

13. Tamura, *The Principles and Practice of Religious Education,* p. 11.

14. Tamura, *The Principles and Practice of Religious Education,* p. 11.

15. Gerben Heitink, *Practical Theology: History, Theory, Action Domains* (Grand Rapids: Eerdmans, 1999), pp. 29-30 (see chap. 1, n. 83).

16. Tamura, *The Principles and Practice of Religious Education,* pp. 15-16.

17. In place of reason, emotion, and will, Augustine found psychological vestiges of the Trinity in human memory, understanding, and will. See Edmund Hill's translation of Saint Augustine, *The Trinity* (Brooklyn: New City Press, 1991), 4:30, 10:17-19, 14:8, 10.

18. See David S. Cunningham, "Toward a Rehabilitation of the Vestigia Tradition," in James J. Buckley and David S. Yeago, eds., *Knowing the Triune God: The Work of the Spirit in the Practices of the Church* (Grand Rapids: Eerdmans, 2001), pp. 179-202.

19. Tamura, *The Principles and Practice of Religious Education,* p. 16.

20. Tamura, *The Principles and Practice of Religious Education,* p. 17.

21. See George A. Coe, *The Psychology of Religion* (Chicago: University of Chicago Press, 1916), pp. 144ff.

22. Tamura, *The Principles and Practice of Religious Education,* pp. 18-19.

23. Tamura, *The Principles and Practice of Religious Education,* p. 21.

24. Tamura, *The Principles and Practice of Religious Education,* pp. 23-24.

25. Tamura, *The Principles and Practice of Religious Education,* p. 24.

26. Tamura, *The Principles and Practice of Religious Education,* pp. 24-25.

27. Tamura, *The Principles and Practice of Religious Education,* p. 26.

28. Tamura's passionate words are particularly poignant considering the fact that they were penned soon after his defeat at the hands of the missionary-led NSSA over his contextualized graded lessons.

29. Tamura, *The Principles and Practice of Religious Education*, p. 25.

30. Tamura, *The Principles and Practice of Religious Education*, p. 29.

31. Tamura Naomi, *Fifty Years of Faith* [in Japanese] (Tokyo: Keiseisha, 1924), p. 313.

32. See George A. Coe, *A Social Theory of Religious Education* (New York: Charles Scribner's Sons, 1917), pp. 149ff.

33. Tamura, *The Principles and Practice of Religious Education*, pp. 30-31.

34. Tamura, *The Principles and Practice of Religious Education*, pp. 37-38.

35. George A. Coe, *The Religion of a Mature Mind* (Chicago: Revell, 1902), pp. 170-72.

36. Tamura, *The Principles and Practice of Religious Education*, p. 39. A contemporary comparison between Japanese ethics and Christian doctrine by Harada Tasuku sheds light on Tamura's attraction to the Gethsemane prayer. "The life of Christ is an example of the victory of *giri* (duty) over *ninjo* (natural affection). The temptations of Satan were all addressed to the natural feelings of Christ as a man; but Christ, discerning clearly what duty demanded, overcame them. Again, when Christ prayed: 'O my Father, if it is possible, let this cup pass from me,' He gave expression to His natural feeling; but when He added 'nevertheless not as I will, but as Thou wilt,' He conquered them by His sense of duty. This is an explanation which, I think, is readily understood by the Japanese. Such theological statements as that the cross of Christ is an atonement, offered up for appeasing God's wrath, find very reluctant acceptance from the Japanese. But if we explain the cross from the standpoint of self-sacrifice, it presents no special difficulty to them." Harada Tasuku, "Japanese Character and Christianity: A Study of Japanese Ethical Ideals as Compared with Teaching of Christianity," *Pacific Affairs* 2, no. 11 (November 1929): 693-98.

37. Coe, *The Religion of a Mature Mind*, p. 408.

38. From my critique of the norms of contemporary North American practical theologians in Chapter One, it is clear that the Westerncentric norms of the modernist epistemology still dominate this field.

39. Tamura, *The Principles and Practice of Religious Education*, p. 40.

40. Tamura, *The Principles and Practice of Religious Education*, p. 49.

41. Tamura, *The Principles and Practice of Religious Education*, pp. 43-44.

42. Tamura, *The Principles and Practice of Religious Education*, p. 44.

43. Tamura, *The Principles and Practice of Religious Education*, p. 44.

44. Tamura, *The Principles and Practice of Religious Education*, p. 45.

45. Tamura, *The Principles and Practice of Religious Education*, p. 46.

46. Tamura, *The Principles and Practice of Religious Education*, p. 48.

47. Tamura, *The Principles and Practice of Religious Education*, pp. 49-50.

48. Coe, for example, called the teaching of dogma via the catechism "intellectualistic drill processes." Coe, *A Social Theory of Religious Education*, p. 305.

49. Tamura, *The Principles and Practice of Religious Education*, p. 53.

50. Tamura, *The Principles and Practice of Religious Education*, p. 57.

51. The fact that *The Child the Center of Christianity* was his first book published in English since *The Japanese Bride* suggests that the aging Tamura wanted to take his more mature practical theological research, criticisms, experiments, and proposed "rules of art" to the bar of a broader, ecumenical reading public.

52. In his characteristically polemical approach, Tamura does not mince words in his descriptive/interpretive account of the missionary-founded churches. "Child nurture has in

NOTES TO PAGES 124-25

NOTES TO PAGES 124-25

large measure been neglected in the Christian work in Japan. Missionaries and native teachers and preachers, lacking a strong conviction of the importance of this work for children, have devoted time and money to hardened sinners. They preach only a negative gospel. What is the result? Come and see in our churches." Tamura, *The Child the Center of Christianity* (Tokyo: Taisho Kindergarten Publishing, 1926), p. 4. He also said, "Sad to say, our Japanese churches are not paying their debt to childhood. Where is there the Christian church in Japan that looks carefully after their spiritual welfare? Native preachers and missionary are alike cool toward children. They will pray and even fast for the conversion of grown people, but how seldom do we hear in our pulpits prayers for children!" (p. 23). Reflecting the strong teacher-disciple tradition of East Asia, Tamura tellingly does not lay the entire blame for this lack of interest in children with the missionaries, but goes beyond them to criticize the seminary professors of the missionaries. For example, he recalls reading Renan's *Life of Jesus* when he was a seminarian in the United States, but confesses that he didn't even notice Renan's positive appraisal of the child and child-like people. Blaming his Auburn and Princeton seminary professors for this blatant oversight, he says, "We were taught by learned professors who emphasized the 'Narrow Gate' and the importance of inducing adult sinners to enter" (p. 33).

53. Tamura, *The Child the Center of Christianity,* p. 57.

54. Tamura, *The Child the Center of Christianity,* p. 57.

55. Tamura, *The Child the Center of Christianity,* p. 57.

56. Tamura, *The Child the Center of Christianity,* p. 58.

57. Tamura, *The Child the Center of Christianity,* p. 58.

58. W. Robertson Nicoll, *The Incarnate Saviour: A Life of Jesus Christ* (Edinburgh: T. & T. Clark, 1897).

59. Tamura, *The Child the Center of Christianity,* p. 59.

60. Of course, the concept of habit is treated extensively by Coe. See Coe, *A Social Theory of Religious Education,* pp. 32, 69, 133ff., 151ff., 165, 170ff., 306ff., 331ff. Tamura's emphasis on the cultivation of a devotional habit as a central task of religious education is ultimately indebted to the New England theology of Jonathan Edwards, as mediated by Horace Bushnell, the evangelical missionaries, and the religious education movement. Written in the aftermath of the revivals of the eighteenth century, Edwards's classic *The Religious Affections,* which sets out to discern, on biblical, theological, and philosophical grounds, the false from the "truly gracious and holy affections" is a forerunner to Bushnell and the psychology of religion literature which gave empirical credence to the religious education movement. See Jonathan Edwards, *The Religious Affections* (Edinburgh: Banner of Truth, 2001).

61. Smart's summary of Coe's theology could easily be applied to Tamura: "a rather thin doctrine of divine immanence, a belief in the naturalness of Christian growth, a blissful confidence in the goodness of man, and a Unitarian conception of Jesus Christ." James Smart, *The Teaching Ministry of the Church* (Philadelphia: Westminster, 1954), p. 58. As a testimony to the degree to which Japanese Protestant theology was current with global ecumenical developments, it is worth noting that the German dialectical critique of *Evangelisch Pädagogik* was articulated in 1935 by Kuwata Hidenobu, one year after Tamura's death. Kuwata based his critique mainly on Emil Brunner's *Das Gebot und Die Ordnungen: Entwurf Einer Protestantisch-Theologischen Ethik.* Kuwata Hidenobu, "Religious Education in Evangelical Perspective: In Search of Principles for Christian Religious Education," in *Collected Works of Kuwata*

Hidenobu [in Japanese] (Tokyo: Kirisutokyo Shinbunsha, 1977), 4:242-56. I still think that the most enduring, comprehensive, and balanced North American critique of the REM's theology is H. Shelton Smith's *Faith and Nurture.* However, while Smith brilliantly criticizes the romantic personalism and immanentalism of the REM, his own neo-Orthodox views are not untainted by the North American *habitus.* For example, while criticizing Coe and the REM for reducing sin to a social phenomenon, he says that the real source of sin is "in the private order of the human self." While the REM's view of sin erred in the social direction, Smith's "private" "self" exegesis is also theologically anachronistic. Also, while his stinging critique of the North American church sounds surprisingly contemporary, he fails to consider the missional charter of the church and perpetuates the fatal dualism between the church's "essential nature and its empirical condition." This shows that the church in North America was just as much of a social, political, and cultural given to the neo-Orthodox Smith as it was to the liberal leaders of the REM. Thus, the modernist *ethos* of individualism and the social, political, and cultural situation of Protestant hegemony subtly colors Smith's biblical exegesis. H. Shelton Smith, *Faith and Nurture* (New York: Charles Scribner's Sons, 1942), pp. 97, 151.

62. Tamura, *The Child the Center of Christianity,* p. 13. While granting that the Pauline *paranesis* on child-rearing in Ephesians 6 and Colossians 3 is helpful, Tamura says, "If this were all the attention our New Testament gave to children the book would lose its attractiveness to both child and parent." Tamura concludes that Paul, in sharp contrast to Jesus, had almost no interest in the life of the child. While the textual comparison between the synoptics and the epistles may support such a claim, Tamura also naïvely projects his own polemic against revivalism onto the Pauline opus, saying, "Paul's theology treats children as wicked sinners for whom hell fires are waiting. His heart is not warm toward pure and loving childhood" (p. 14). Next, borrowing from David Smith's psychological portrait of the pre-conversion Paul in his *The Life and Letters of Paul* (London: Hodder & Stoughton, 1919), Tamura speculates that Paul's personal "bitter and tragic" family experiences may account for his almost total neglect of the family. He also draws on G. Oswald Griffith's *St. Paul's Life of Christ* (London: George Dornan, 1924), which argues the existence of a "striking contrast between the Christ of Paul and the Christ of the gospels." He draws on R. H. Fisher's *Religious Experience,* saying, "Jesus said little about sin with a capital 'S,' though he has much to say about particular sins. The word sin occurs 40 times in Paul's *Romans* and only three times in the synoptic gospels. As we approach the mind of the Master we are impressed with the feeling that he did not brood over the sinfulness of human nature with half the intensity of Paul's brooding. His look was forward, not backward; not forgiveness of the past so much as bringing in the Kingdom of God in the future" (p. 15). On the one hand, Tamura's personal painful childhood experience likely sensitized him to the complex psychological dynamics operative in families. On the other hand, Tamura's tendency to resort to anachronism to score rhetorical points for his cause undermines his so-called "scientific" approach.

63. His reading of the Great Commission of Matthew 28 underlines this opposition between preaching and teaching. "It is a pity that the Christian church did not catch the full import of this commandment. It was more than 'preach the gospel to all nations.' Twice He commands to 'Teach.' Christian education was the heart of His commandment. Renan says that 'Disciple' and 'Child' in Aramaic are very nearly synonymous. We cannot successfully train disciples until we begin with the children. Childhood is the golden time for teaching devotion to Jesus. We must not miss this epochal period. Christ's last injunction is to teach the

child and make him a disciple. Jesus thus lays stress on this task from the very beginning of his public ministry to its close. Teaching and nurturing the child is the burden of his thought. The child is the center of Christianity." Tamura, *The Child the Center of Christianity,* pp. 99-100. Tamura's reading of the Great Commission may not sound particularly controversial or even novel to readers today; however, we can easily imagine how it might have offended many of Japan's Protestant missionaries and native pastors in 1925. Since Japan had been a coveted objective of missionary aspirations since the 1860s, Tamura's claim that educating children was a higher priority to Jesus than evangelizing adults would surely have agitated his adversaries. Mission historian David Bosch carefully examines the complex exegetical history of Matthew's Great Commission, the *ur text* for the modern missionary movement. He says that especially during the late nineteenth century, as conservative reaction to the rationality of the Enlightenment was gaining momentum, "the theme of obedience to the 'Great Commission' indeed tended to drown all other motifs." David J. Bosch, *Transforming Mission: Paradigm Shifts in Theology of Mission* (New York: Orbis, 1991), p. 341. While many of the missionaries in Japan would have read the Great Commission as the unambiguous biblical summons to overseas mission, and many of the native pastors would have read it as a call to evangelize Japanese adults, Tamura's admittedly somewhat anachronistic reading may be more contextually appropriate, especially when you remember that he always linked building up the church to the Christianization of the nation. Commenting on the exegetical latitude in interpreting the Great Commission, Andrew Walls says, "The associations of such words will be different in different parts of the human auditorium." Andrew Walls, "The Transmission of Christian Faith," in *The Missionary Movement in Christian History: Studies in the Transmission of Faith* (Maryknoll, NY: Orbis, 1996), pp. 48-49.

64. Tamura rejects such a view on the basis of his own experience and his reading of the psychology of religion literature, countering that "Difference in temperament, environment, and spiritual perceptions create different types of conversion, but we have been slow to discover this." Tamura, *The Child the Center of Christianity,* p. 69.

65. While praising the work of evangelists, he quotes Henry Drummond who says, "Christianity is not simply a religion for rebuilding human ruins, but even more emphatically and essentially a religion for preventing men and women from becoming ruined." Again, he quotes Gladstone who says, "To reform is a noble work, but to form is nobler." He criticizes the Japanese churches for allocating more resources to the "noble" work of evangelism than to the "nobler" work of education. Tamura, *The Child the Center of Christianity,* pp. 17, 19.

66. This liberal view of sin was more in keeping with Tamura's ethical Confucian heritage than with the Reformed faith of the missionaries or his theological professors at Auburn and Princeton. Chapter fourteen, "The Child is the Son of God," sheds more light on Tamura's struggle with the Pauline view of sin. He naïvely asserts that while Paul (and Augustine, Luther, and Wesley) made no distinctions between children and adults, "Jesus never called children sinners. He respected them as Sons of God" (p. 51). I will touch on his Confucian interpretation of this phrase, "Sons of God," later. For a helpful contemporary comparison of Japanese ethics and Christian doctrine, see Harada, "Japanese Character and Christianity," pp. 693-98.

67. As James Smart says in his nuanced critique of the REM, "We shall be more charitable in our attitude toward their theological delinquencies if we recollect that, in the American Church of 1903, the only clear-cut theologies in which men believed with passion were

the two extremes of liberalism and fundamentalism. Those who stood somewhere between had, as yet, no spokesman who could make his voice heard on behalf of a valid third possibility." Smart, *The Teaching Ministry of the Church,* p. 59.

68. Tamura, *The Child the Center of Christianity,* p. 2.

69. In a fanciful isogetical excursus, Tamura says that Jesus "was a frequent visitor in the home of Peter in Capernaum. Coming here, weary from a day of teaching and healing and improving the multitude of opportunities for doing good, He was greeted at the door by Peter's children. They climbed upon His knees, and were happily, childishly familiar with their dear Friend. A home full of children was a Paradise to Jesus." *The Child the Center of Christianity,* p. 11.

70. Tamura, *The Child the Center of Christianity,* p. 5.

71. He expresses great interest in the post–World War I appearance in Europe and North America of numerous books on the life of Christ, because this popular genre tends to portray him in a much brighter light than the missionaries' version. The historical Jesus was such a passion to Tamura that, while he was not a biblical scholar per se, in his final years he took on the task of presenting Jesus in this "more scientific," historical light in *The Figure of Jesus of Nazareth* [in Japanese] (Tokyo: Keiseisha, 1930) and *The Background of Jesus of Nazareth* [in Japanese] (Tokyo: Keishosha, 1931). Not unlike other contemporary books in this genre, in *The Figure of Jesus of Nazareth,* Tamura readily dismisses the miraculous birth, the logos doctrine, the Trinity, and the new life as the dressing up of Jesus in the alien conceptualities of Greek philosophy. For example, referring to the recent visit to Japan of "the famous British scholar Stretcher," Tamura says, "His argument that, within Christology, the Father, Son, and Holy Spirit are three in one and one in three is completely ridiculous." *The Figure of Jesus of Nazareth,* p. 136.

Besides the devastating theological problems with this view of Jesus, Tamura's unambiguous support of the so-called "Liberal Lives of Jesus" genre makes him an easy target of Schweitzer's classical critique that this approach limited "the explanation of Jesus' actions and the events of his life to natural, psychological causes and motivations and completely ignored the profoundly eschatological setting of Jesus' teachings and actions." Richard N. Soulen, *Handbook of Biblical Criticism* (Atlanta: John Knox, 1976), p. 139.

72. Tamura, *The Child the Center of Christianity,* p. 8.

73. He writes, "It is a sad fact that although Christ discovered the child's true value nearly 2000 years ago, men have so generally lost interest in children and crowded them back into the shadow. Today the child is coming to the front. Great universities have professorships of child psychology" (*The Child the Center of Christianity,* pp. 7-8). Reflecting the religious education movement's positive view of the relation between science and religion, Tamura sees modern trends in biblical studies and the social sciences as supporting a reconsideration of this long-forgotten aspect of Jesus. A North American exemplar of this approach was William Rainey Harper who, according to Stephen Schmidt, "spent the majority of his adult life concerned with developing an agreeable scientific partnership between biblical criticism and traditional Christian understandings and pieties." Schmidt, *A History of the Religious Education Association* (Birmingham, AL: Religious Education Press, 1983), pp. 11-12.

74. James E. Loder, *The Transforming Moment* (Colorado Springs: Helmers & Howard, 1989), pp. 161-66, and *The Logic of the Spirit: Human Development in Theological Perspective* (San Francisco: Jossey-Bass, 1998), pp. 118-22. Interestingly, in contrast to Tamura, who fo-

cuses on the gospel accounts of Jesus, Loder's transformational model unwittingly emphasizes the Pauline strata of the New Testament. Thus, in very different material, or missional conditions, both Loder and Tamura give in to the either/or modernist rationality that undermines the rich integrity and complexity of the Christian canon.

75. Tamura, *The Child the Center of Christianity,* p. 31.

76. Tamura, *The Child the Center of Christianity,* p. 88. This portrayal sounds surprisingly similar to James Fowler's description of those who have attained the "universalizing faith" of stage six according to his theory of faith development. "The rare persons who may be described at this stage have a special grace that makes them seem more lucid, more simple, and yet somehow more fully human than the rest of us. Their community is universal in extent." Fowler, *Stages of Faith: The Psychology of Human Development and the Quest for Meaning* (San Francisco: Harper & Row, 1981), p. 201. Tamura also considers Jesus' poetical ideas from a developmental perspective, saying that Jesus poetically addresses childhood, youth, and adulthood in order. "The child floats in a lyric world; the youth lives in the epic of the heroism of humanity; and the man (adult) lives his destiny tragically and dramatically." Tamura, *The Child the Center of Christianity,* p. 88.

77. He says, "We delight to see Him walking the radiant countryside of Palestine. He approaches the shore of Galilee and watches the fishers engaged in their daily task. 'Come after me and I will make you fishers of men.' Pointing to an oriental town on a hill crest he exclaims, 'A city set on a hill cannot be hid, neither do men light a candle and put it under a bushel.' 'Ye are the light of the world.' Seeing how strenuously men labor to accumulate a fortune he says 'Behold the fowls of the air; they sow not neither do they reap nor gather into barns, yet your Heavenly Father feeds them.' 'Consider the lilies of the field how they grow; They toil not neither do they spin, and yet I say unto you that Solomon in all his glory was not arrayed like one of these. Are ye not much better than they?'" Tamura, *The Child the Center of Christianity,* pp. 88-89.

78. Tamura, *The Child the Center of Christianity,* p. 89.

79. Tamura, *The Child the Center of Christianity,* p. 90.

80. Tamura tells the touching story of a Boston kindergartner who introduced herself as "Don't" on the first day of school. Over and over, she had heard her mother say "Don't do that," "Don't spoil that book," "Don't talk so loud," "Don't! Don't! Nothing but Don't" (*The Child the Center of Christianity,* p. 91). Loder has beautifully described the function of negation in developmental terms and the "negation of negation" in theological terms in *The Logic of the Spirit.*

81. Tamura, *The Child the Center of Christianity,* p. 91.

82. Such testimony was not unusual among the first generation of Japanese Protestants, who sometimes equated the Bushido heritage with the Old Testament law. Tamura refers to the Golden Rule as an example of the incongruities between the old and new ways, saying, "Confucius' rendering of the Golden Rule is prohibitive" while Jesus "puts it positively. 'Whatsoever ye would that men should do unto you, do ye even so unto them'" (*The Child the Center of Christianity,* pp. 91-92).

83. Tamura, *The Child the Center of Christianity,* p. 92.

84. Tamura, *The Child the Center of Christianity,* p. 92.

85. Tamura, *The Child the Center of Christianity,* p. 93.

86. Tamura, *The Child the Center of Christianity,* p. 94.

87. Tamura, *The Child the Center of Christianity*, p. 95.

88. Tamura's exegesis may be read as a proto-example of the contemporary post-critical, "cultural hermeneutic" approach in biblical studies that focuses on the social, cultural, ethnic, or gender "location" of the reader. See Fernando F. Segovia and Mary Ann Tolbert, eds., *Reading from This Place: Social Location and Biblical Interpretation in the United States* (Minneapolis: Fortress, 1995).

89. Tamura, *The Child the Center of Christianity*, p. 95.

90. Tamura, *The Child the Center of Christianity*, p. 96.

91. In Tamura's focus on the Son-Father relation in the passion narrative, he anticipates Kitamori Kazoh's post–World War II *The Theology of the Pain of God* (Richmond, VA: John Knox Press, 1965). See also Thomas John Hastings, "Kitamori Kazoh," in *A Dictionary of Asian Christianity*, ed. Scott W. Sunquist (Grand Rapids: Eerdmans, 2001).

92. Tamura, *The Child the Center of Christianity*, p. 97.

93. Tamura, *The Child the Center of Christianity*, p. 97.

94. Tamura, *The Child the Center of Christianity*, p. 97.

95. Tamura, *The Child the Center of Christianity*, p. 98.

96. Αληθησ Λογοσ, or *True Discourse* (c. 178 CE), is the oldest literary attack on Christianity. F. L. Cross, ed., *The Oxford Dictionary of the Christian Church* (Oxford: Oxford University Press, 1990), p. 260.

97. Tamura, *The Child the Center of Christianity*, p. 28. I have already mentioned the way that Japanese Buddhists had borrowed the Sunday School theories and methods from Tamura and other leaders.

98. Tamura, *The Child the Center of Christianity*, p. 37.

99. Tamura, *The Child the Center of Christianity*, p. 38.

100. Tamura, *The Child the Center of Christianity*, pp. 39-40.

101. One year before his death, Tamura wrote a fascinating article titled "Barthian Theology and Religious Education." See my translation in Appendix D.

102. This sounds very much like the "slow, vegetative growth" which is, according to Jaeger, exactly what the Greeks had in mind by their notion of *paideia*. Werner Jaeger, *Paideia*, trans. Gilbert Highet (Oxford: Basil Blackwell, 1939-1963), 2:228.

103. In spite of his sharp polemic against dramatic emotional conversions and his organic conception of the parent-child relation, Bushnell, in *Christian Nurture*, continued to hold to a strong Reformed doctrine of depravity, saying, for example, "The growth of Christian virtue is no vegetative process, no mere onward development. It involves a struggle with evil, a fall and a rescue." Horace Bushnell, *Christian Nurture* (Grand Rapids: Baker, 1979), p. 23.

104. Matsunaga Kikuo, "Theological Education in Japan," in *Preparing for Witness in Context: 1998 Cook Theological Seminar*, ed. Jean Stoner (Louisville: Presbyterian Church, 1999), p. 299.

Notes to Chapter Six

1. Again, for the most comprehensive neo-Orthodox critique of those theological norms, see H. Shelton Smith, *Faith and Nurture* (New York: Charles Scribner's Sons, 1942).

2. Thomas F. Torrance, *The Mediation of Christ* (Colorado Springs: Helmers & Howard, 1992), pp. 3-4.

3. Torrance, *The Mediation of Christ,* pp. 3-4.

4. Lamin Sanneh, *Translating the Message: The Missionary Impact on Culture* (New York: Orbis, 1989).

5. The laboratory school at Union may have been an honest attempt to bring the church to the academy, but the epistemology underlying this non-contextual approach is problematic.

6. See Chapter Three, note 97, above.

7. See Chapter Three, note 91, above.

8. Dohi Akio, "The First Generation: Christian Leaders in the First Period," in *A History of Japanese Theology,* ed. Furuya Yasuo (Grand Rapids: Eerdmans, 1997), p. 25.

9. Dohi, "The First Generation," pp. 25-26.

10. Dohi, "The First Generation," p. 26.

11. See Tamura Naomi, *Uemura Masahisa and Uchimura Kanzo as I Remember Them* [in Japanese] (Tokyo: Mukoyamadoshobo, 1932).

12. Samuel P. Huntington, *The Clash of Civilizations and the Remaking of World Order* (New York: Simon & Schuster, 1996).

13. Schleiermacher, *Brief Outline of Theology as a Field of Study,* p. 133.

14. On this point, I must confess that Roman Catholic theologians have been much more ecumenical than Protestant theologians.

15. The concluding section of this chapter is an attempt to tease out some of the differences in how the self is construed in Japan and the United States.

16. John Calvin, *Institutes of the Christian Religion* (Philadelphia: Westminster Press, 1960), p. 35.

17. Calvin, *Institutes,* p. 36.

18. See Robert Jay Lifton's comments on Adler, Rank, and Jung, the so-called "disciples-turned-heretics" of Freud. Robert Jay Lifton, *The Protean Self: Human Resilience in an Age of Fragmentation* (San Francisco: Basic, 1993), pp. 24ff.

19. As an example of how Western theories don't quite fit the Japanese context, Alan Roland offers the following criticism of Erik Erikson's theory: "Erik Erikson interrelates social, cultural, and historical dimensions with the varied needs and challenges of the psychosocial dimensions of development throughout the life cycle, as he systematically elaborated these in his developmental schema. There is much to commend in this approach. The only problem is that in cross-cultural and psychohistorical interdisciplinary work in India and Japan it doesn't fully work. The tightly organized sections don't fit together. Why? Because Erikson systematized and universalized a developmental schema that is completely based on the data of Western personality. Strivings for autonomy and initiative in young children, or the identity crises, moratoria, and syntheses of adolescence and young adulthood may be central to American, and even Western development, but they certainly are not to Indian and Japanese development. His schema not only emphasizes what is not central to their development, but completely omits what is paramount — such as the child's reactions to the active encouragement of dependency needs in the earlier phases of childhood, and the child's negotiation of the severe crackdown on behavior in familial hierarchical relationships from ages four or five through adolescence. In effect, Erikson has kept his section of the pot

too intact to fit in with the cultural, social, and historical dimensions of these societies. In psychohistorical and cross-cultural work in India and Japan, the psychological section has to be considerably modified in order to interrelate with other dimensions of reality." Roland, *In Search of Self in India and Japan: Toward a Cross-Cultural Psychology* (Princeton: Princeton University Press, 1988), p. 314.

20. Kohlberg's theory of moral development and Fowler's theory of faith development are examples of theories that seem to have made premature claims to universality. See Yamagishi Akiko, "A Moral Judgment Scale for the Adolescent," *Japanese Journal of Psychology* 51 (1980); and Thomas Hastings, "Parameters of Faith Among Japanese Junior College Women: An Initial Inquiry Based on Fowler's Theory of Faith Development," *Japanese Religions* 16, no. 4 (1991): 49-81, and "Beyond Autonomy and Belonging: Toward a Global Vision for Christian Nurture," *Japan Christian Review* 60 (1994): 79-95.

21. This kind of intercultural teaching experience can be compared to Winnicott's description of the child playing in the presence of the mother. Though I teach in Japanese, I, the foreigner, am, in many ways, the child and my Japanese students, in whose language I am introducing Erikson, Kohlberg, and Fowler, are my holding environment. We playfully test the reality of these theories of human development in the charged intermediate space of the classroom. Though their body language is subtle, I can pretty much read it after all of these years and I know almost at once when a concept is alien and when it rings true.

22. Christopher Bollas, *Being a Character: Psychoanalysis and Self Experience* (New York: Hill & Wang, 1992), p. 15.

23. Robert H. Stein, "Judas," in *Harper's Bible Dictionary,* ed. Paul J. Achtemeier (San Francisco: Harper & Row, 1985), p. 552.

24. See James E. Loder, *The Transforming Moment* (Colorado Springs: Helmers & Howard, 1989).

25. This is the kind of dualistic thinking that, until the Einsteinian revolution, has dominated the modern Western intellectual tradition. It assumes a radical distantiation between subject and object, a rupture between ontology and epistemology, and moves from disembodied principle to specific, and often hypothetical cases. I will return to this problem later.

26. See Ivan Morris, *The Nobility of Failure: Tragic Heroes in the History of Japan* (New York: Noonday, 1975).

27. Malcolm Waters, *Globalization* (London: Routledge, 1995), p. 62.

28. Maruyama Masao, *Japanese Thought* [in Japanese] (Tokyo: Iwanami Shinsho, 1961).

29. Gerben Heitink, *Practical Theology: History, Theory, Action Domains* (Grand Rapids: Eerdmans, 1999), pp. 29-30.

30. Nakamura Hajime, *Ways of Thinking of Eastern Peoples: India-China-Tibet-Japan* (Honolulu: University of Hawaii Press, 1964), p. 574.

31. Furuya, *A History of Japanese Theology.*

32. Bollas, *Being a Character*, p. 65.

33. Joseph Tobin, "Japanese Preschools and the Pedagogy of Selfhood," in *Japanese Sense of Self,* ed. Nancy Rosenberger (Cambridge: Cambridge University Press, 1992), p. 24.

34. Bollas, *Being a Character*, p. 19.

35. Wolfhart Pannenberg, *Anthropology in Theological Perspective* (Philadelphia: Westminster Press, 1985), pp. 321-22.

36. D. W. Winnicott, *Playing and Reality* (London: Routledge, 1971), p. 14.

37. Jeff Astley, "The Role of Worship in Christian Learning," in *Theological Perspectives on Christian Formation*, ed. Astley et al. (Grand Rapids: Eerdmans, 1996), p. 245.

38. Bollas, *Being a Character*, p. 59.

39. In the Judeo-Christian tradition, all three dimensions of the self are integrated in the two great commandments. "'You shall love the Lord your God with all your heart, and with all your soul, and with all your mind.' This is the greatest and first commandment. And a second is like it: 'You shall love your neighbor as yourself.' On these two commandments hang all the law and the prophets" (Matt. 22:37-40).

40. Winnicott, *Playing and Reality*, p. 14.

41. Winnicott, *Playing and Reality*, p. 2.

42. Erik H. Erikson, *Identity: Youth and Crisis* (New York: Norton, 1968), p. 217.

43. Thomas F. Torrance, *The Ground and Grammar of Theology* (Charlottesville: University of Virginia Press, 1980), p. 105.

44. Pannenberg, *Anthropology in Theological Perspective*, p. 409.

45. Pannenberg, *Anthropology in Theological Perspective*, p. 409.

46. The individual and communal relation to the context of ultimacy may, in turn, significantly influence one's understanding of the other modalities of the self. In overcoming the despair that haunts human experience, Søren Kierkegaard recognized both the I's intrinsic other and self-relationality and our common exocentric longing for an ultimate ground beyond our self(ves). In *Sickness unto Death*, Kierkegaard writes, "The formula that describes the state of the self when despair is completely rooted out is this: in relating itself to itself and in willing to be itself, the self rests transparently in the power that established it." For Kierkegaard, the Creator God who is revealed in the God/man Jesus Christ is the context of ultimacy that gives new order and meaning to the other modalities of the self. Søren Kierkegaard, *The Sickness unto Death*, ed. and trans. Howard Hong and Edna Hong (Princeton: Princeton University Press, 1980), p. 14.

47. See Thomas J. Hastings, "What Is the Future of Japan's Past? Negotiating Japanese Identity in a Global Age" [in Japanese], *Journal of Theology* 61 (1999).

48. Pierre Bourdieu, *The Logic of Practice*, trans. Richard Nice (Stanford, CA: Stanford University Press, 1990), p. 53.

49. Though I find the core insights of Bourdieu's theory of *habitus* applicable to Japan as well as the United States, his description borders at times on an extreme determinism, as when he claims that the schemes of *habitus* are "beyond the reach of introspective scrutiny or control by the will." This seems a contradiction in Bourdieu, a politically concerned thinker who is concerned with exposing the sources of social domination as a path toward individual and social transformation. While not wanting to deny the daunting power of *habitus*, I want to also hold on to the New Testament's eschatological vision of *koinonia*, expressed so eloquently by the Christian ethicist Paul Lehmann. "The penultimate chapter of the biblical story is the story of the eucharistic community in the world. Here is a *laboratory* of maturity in which, by the operative (real) presence of the Messiah-Redeemer in the midst of his people, and through them of all people, the will to power is broken and displaced by the power to will what God wills. . . . Maturity is the full development in a human being of the power to be truly himself in being related to others who also have the power to be truly and fully themselves. The Christian koinonia is the foretaste and the sign in the world that God has always been and is contemporaneously doing what it takes to make and to keep human life human.

This is the will of God 'as it was in the beginning, is now, and ever shall be, world without end.'" Paul Lehmann, *Ethics in a Christian Context* (New York: Harper & Row, 1963), p. 155.

50. See Thomas Hastings, "Theologie, Praxis und kultureller Habitus, Fragen zur japanischen Situation," in *Christentum und Spätmoderne, Ein internationaler Diskurs über Praktische Theologie und Ethik,* ed. Wilhelm Gräb, Gerhard Rau, Heinz Schmidt, and Johannes A. Van der Ven (Berlin: Kohlhammer, 2000), pp. 170-78.

51. "The contemporary definition of spirituality falls short on two counts. All too often it serves to comfort people — allowing them to feel better about things as they are and helping them to be happy — than to challenge them to move significantly beyond their present situation, especially if such movement involves definite sacrifices or discomforts. Rather than encouraging people to seek higher goals, it can inoculate them against taking the risks that may be necessary for true growth. A small group helps its members adapt to the demands of everyday life rather than providing a sense of transcendence that casts a new perspective on everyday life. It also makes the individual the measure of all things. At one time, theologians argued that the chief purpose of humankind was to glorify God. Now it would seem that the logic has been reversed: the chief purpose of God is to glorify humankind. Spirituality no longer is true or good because it meets absolute standards of truth or goodness but because it helps us get along. We are the judge of its worth. If it helps us find a vacant parking space, we know that our spirituality is on the right track. If it leads us into the wilderness, calling on us to face dangers we would rather not deal with, then it is a form of spirituality we are unlikely to choose. To be sure, there are significant exceptions to these patterns. Small groups sometimes challenge their members to undertake painful processes of spiritual growth. But the more common pattern seems to be a kind of faith that focuses heavily on feelings and on getting along rather than encouraging worshipful obedience to or reverence toward a transcendent God." Robert Wuthnow, *Sharing the Journey: Support Groups and America's New Quest for Community* (New York: Free Press, 1996), pp. 18-19.

52. See Furuya Yasuo and Ohki Hideo, *A Theology of Japan* [in Japanese] (Tokyo: Yorudansha, 1989).

53. By participating in Christ by the power of the Spirit and belonging to his people, we are gifted with an inexhaustibly rich knowledge of God through Word and Sacrament which, continually and over a lifetime, turns us in the direction of our true self "in Christ." Torrance says, "It is not a Word that we can hear by our clear-sightedness or master by our reason, but one that we can only hear through judgment of the very humanity in which it is clothed and to which it is addressed and therefore only through crucifixion and repentance. It is because the Word of God comes to us in this way that either we are offended at it and reject it in order to cling to ourselves, or we believe in it through a decision against ourselves and so hear it by committing ourselves to its action upon us." Thomas F. Torrance, *Divine Meaning: Studies in Patristic Hermeneutics* (Edinburgh: T. & T. Clark, 1995), pp. 8-9.

Note to Appendix D

1. A Buddhist monk (lived 1222-1282) who founded one of the major sects of Japanese Buddhism.

Bibliography

Achtemeier, Paul J., ed. *Harper's Bible Dictionary.* San Francisco: Harper & Row, 1985.

Akiyama Shigeo. *Stories of Meiji-era Personalities: A Genealogy of Christianity* [in Japanese]. Tokyo: Shinkyo, 1982.

Aoyoshi Katsuhisa. *Dr. Uemura Masahisa: A Christian Leader.* Tokyo: Kyobunkan, 1941.

Astley, Jeff. "The Role of Worship in Christian Learning." In *Theological Perspectives on Christian Formation,* edited by Jeff Astley, Leslie J. Francis, and Colin Crowder, pp. 244-50. Grand Rapids: Eerdmans, 1996.

Augustine. *The Trinity.* Translated by Edmund Hill. Brooklyn: New City Press, 1991.

Barclay, William. *Educational Ideals in the Ancient World.* Grand Rapids: Baker, 1974.

Barth, Karl. *Church Dogmatics* IV/I. Edited by Geoffrey W. Bromiley and Thomas F. Torrance. Edinburgh: T. & T. Clark, 1956.

————. *Der Römerbrief.* Abdruck der neuen Bearb. Munich: Kaiser, 1926.

Bellah, Robert Neelly. *Habits of the Heart: Individualism and Commitment in American Life.* Berkeley: University of California Press, 1996.

Berling, Judith A., ed. "Incarnating Globalization in ATS Schools: Issues, Experiences, Understandings, Challenges." *Theological Education* 35 (Spring 1999): i-vii, 1-189.

Bollas, Christopher. *Being a Character: Psychoanalysis and Self-Experience.* New York: Hill & Wang, 1992.

Bosch, David J. *Transforming Mission: Paradigm Shifts in Theology of Mission.* New York: Orbis, 1991.

Bourdieu, Pierre. *The Logic of Practice.* Translated by Richard Nice. Stanford, CA: Stanford University Press, 1990.

Boys, Mary C. *Educating in Faith: Maps and Visions.* Kansas City: Sheed & Ward, 1989.

Brueggemann, Walter. *The Creative Word: Canon as a Model for Biblical Education.* Philadelphia: Fortress Press, 1982.

Brunner, Emil. *Das Gebot und die Ordnungen: Entwurf einer protestantisch-theologischen Ethik.* Tübingen: J. C. B. Mohr, 1932.

Buckley, James J., and David S. Yeago, eds. *Knowing the Triune God: The Work of the Spirit in the Practices of the Church.* Grand Rapids: Eerdmans, 2001.

Buell, Frederick. *National Culture and the New Global System.* Baltimore: Johns Hopkins University Press, 1994.

Bühlmann, Walbert. *The Coming of the Third Church: An Analysis of the Present and Future of the Church.* Slough, UK: St. Paul, 1974.

Burton, Edwin. "Evangelical Alliance." *Catholic Encyclopedia.* http://www.newadvent.org/cathen/05641a.html.

Bushnell, Horace. *Christian Nurture.* Grand Rapids: Baker, 1979.

Calvin, John. *Institutes of the Christian Religion.* Philadelphia: Westminster Press, 1960.

Chan Wing-Tsit, trans. *A Sourcebook in Chinese Philosophy.* Princeton: Princeton University Press, 1963.

Chopp, Rebecca S. "Practical Theology and Liberation." In *Formation and Reflection: The Promise of Practical Theology,* edited by Lewis S. Mudge and James N. Poling, pp. 120-38. Philadelphia: Fortress, 1987.

Christian Yearbook [in Japanese]. Tokyo: Kirisuto Shinbunsha, 2003.

Coe, George A. *A Social Theory of Religious Education.* New York: Charles Scribner's Sons, 1917.

———. *The Psychology of Religion.* Chicago: University of Chicago Press, 1916.

———. *The Religion of a Mature Mind.* Chicago: Revell, 1902.

———. "The Religious Education Movement in Retrospect." *Religious Education* 39 (July-August 1944): 223.

———. *The Spiritual Life.* New York: Eaton & Mains, 1900.

Colyer, Elmer M. *How to Read T. F. Torrance: Understanding His Trinitarian and Scientific Theology.* Downers Grove, IL: InterVarsity Press, 2001.

The Constitution of the Presbyterian Church (U.S.A.): Part One, Book of Confessions. Louisville: Office of the General Assembly, 1996.

Cross, F. L., ed. *The Oxford Dictionary of the Christian Church.* Oxford: Oxford University Press, 1990.

Dennis, James. *Foreign Missions After a Century,* Students' Lectures on Missions, Princeton Theological Seminary, 1893. New York: Revell, 1893.

Dohi Akio. "The First Generation: Christian Leaders in the First Period." In Furuya, *A History of Japanese Theology,* pp. 11-42.

Drummond, Richard. *A History of Christianity in Japan.* Grand Rapids: Eerdmans, 1971.

Dudley, Carl S., and James D. Anderson. *Building Effective Ministry: Theory and Practice in the Local Church.* San Francisco: Harper & Row, 1983.

Dykstra, Craig R., and Sharon Parks, eds. *Faith Development and Fowler.* Birmingham, AL: Religious Education Press, 1986.

Edwards, Jonathan. *The Religious Affections.* Edinburgh: Banner of Truth, 2001.

Enns, Robert. "'Slander Against Our People': Tamura Naomi and the Japanese Bride Incident." *Japanese Religions* 18 (January 1993): 15-46.

Erikson, Erik H. *Identity: Youth and Crisis.* New York: Norton, 1968.

Faris, John T., ed. *The Sunday School and World Progress: The Official Book of the Eighth World's Sunday School Convention, Held in Tokyo, Japan, October 5-14, 1920.* New York: World's Sunday School Association, 1921.

Farley, Edward. *Theologia: The Fragmentation and Unity of Theological Education.* Philadelphia: Fortress, 1983.

Fowl, Stephen E. *Engaging Scripture: A Model for Theological Interpretation.* Malden, MA: Blackwell, 1998.

Fowler, James W. "Practical Theology and Theological Education: Some Models and Questions." *Theology Today* 42, no. 1 (1985): 43-58.

———. *Stages of Faith: The Psychology of Human Development and the Quest for Meaning.* San Francisco: Harper & Row, 1981.

Fowler, James W., Sam Keen, and Jerome Berryman. *Life Maps: Conversations on the Journey of Faith.* Waco: Word Books, 1978.

Furuya Yasuo. *Japanese Christianity* [in Japanese]. Tokyo: Kyobunkan, 2003.

Furuya Yasuo, ed. *A History of Japanese Theology.* Grand Rapids: Eerdmans, 1997.

Furuya Yasuo and Ohki Hideo. *A Theology of Japan* [in Japanese]. Tokyo: Yorudansha, 1989.

Gallup, George, Jr., and Sarah Jones. *100 Questions and Answers: Religion in America.* Princeton: Princeton Religion Research Center, 1989.

Griffith, Gwilym Oswald. *St. Paul's Life of Christ.* London: George Dornan, 1925.

Groome, Thomas. *Christian Religious Education: Sharing Our Story and Vision.* San Francisco: Harper & Row, 1980.

Hall, Robert. *Education for a New Japan.* New Haven: Yale University Press, 1963.

Hane Mikiso. *Modern Japan: A Historical Survey.* Boulder and London: Westview, 1986.

Harada Tasuku. "Japanese Character and Christianity: A Study of Japanese Ethical Ideals as Compared with Teaching of Christianity." *Pacific Affairs* 2, no. 11 (November 1929): 693-98.

Hardacre, Helen. *Shinto and the State, 1868-1988.* Princeton: Princeton University Press, 1989.

Harvey, Barry. *Another City: An Ecclesiological Primer for a Post-Christian World.* Harrisburg, PA: Trinity Press International, 1999.

Hastings, Thomas John. "Beyond Autonomy and Belonging: Toward a Global Vision for Christian Nurture." *Japan Christian Review* 60 (1994): 79-95.

————. "Japan's Protestant Schools and Churches in Light of Early Mission Theory and History." In Mullins, *Handbook of Christianity in Japan,* pp. 101-23.

————. "Parameters of Faith Among Japanese Junior College Women: An Initial Inquiry Based on Fowler's Theory of Faith Development." *Japanese Religions* 16, no. 4 (1991): 49-81.

————. "Protestantism's Perduring Preoccupation with Western Theological Texts: Japan." *Theology Today* 62, no. 1 (2005): 49-57.

————. "Theologie, Praxis und kultureller Habitus, Fragen zur japanischen Situation." In *Christentum und Spätmoderne, Ein internationaler Diskurs über Praktische Theologie und Ethik,* edited by Wilhelm Gräb, Gerhard Rau, Heinz Schmidt, and Johannes A. Van der Ven, pp. 170-78. Berlin: Kohlhammer, 2000.

————. "What Is the Future of Japan's Past? Negotiating Japanese Identity in a Global Age" [in Japanese]. *Journal of Theology* 61 (1999): 28-56.

Hauerwas, Stanley. *With the Grain of the Universe: The Church's Witness and Natural Theology.* Grand Rapids: Brazos, 2001.

Hays, Richard B. *First Corinthians.* Louisville: John Knox Press, 1997.

————. *The Moral Vision of the New Testament: Community, Cross, New Creation: A Contemporary Introduction to New Testament Ethics.* San Francisco: Harper, 1996.

Heitink, Gerben. *Practical Theology: History, Theory, Action Domains.* Grand Rapids: Eerdmans, 1999.

Hiyane Antei. *History of Modern Japanese Christians* [in Japanese]. Tokyo: Kirisutokyo Shisogyosho, 1935.

Hoffman, Stuart D. "School Texts, the Written Word, and Political Indoctrination: A Review of Moral Education Curricula in Modern Japan (1886-1997)." *History of Education* 28, no. 1 (1999): 87-97.

Hoge, Dean R., Benton Johnson, and Donald A. Luidens. *Vanishing Boundaries: The Religion of Mainline Protestant Baby Boomers.* Louisville: Westminster/John Knox Press, 1994.

Howard, Philip E., ed. *Sunday Schools the World Around: The Official Report of the World's Fifth Sunday-School Convention, in Rome, May 18-23, 1907.* Philadelphia: The World's Sunday-School Executive Committee, 1907.

Hunsinger, George R. *Disruptive Grace: Studies in the Theology of Karl Barth.* Grand Rapids: Eerdmans, 2000.

————. "The Newbigin Gauntlet: Developing a Domestic Missiology for North America." In Hunsberger and Van Gelder, *The Church Between Gospel and Culture,* pp. 3-25.

Hunsberger George R., and Craig Van Gelder, eds. *The Church Between Gospel and Culture: The Emerging Mission in North America.* Grand Rapids: Eerdmans, 1996.

Huntington, Samuel P. *The Clash of Civilizations and the Remaking of World Order.* New York: Simon & Schuster, 1996.

Hütter, Reinhard. "The Knowledge of the Triune God: Practices, Doctrine, Theology." In Buckley and Yeago, *Knowing the Triune God,* pp. 23-47.

———. *Suffering Divine Things: Theology as Church Practice.* Grand Rapids: Eerdmans, 2000.

Igleheart, Charles, ed. *The Japan Christian Yearbook 1938.* Tokyo: Kyobunkan, 1938.

Jaeger, Werner. *Paideia.* Translated by Gilbert Highet. Oxford: Basil Blackwell, 1963.

Jenson, Robert. "How the World Lost Its Story." *First Things* 36 (1993): 20.

Katakozawa Chiyomatsu, Mizuno Makoto, Okamura Shoji, Matsukawa Shigeo, Mizutani Mitsuko, and Yoshioka Harue, eds. *The Journey of the Church School in Japan* [in Japanese]. Tokyo: The Educational Division of the National Christian Council, 1977.

Katoh Masao. *The Spirit of the Meiji Christians and Modernity: The Christian Schools Are Founded* [in Japanese]. Tokyo: Kindai Bungeisha, 1996.

Kelly, Robert A. "Oratio, Meditatio, Tentatio Faciunt Theologum: Luther's Piety and the Formation of Theologians." *Consensus* 19, no. 1 (1993): 9-27.

Kelsey, David H. *Proving Doctrine: The Uses of Scripture in Modern Theology.* Harrisburg, PA: Trinity Press International, 1999.

Kierkegaard, Søren. *Attack upon Christendom.* Translated by Walter Lowrie. Princeton: Princeton University Press, 1972.

———. *The Sickness unto Death.* Edited and translated by Howard Hong and Edna Hong. Princeton: Princeton University Press, 1980.

Kitamori Kazoh. *The Theology of the Pain of God.* Richmond, VA: John Knox Press, 1965.

Kitoku Kazuo. *The Principles of Religious Education* [in Japanese]. Tokyo: Bunkawado, 1932.

Knoff, Gerald E. *The World Sunday School Movement: The Story of a Broadening Mission.* New York: Seabury, 1979.

Kobayashi Koichi. *The Background of Christian Education* [in Japanese]. Tokyo: Yorudansha, 1979.

———. "Japanese Education and Christian Education." In *Dictionary of Christian Education* [in Japanese]. Tokyo: Kyodan, 1969.

Koizumi Takashi. "Fukuzawa Yukichi and Religion." *Asian Philosophy* 4, no. 2 (1994): 109-19.

Kuwata Hidenobu. "Religious Education in Evangelical Perspective: In Search of Principles for Christian Religious Education." In *Collected Works of Kuwata Hidenobu* [in Japanese], 4:242-56. Tokyo: Kirisutokyo Shinbunsha, 1977.

LaCugna, Catherine Mowry. *God for Us: The Trinity and Christian Life.* San Francisco: HarperCollins, 1991.

Lamb, Mathew L. *Solidarity with the Victims.* New York: Crossroad, 1982.

Lehmann, Paul. *Ethics in a Christian Context.* New York: Harper & Row, 1963.

Lewis, Robert E. *The Educational Conquest of the Far East.* New York: Revell, 1903.

Lifton, Robert Jay. *The Protean Self: Human Resilience in an Age of Fragmentation.* San Francisco: Basic, 1993.

Lindbeck, George. *The Nature of Doctrine: Religion and Theology in a Postliberal Age.* Philadelphia: Westminster Press, 1984.

Loder, James E. "The Dominance of Socialization." In unpublished manuscript titled *Educational Ministry in the Logic of the Spirit.* Computer Printout, Princeton Theological Seminary, 2001, pp. 1-66.

————. *The Logic of the Spirit: Human Development in Theological Perspective.* San Francisco: Jossey-Bass, 1998.

————. "Normativity and Context in Practical Theology: The Interdisciplinary Issue." In *Practical Theology: International Perspectives,* edited by Friedrich Schweitzer and J. A. Van der Ven, pp. 359-81. Frankfurt am Main and New York: Peter Lang, 1999.

————. *The Transforming Moment.* Colorado Springs: Helmers & Howard, 1989.

Loder, James E., and James W. Fowler. "Conversations on 'Stages of Faith' and 'The Transforming Moment.'" *Religious Education* 77, no. 2 (1982): 133-48.

Loder, James E., and W. Jim Neidhardt. *The Knight's Move: The Relational Logic of the Spirit in Theology and Science.* Colorado Springs: Helmers & Howard, 1992.

Löwith, Karl. *Sämtliche Schriften.* Stuttgart: Metzler, 1981.

Luhmer, Klaus. "Moral Education in Japan." *Journal of Moral Education* 19, no. 3 (October 1990): 172-82.

Luther, Martin. *Luther's Works: The American Edition.* Philadelphia and St. Louis: Fortress & Concordia, 1955.

Marrou, H. I. "The Old Roman Education." Part 3, Chapter 1 in *A History of Education in Antiquity.* Madison: University of Wisconsin Press, 1956.

Maruyama Masao. *Japanese Thought* [in Japanese]. Tokyo: Iwanami Shinsho, 1961.

Matsumoto Sannosuke. "The Significance of Nationalism in Modern Japanese Thought: Some Theoretical Problems." *Journal of Asian Studies* 31, no. 1 (November 1971): 49-56.

Matsunaga Kikuo. "Theological Education in Japan." In *Preparing for Witness in Context: 1998 Cook Theological Seminar,* edited by Jean Stoner, pp. 295-311. Louisville: Presbyterian Church, 1999.

McKim, Donald. *Theological Turning Points: Major Issues in Christian Thought.* Atlanta: John Knox, 1988.

Miura Tadashi, ed. *Research on the Tsukiji Band* [in Japanese]. Tokyo: UCCJ Sugamo Church, 1986.

————. "'The Children of Jesus': Tamura Naomi, The Father of Japanese Modern Religious Education." In Miura, *Research on the Tsukiji Band,* pp. 6-17.

Moltmann, Jürgen. *Theology of Hope.* London: SCM Press, 1967.

————. *The Crucified God: The Cross of Christ as the Foundation and Criticism of Christian Theology.* London: SCM, 1974.

Morris, Ivan. *The Nobility of Failure: Tragic Heroes in the History of Japan.* New York: Noonday, 1975.

Mullins, Mark R. *Christianity Made in Japan: A Study of Indigenous Movements.* Honolulu: University of Hawaii Press, 1998.

Mullins, Mark R., ed. *Handbook on Christianity in Japan.* Leiden: Brill, 2003.

Nakamura Hajime. *Ways of Thinking of Eastern Peoples: India-China-Tibet-Japan.* Honolulu: University of Hawaii Press, 1964.

Newbigin, Lesslie. "Christ and the Cultures." *Scottish Journal of Theology* 31 (1978): 11-12.

————. *Foolishness to the Greeks: The Gospel and Western Culture.* Grand Rapids: Eerdmans, 1986.

————. *The Gospel in a Pluralist Society.* Grand Rapids: Eerdmans, 1989.

————. *The Other Side of 1984: Questions for the Churches.* Geneva: World Council of Churches, 1983.

————. *Proper Confidence: Faith, Doubt, and Certainty in Christian Discipleship.* Grand Rapids: Eerdmans, 1995.

Niebuhr, H. Richard. *Christ and Culture.* New York: Harper, 1951.

Nishikawa Yuko. "The Changing Form of Dwellings and the Establishment of the Katei (Home) in Modern Japan." *U.S.-Japan Women's Journal* 3 (1995): 3-36.

Osmer, Richard Robert., ed. *Developing a Public Faith: New Directions in Practical Theology — Essays in Honor of James Fowler.* St. Louis: Chalice Press, 2003.

Osmer, Richard Robert, and Friedrich Lutz Schweitzer. *Religious Education between Modernization and Globalization: New Perspectives on the United States and Germany.* Grand Rapids: Eerdmans, 2003.

Pannenberg, Wolfhart. *Anthropology in Theological Perspective.* Philadelphia: Westminster Press, 1985.

Parker, Harris H. "The Union School of Religion, 1910-1929: Embers from the Fires of Progressivism." *Religious Education* 86, no. 4 (Fall 1991): 597-607.

Pazmino, Robert. *God Our Teacher: Theological Basics in Christian Education.* Grand Rapids: Baker Academic, 2001.

Polanyi, Michael. *Personal Knowing.* Chicago: University of Chicago Press, 1958.

————. *The Tacit Dimension.* Gloucester, MA: Peter Smith, 1983.

Proceedings of the General Conference of the Protestant Missionaries in Japan Held at Osaka, April, 1883. Yokohama: R. Meiklejohn, 1883.

Proceedings of the General Conference of Protestant Missionaries in Japan Held in Tokyo, October, 1900. Tokyo: Methodist Publishing House, 1901.

Reischauer, August Karl. *The Task in Japan.* New York: Revell, 1926.

Robertson, Roland. *Globalization: Social Theory and Global Culture.* London: Sage Publications, 1992.

Robertson, Nicoll W. *The Incarnate Saviour: A Life of Jesus Christ.* Edinburgh: T. & T. Clark, 1897.

Roland, Alan. *In Search of Self in India and Japan: Toward a Cross-Cultural Psychology.* Princeton: Princeton University Press, 1988.

Sanneh, Lamin. *Translating the Message: The Missionary Impact on Culture.* New York: Orbis, 1989.

Schleiermacher, Friedrich. *Brief Outline of Theology as a Field of Study.* Translated by Terrence N. Tice. Lewiston, NY: Edward Mellen Press, 1988.

Schmidt, Stephen A. *A History of the Religious Education Association.* Birmingham, AL: Religious Education Press, 1983.

Schwantes, Robert S. "Christianity Versus Science: A Conflict of Ideas in Meiji Japan." *The Far Eastern Quarterly* 12, no. 2 (February 1953): 123-32.

Seat, Karen. "Mission Schools and Education for Women." In Mullins, *Handbook of Christianity in Japan,* pp. 321-42.

Segovia, Fernando F., and May Ann Tolbert, eds. *Reading from This Place: Social Location and Biblical Interpretation in the United States.* Minneapolis: Fortress, 1995.

Shenk, Wilbert R. "The Culture of Modernity as a Missionary Challenge." In Hunsberger and Van Gelder, *The Church Between Gospel and Culture,* pp. 69-78.

Smart, James. *The Teaching Ministry of the Church.* Philadelphia: Westminster, 1954.

Smith, David. *The Life and Letters of St. Paul.* Hodder and Stoughton, 1919.

Smith, H. Shelton. *Faith and Nurture.* New York: Charles Scribner's Sons, 1942.

Soltau, Addison. "Uemura Masahisa (1857-1925): First Generation Pastor, Christian Leader and Instinctive Proponent of Indigenized Christianity in Japan." Th.D. diss., Concordia Seminary, St. Louis, 1982.

Soulen, Richard N. *Handbook of Biblical Criticism.* Atlanta: John Knox, 1976.

Stark, Rodney. *The Rise of Christianity.* Princeton: Princeton University Press, 1996.

Sunquist, Scott W., ed. *A Dictionary of Asian Christianity.* Grand Rapids: Eerdmans, 2001.

Takakusu Junjiro. "The Social and Ethical Value of the Family System in Japan." *International Journal of Ethics* 17, no. 1 (October 1906): 100-106.

Takeda Kiyoko. *The Yokohama Band's View of Women: Reflections on the Japanese Bride Incident* [in Japanese]. Tokyo: Meiji Gakuin University Institute for Christian Studies, 1997.

Tamura Naomi. *The Background of Jesus of Nazareth* [in Japanese]. Tokyo: Keiseisha, 1931.

———. "Barthian Theology and Religious Education." *Sunday School* [in Japanese]. April 1933.

———. *Fifty Years of Faith* [in Japanese]. Tokyo: Keiseisha, 1924.

———. *Miscellaneous Thoughts on Pastoral Ministry* [in Japanese]. Tokyo: Taisho Kindergarten Publishing, 1928.

————. *Sunday School Lessons Graded Series: Outline of Bible Stories, Primary Course First Year* [in Japanese]. 4th ed. Tokyo: Kyobunkan, 1912.

————. *The Child the Center of Christianity.* Tokyo: Taisho Kindergarten Publishing, 1926.

————. *The Figure of Jesus of Nazareth* [in Japanese]. Tokyo: Keiseisha, 1930.

————. *The Guide of Religious Education* [in Japanese]. Tokyo: Taisho Kindergarten Publishing. 1928.

————. *The Japanese Bride.* New York: Harper & Brothers, 1893.

————. *The Principles and Practice of Religious Education* [in Japanese]. Tokyo: Keiseisha, 1920.

————. *The Rights of Children* [in Japanese]. Tokyo: Keiseisha, 1907.

————. *Twentieth-Century Sunday School* [in Japanese]. Tokyo: Keiseisha, 1907.

————. *Uemura Masahisa and Uchimura Kanzo as I Remember Them* [in Japanese]. Tokyo: Mukoyamadoshobo, 1932.

Taylor, John. "The Future of Christianity." In *The Oxford Illustrated History of Christianity,* edited by John McManners, pp. 628-65. Oxford: Oxford University Press, 1990.

Tobin, Joseph. "Japanese Preschools and the Pedagogy of Selfhood." In *Japanese Sense of Self,* edited by Nancy Rosenberger, pp. 21-39. Cambridge: Cambridge University Press, 1992.

Torrance, Thomas F. *Divine Meaning: Studies in Patristic Hermeneutics.* Edinburgh: T. & T. Clark, 1995.

————. *Space, Time and Resurrection.* Grand Rapids: Eerdmans, 1976.

————. *The Ground and Grammar of Theology.* Charlottesville: University of Virginia Press, 1980.

————. *The Mediation of Christ.* Colorado Springs: Helmers & Howard, 1992.

————. *The School of Faith.* New York: Harper & Brothers, 1959.

————. *Transformation and Convergence in the Frame of Knowledge: Explorations in the Interrelations of Scientific and Theological Enterprise.* Eugene, OR: Wipf & Stock, 1980.

Tracy, David. *Blessed Rage for Order: The New Pluralism in Theology.* New York: Seabury Press, 1975.

————. *The Analogical Imagination: Christian Theology and the Culture of Pluralism.* New York: Crossroad, 1981.

Uchimura Kanzo. "Can Americans Teach Us Religion?" *Japan Christian Intelligencer* 1 (1926): 352-62.

Uemura Masahisa. *Collected Works of Uemura Masahisa.* Edited by Kumano Yoshitaka, Ishihara Ken, Saito Isamu, Ouchi Sabura [in Japanese]. Tokyo: Shinkyo Shuppansha, 1932.

Van Gelder, Craig. "A Great New Fact of Our Day: America as Mission Field." In Hunsberger and Van Gelder, *The Church Between Gospel and Culture,* pp. 57-68.

Walls, Andrew F. *The Cross-Cultural Process in Christian History.* New York: Orbis, 2002.

————. "The Expansion of Christianity: An Interview with Andrew Walls." *Christian Century* 117, no. 22 (August 2-9, 2000): 795.

————. *The Missionary Movement in Christian History: Studies in the Transmission of Faith.* New York: Orbis, 1996.

Waters, Malcolm. *Globalization.* London: Routledge, 1995.

Winnicott, D. W. *Playing and Reality.* London: Routledge, 1971.

World-Wide Sunday School Work: The Official Report of the World's Sixth Sunday-School Convention, Held in the City of Washington, U.S.A. May 19-24, 1910. Chicago: The Executive Committee of the World's Sunday-School Association, 1910.

Wuthnow, Robert. *Sharing the Journey: Support Groups and America's New Quest for Community.* New York: Free Press, 1996.

————. *The Restructuring of American Religion: Society and Faith Since World War II.* Princeton: Princeton University Press, 1988.

Yamagishi Akiko. "A Moral Judgment Scale for the Adolescent." *Japanese Journal of Psychology* 51 (1980).

Yamaji Aizan. *Essays on the Modern Japanese Church.* English translation of 1906 Japanese version. Ann Arbor: Center for Japanese Studies, University of Michigan, 1999.

Yeago, David. "The Spirit, the Church, and the Scriptures: Biblical Inspiration and Interpretation Revisited." In Buckley and Yeago, *Knowing the Triune God,* pp. 49-93.

————. "The New Testament and the Nicene Dogma: A Contribution to the Recovery of Theological Exegesis." In *The Theological Interpretation of Scripture: Classic and Contemporary Readings,* edited by Stephen Fowl, pp. 87-100. Malden, MA: Blackwell, 1997.

Young, Frances. *From Nicaea to Chalcedon.* Philadelphia: Fortress, 1983.

Index